RAINSFORD ISLAND

A Boston Harbor Case Study in Public Neglect and Private Activism

First Printing

September 3, 2019

Revision

December 6, 2020

William A. McEvoy Jr, & Robin Hazard Ray

Dedicated to my wife, Lucille McEvoy

Table of Contents

Cover illustration:

Sweetser, M. F. (Moses Foster), 1848-1897, Charles George Copeland, illustrator, and Moses King. King's Handbook of Boston Harbor. Cambridge Mass. Moses King, publisher, p 181

Preface by Bill McEvoy

I first became acquainted with Rainsford Island, located in Boston Harbor, during my research on the Catholic Mount Auburn Cemetery, also known as the Sand Banks Cemetery, located in Watertown, MA. That four-year study, which began in February 2012, included recording the cemetery's history, as well as gleaning all available vital statistical information on the 23,205 people interred there.

Nearly all of the 5,311 Catholic Mount Auburn Cemetery's burial lots were sold between 1854 and 1864. From 1854 to 1881, 81 percent of those buried there died in Boston. With a few exceptions, all were Irish immigrants who had fled the great famine of the late 1840s, or their descendants.

That research made me aware of the hardships that newly arrived immigrants faced: poor living conditions; scanty health care; a lack of skills that allowed most to only work as laborers; dangerous working conditions; a prejudiced press, law-enforcement, and judicial system; and an extremely high rate of childhood mortality. Between 1854 and 1881, 49 percent of the 15,562 people buried at Catholic Mount Auburn died before age 6; 44 percent were under 4. The cause of death for 306 was listed as "teething."

Between 1856 and 1893, thirty-six of the people buried at the Catholic Mount Auburn Cemetery were noted as dying at Rainsford Island. Their ages ranged from nine months to eighty-six years. James Tubman, nine months old, died in 1863 at Rainsford Island from starvation. Prior to going to Rainsford, he had been Baptized at St. Joseph Church, Boston. Mary E. Sullivan, died in 1858 at Bennett Avenue [sic], Boston, from lung inflammation. She was born at Rainsford Island.

What was Rainsford Island and why did so many indigent Irish immigrants die there? After a cursory review of the City of Boston Records of Death, as well as an attempt to determine the extent of work done by other researchers, I put those questions on hold while working on the Catholic Mount Auburn Cemetery project. With that work completed in February 2016, I was at last able to turn to Rainsford.[1]

Methodology

My research on Rainsford Island involved many sources. Using online resources, I found over 1,000 newspaper articles and scholarly articles from the early 1800s to 1984 that included the words "Rainsford Island". I reviewed all the City of Boston's Records of deaths from 1800 to 1920 for mentions of the island, and I read every available governmental report from the City of Boston and the Commonwealth of Massachusetts that mentioned it. I searched the Military records of Ancestry.com to discover the names of Civil War Veterans connected with the place and any who may have been buried there while still on active duty. Photographs and illustrations gleaned from various archives and databases helped to visualize the changing island landscape.

I visited the City of Boston Archives for information on Rainsford Island, and I wrote to, as well as, personally searched the City of Boston cemeteries to see whether anyone originally buried at Rainsford Island may have been reinterred at another cemetery. The collections of the Boston Public Library turned up a limited amount of information on Rainsford Island, including historical maps. The City of Boston's Archaeologist, Joseph Bagley, and other written sources, helped me figure out the former placement of buildings on the island. With the exception of the base foundation of the former piggery and the scattered foundations of one old hospital, no structures remain.

Rainsford Island changed hands and uses many times. It was owned privately from 1636 to 1736. Thereafter it passed through various forms of governmental ownership, beginning with the Province of the Massachusetts Bay, followed by the Commonwealth of Massachusetts and the City of Boston. Today the island is part of a National and State Park.

---

[1] The database, methodology, and PowerPoint presentation from that project are available on the website of Historical Society of Watertown, MA. The database is also held at Boston College's Irish Studies Collection. All are welcome to utilize it. I request only that I be acknowledged as the source.

Per the National Park Service's Boston Harbor Islands web page:

> "The Boston Harbor Islands Partnership, together representatives from nonprofit organizations, federal agencies, and city and state government oversee the day-to-day operations of the Boston Harbor Islands. The Partnership meets regularly to report on island activities and develop overall strategies for this national and state park area."

The island's complex history is best told by segmenting the various uses of the island, from fishing spot to summer retreat to sanitorium. Its story took a sinister turn in 1854, when the island started to be used as an off-shore dumping ground to deal with the mass immigration from Ireland. At first, the term "quarantine" was used to justify the segregation of unwanted persons far from any family or civic oversight. Later this exile became a matter of course, with hundreds shipped to the island "hospital"—a great misnomer.

Though historic anecdotes allude to the later removal of the dead from Rainsford Island, I believe that more than 1,777 bodies remain there in unmarked graves (see Chapter 7). That total includes a War of 1812 Sailor; 9 Civil War soldiers who died on active duty; and 109 Veterans of the Civil War who died between 1873 and 1893. Fourteen of those were African American Veterans.

One of those African American Veterans was Stephen Ennis, a musician from Montrose, PA. He was paid $50 for enlisting in the famous 54th Massachusetts Regiment—the first in the Union to recruit African Americans—joining the Regiment on March 27, 1863, and serving until August 20, 1865. He died at Rainsford on August 12, 1882. One can look at the magnificent Memorial to the 54th Regiment on Boston Common by sculptor Augustus Saint-Gaudens and think, perhaps, Ennis is the drummer portrayed leading the marching soldiers. It is bitter to conclude that Ennis died forgotten at a place like Rainsford and lies there still in an unmarked grave. To quote another man who died on a different "godforsaken island" (Napoleon Bonaparte), "Glory is fleeting, but obscurity is forever."

* * *

There are two heroes whose efforts resulted in the City of Boston terminating the use of the Rainsford Island as a warehouse for the poor, the unwanted, and the mentally ill. Alice North Towne Lincoln (1853–1926) began her efforts to provide proper housing for the poor in 1879, at the age of 26, the year before she married. In 1890, she stepped up her efforts to reform Boston's Public Institutions, including Rainsford Island and the Long Island Hospital, which opened in late 1887.

Her dogged complaints at board meetings and letters to the editors of Boston newspapers resulted in the Boston Board of Aldermen holding fifty-eight days of hearings between May 15, 1894, and December 28, 1894. The record of those hearings totals 3,700 pages (see Chapter 4).

Mrs. Lincoln was represented, pro-bono, by our second hero, Attorney Louis Dembitz Brandeis (1856–1941), later an associate justice on the U.S. Supreme Court. He remained for all of the hearings and actively participated in the presentation of witnesses and evidence to support Mrs. Lincoln's charges. His deft cross-examination of the Board of Aldermen's witnesses, most of whom simply wanted Mrs. Lincoln to go away, make great reading even a century later.

By January 31, 1895, as a result of Lincoln's complaints, Rainsford Island Hospital was finally closed. As we shall see in Chapter 6, however, that was not the end of its sordid history.

I dedicate this work to the memory of all who were sent to Rainsford Island, especially those who remain buried there, still neglected and forgotten. Their names, dates and causes of death, as well place of birth is listed in **Appendix 7.2**

My thanks to:

Robin Hazard Ray for her excellent editing of my lengthy first draft, as well as her written contributions.
Robert F. DeVellis, James F. Smith, James Gorman, Gail Peterson, Joyce M. Kelly, B. Steven Willis, Joseph M. Bagley, Doc Searls, and Holly Sullo of the Harvard Book Store for their support, advice and encouragement.

Finally, my wife Lucille H. McEvoy for her enduring support and patience that have never failed since our first meeting, February 12, 1966, when we were 16.

Introductory Note by Robin Hazard Ray

Bill McEvoy's extraordinary gift for research is something of a legend among the docents at Mount Auburn Cemetery. In addition to the Catholic Mount Auburn Cemetery project, to which Bill alludes above, he also researched every individual buried in Mount Auburn's "public lots"—named after the four Evangelists of the New Testament, Saints John, James, Luke, and Matthew. We now have thick volumes to which to refer when visitors come to us with questions about the people buried there. When Bill was looking for someone to help him tell the story of Rainsford Island, whose dramatic turns of fortune we recount, I volunteered.

Each of the 34 Harbor Islands has its unique history, but the fact that they are islands adds a layer of secrecy to their pasts. Islands, which are so difficult and costly to get to and to survive upon, end up being great places to dump the unwanted, to hide the embarrassing, and to deceive others about what is actually transpiring. For this reason, islands become prisons, landfills, slaughtering grounds, and places of exile. Out of sight and hearing, out of mind.

Thus, the disturbing history of Rainsford Island, which lies 5.2 miles off of South Boston. At various times, the island boasted grand buildings with impressive facades. But almost always at work in the background were decay, neglect, and malfeasance.

Its history is unique, and yet it is not. A similar history could be written about Long Island in Boston Harbor, or Riker's Island in New York, or a dozen other places. If I wish readers to take away one thing from this work, it is that citizens need to pay attention to places that are off the main track. Visit them. Take a flashlight, a notebook, and a camera. And leave a record for the generations that follow.

Chapter 1: The Island to 1854

Rainsford Island lies about halfway between the City of Boston and the town of Hull in Boston Harbor. A series of geologic faults run in an east-northeasterly direction from the heart of Milton, MA, out into the Atlantic Ocean. They are the lasting remnants of a tectonic collision hundreds of millions of years ago that slivered the older local rocks, late Pre-Cambrian and Early Cambrian in age, which were themselves products of long-ago volcanoes. The faults mark a physical severing of the continuity between the more solid shore region of Boston Harbor and the scattered Harbor Islands.

Rainsford itself comprises about 11 acres, with two irregular halves pinched in the middle. The western half shows rocky outcrops of the Cambridge Formation, an ancient non-fossiliferous mudstone that underlies much of the Boston Basin. The eastern half is entirely composed of glacial sediments, rucked up during the last Ice Age to form a drumlin. The halves are connected by a relatively narrow spit of sand and gravel. According to a Rainsford Island Archaeology Survey, the highest point of the island as of 2001 was 16.7 meters (54 feet) above Mean Sea Level.[2]

Early Uses of the Island

The prehistory of the island is unknown, as thus far no archaeological evidence of Native American use has come to light. However, the evidence of shellfish middens and projectile points on neighboring Harbor Islands would suggest pre-European use of the place as a fishing and hunting spot, and possibly a burial place as well.

Soon after the establishment of the Massachusetts Bay Colony, in 1636, one Edward Raynsford, at the request of Owen Rowe, was granted the island, and it began to appear on maps with his name attached. It seems to have served a number of functions in the following centuries: timber lot, rock quarry, fishing station, cattle pasture, and summer retreat.

---

[2] Stefan Claesson, "Rainsford Island Archaeological Survey," Institute of Maritime History, ca. 2002.

Pest House Island

According to a useful summary published in 1876, the Province of Massachusetts purchased the island in 1736 or 1737 (sources disagree) for the sum of £570 for use as a quarantine station.[3] It was "to be used and improved for a publick [sic] hospital for the reception and accommodation of such sick and infectious persons as shall be sent there by order."[4] From time to time, it appears on early maps as "Hospital Island," "Pest House Island", or "Quarantine Island."[5] Ships entering the harbor were required to stop there for inspection, to see if any aboard showed signs of smallpox or other communicable diseases. If there were signs of disease, the entire crew was waylaid for a period of weeks. The combination of sailors and idleness created the usual market for the usual vices.

After the Revolutionary War, the Province of Massachusetts became the Commonwealth of Massachusetts, and it retained title to the Rainsford property. The island in this period doubled as both quarantine station and summer resort. Moses F. Sweetser, in his late nineteenth-century guide to the Harbor Islands, writes:

> On Great Head [the northeast bluff of the island] stands the Old Mansion House built in 1819, which was for many years the chief summer resort in the harbor, and has given comfortable shelter to many well-known Bostonians of the old *régime*. The town authorities allowed the keepers to take boarders, when no infectious diseases were upon the island; and the fever and small-pox hospitals were often crowded, besides the old mansion. It must have been a grewsome [sic] summer-resort, and abounding in suggestions not conducive to hilarity; yet our grandfathers appear to have found real and lively pleasure here.[6] See pictures at pages 156-157.

Though the advent of the smallpox vaccine—being first administered in this country, at Boston, in 1800—made that contagion less of a menace, the quarantine function of Rainsford

---

[3] F. B. Sanborn, "The Public Charities of Massachusetts during the Century Ending Jan. 1, 1876," Report Made to the Massachusetts Centennial Commission, Feb. 1, 1876 (Boston: Wright & Potter, 1876), pp. 22–28;

[4] M. F. Sweetser, *King's Handbook of Boston Harbor* (1882), p. 179.

[5] Osgood Carleton, "A Chart of the Harbour of Boston : with soundings, sailing marks, &c. taken from Holland's survey's [sic]." Boston: Republished and sold by W. Norman, book and chart-seller [ca. 1800?], Harvard Map Collection.

[6] M. F. Sweetser, *King's Handbook of Boston Harbor* (1882), 180.

remained critical. Typhus and cholera raged through Boston at various points,[7] and though the microbiological causes of these contagions had yet to be discovered, it was known that they spread from person to person and could be arrested by isolating those affected. Developments on the island may have reflected alarming trends onshore: in 1832, cholera swept through the crowded neighborhoods of Boston. In 1837, the repeal of the 1800 law requiring mandatory smallpox vaccinations lent a new urgency to quarantine efforts.[8]

The Commonwealth authorized the construction of a handsome Greek Revival building on Rainsford Island to house the increasing numbers of ill wayfarers and immigrants passing into Boston Harbor. Designed and built by a pair of builder-architect brothers, Josiah and Isaiah Rogers, the building presented a dignified cover to what was often a chaotic and unsanitary facility.[9] An itinerant English artist, Robert Salmon (1775–1845 or after) captured this building in a flattering painting in the early 1840s, as part of a series of South Shore seascapes tailored to the local market. Though the painting emphasizes the fine hospital building, it also reveals the existence of numerous smaller, shabbier buildings on the island, about whose functions we can only speculate.

Robert Salmon (1775–1845 or after), *Rainsford's Island, Boston Harbor,* about 1840. Museum of Fine Arts, Boston. Bequest of Martha C. Karolik for the M. and M. Karolik Collection of American Paintings, 1815-1865.

---

[7] Cholera epidemics occurred in 1832, 1849, and again in 1866. See "The Cholera Epidemic in Boston," *Boston Med. Surg. J.* (1849) 41: 296–299.

[8] Samuel Bayard Woodward, "The Story of Smallpox in Massachusetts," *New England Journal of Medicine*, vol. 206, no. 23 (June 9, 1932).

[9] Stefan Claesson, "Rainsford Island Archaeological Survey," Institute of Maritime History, ca. 2002.

Sweetser mentions a superintendent's house and "the old dead house," as well as the extensive graveyard:

> Here are buried most of the old keepers of the island, and many sailors and officers of foreign ships, who have ended their voyages here. Up to a date well within the present century, it was the custom for Boston families to send their members when taken with dangerous infectious diseases to the island, whence they were tolerably certain never to return.[10]

Disposal to the island meant not only separating the family from the contagion but also free burial, which for many of Boston's poor was not an idle consideration.

According to a Boston City Document, published in 1841 by a Special Joint Committee, legislation in 1833 had decreed that a Resident Physician should be chosen for the quarantine island, who was to live on the island from June 1 to October 1 "and at other times, as the Mayor and Alderman may direct." This doctor was to visit every ship "liable to Quarantine," to direct its cleaning and the disposal of tainted goods, and to care for anyone aboard who was "sick of any contagious, infectious, or malignant disease during the passage to Boston."[11] The report noted, however, that fewer and fewer ships were inspected for quarantine, perhaps because the health of passengers was better regulated at the departure ports, perhaps because the resident doctor was using "free judgment" in determining which ships were to be inspected. It is hard at this distance to interpret the phrase "free judgment", but it may correspond to laziness or corruption. The decision was made to stop waylaying ships on their way in, and only to turn around to Rainsford Island those found to be "foul and infected" once they had landed in Boston. A great deal of money could be saved this way, though of course it laid the city open to escapees carrying disease with them. Dr. John C. Warren, Chairman of the Boston Board of Consulting Physicians, wrote complacently at the close of the Committee's Report:

> We are happy in the belief that our community is too well informed to require to be amused by fictitious appearances and unnecessary regulations. The best protection we are able to obtain against the ravages of those tremendous visitations [of disease], which are now and then sent to scourge our race, is to be found neither in Cordons nor Quarantines: but in the removal . . . of substances which vitiate the atmosphere; in the

---

[10] M. F. Sweetser, *King's Handbook of Boston Harbor* (1882), p. 181.
[11] City of Boston Document No. 16, "Quarantine" (May 13, 1841), p. 2.

> preservation of personal cleanliness; in the cultivation of temperate habits of living; in a fearless performance of our duties whenever they call us; and in a perfect confidence in an all-wise overruling power.[12]

The measure adopted by the City no doubt saved a great deal of money at least in the short term. It was to show its defects when the cholera returned aboard a ship of starving Irish immigrants in 1849.

In nineteenth-century Massachusetts, the poor were the responsibility of the town from which they hailed. But with increasing levels of immigration came increasing numbers of individuals who had no place in America to call home and therefore no place to take responsibility for keeping them from total starvation. The "unsettled poor" were sorted into categories, with some deemed able-bodied—and therefore capable of being put to work—and others either too ill physically or mentally to repay the state with labor. According to a report written in 1876 on the history of public charities in Massachusetts:

> [In] 1852 . . . an Act was passed establishing a hospital for sick state paupers [at Rainsford]. This Act provided for the building of three state almshouses with farms and other facilities for employing the able-bodied poor who had no town settlement, and directed that all the unsettled poor should be removed to these almshouses on their completion, except such foreign paupers, arriving by water, as could not on account of sickness be so removed. These were to be left at the hospital on Rainsford Island, "during the continuance of such inability."
>
> Under this Act, extensive repairs and additions were made at Rainsford Island, and the enlarged buildings there were opened as a hospital for the sick state poor who had come into the Commonwealth by water, on the 16th of May 1854.[13]

---

[12] City of Boston Document No. 16, "Quarantine," May 13, 1841, p. 15.

[13] Sanborn, "Public Charities," p. 26.

Chapter 2: The Hospital under the Commonwealth, 1854–67

Although originally established as a hospital for the isolation of sick passengers, arriving by ship, its use drifted from that purpose to any use designated by the governing body. First the Commonwealth of Massachusetts; then the City of Boston.

The Commonwealth once again opened Rainsford Island for use as a hospital in 1854. The Commission on Alien Passengers and State Paupers, and the Office of Superintendent of Alien Passengers in the city of Boston, which had been established by Acts of 1856, had nominal oversight.[14] But the first detailed report of its activities by the City of Boston Board of Charities, cited in Chapter 1, was not published until 1865, allowing a full decade of neglect to pass virtually unchecked. The island's original purpose of taking sick passengers from incoming ships was in such decline that, according to the *Boston Post*, only two passengers—both suffering from "ship fever" (typhus)—were treated on Rainsford Island in the whole of the year 1857.[15] Despite the fact that the island appears to have been mostly neglected in this period, it was enumerated by John Hayward in 1857 as "Among the numerous charitable and humane institutions of the city": "the Quarantine Hospital [is] delightfully situated on Rainsford's Island," he wrote.[16]

A Decade of Neglect

The Board of Charities was established in 1863, at the height of the Civil War, to replace the previous oversight bodies; its officers were sworn in October of that year. Their mandate included filing an annual report on the activities of the various institutions under their control, which included "lunatic" and pauper hospitals, almshouses, reforms schools, the "Blind Asylum" and the "Idiot Asylum," and finally the mysterious "School Ship."[17] According to their mandate:

> They shall investigate and supervise the whole system of the public charitable and correctional institutions of the Commonwealth, and shall recommend such changes and additional provisions as they may deem necessary for their economical and efficient

[14] Massachusetts Acts of 1856, Chapter 294, p. 231.
[15] *Boston Post*, January 13, 1858, p. 1.
[16] John Hayward, *New England Gazetteer* (1857), p. 58.
[17] Massachusetts Acts of 1856, Chapter 294, p. 231.

administration. They shall have full power to transfer pauper inmates from one charitable institution or lunatic hospital to another, and for this purpose to grant admittances and discharges to such pauper inmates, but shall have no power to make purchases for the various institutions.[18]

The officers were not paid.

The Board looked into the statutes bearing on Rainsford Island and the deed by which it was conveyed to the Provincial authorities before the Revolution. They found that "the position of the institution was decidedly anomalous." They determined "that the Island, according to the deed, was to be used as a Hospital forever for the benefit of the people of the Province of Massachusetts Bay";[19] "that the Island, if used at all, must be used as a Hospital, and in no sense as an Almshouse or mere infirmary, though no forfeiture was attached by the deed to any violation of this provision"; and finally "that persons retained for useful services should not be reckoned or treated as paupers."[20]

With these guidelines in mind, the Board's General Agent and his assistant visited Rainsford Island on November 2, 1863: it was the first institution that they visited. Though the patients seemed well cared for, the place had "the aspect of an almshouse rather than a hospital." The inspector and his scribe found the island was home to a hodgepodge of inmates, most of them foreign-born: male, female, children and adults, criminals and paupers, the syphilitic and the injured, most of whom were set to work in various capacities (see Appendix 2.1).

It appeared indeed that "during the spring and summer of [1863] nearly 40 persons had been transferred thither from the State Almshouses, and that the authorities of Boston had been requested to send thither during the same period cases of intemperance and syphilitic disease; and that this course had been taken to supply the Island with inmates, although it might be questionable whether it was a literal compliance with the law."[21] The Hospital being anxious "merely to swell its numbers," the definition of "patient" had been loosened to include anyone

---

[18] Public Document 19, First Annual Report of the [Massachusetts] Board of State Charities (January 1865) [hereafter Doc. 19 (1865)], p. iv.

[19] Doc. 19 (1865), p. xxvii.

[20] Doc. 19 (1865), p. xxix.

[21] Doc. 19 (1865), p. xxvii.

who could be compelled by dependence on government to make the move.[22] Legislators, violating the terms of the conveyance, had "authori[zed] certain classes of convicts to be committed to the Island, and permit[ed] the cities and towns to send thither their sick State paupers. . . ."[23] One of the Alien Commissioners had found, on a visit in 1858, "some twenty-five convicts, about two hundred and thirty of the vicious poor of Boston; and not one sick immigrant, or person 'ill with an infectious disease.'" The Board of Charities reported indignantly, "a greater perversion of charitable appropriations was never witnessed. Thieves, strumpets and drunkards were living by the seaside almost in luxurious ease on the bounty of the State."[24]

Many of the "nurses" caring for the indigent sick had no training whatsoever; their practical experience consisted of having been patients themselves. A number of them had syphilis:

> For instance, up to the month of April, the principal male nurse there was Manuel Cunha, Portuguese sailor, who had long been under treatment for syphilis in the hospital, and who is understood to have served without pay until that time. After April, he was a paid nurse, except when his loathsome disease made it necessary for him to be under treatment, when he was removed from the list of hired nurses and put on the sick list of patients.[25]

His place was taken by a Danish sailor, similarly infected. Among the patients were "light syphilitic and bastardy cases, which were sent here in great numbers before 1859."[26]

Many children were born on Rainsford Island in this period, the vast majority of them to foreign-born mothers. According to the 1865 report, "It was formerly charged that persons were sent and received here through favor, and that it became at one time the resort of disreputable persons seeking relief from their peculiar maladies, without expense to themselves and without much publicity. It was also said that young women were sent here by their seducers to undergo or avoid the pains of childbirth, and that a considerable part of the money expended by the State

---

[22] Doc. 19 (1865), p. xxxi.

[23] Public Document 17, Third Annual Report of State Charities of Massachusetts to which are added the Reports of the Secretary, and the General Agent of the Board (January 1867) [hereafter Doc. 17 (1867)], p. lxxv.

[24] Doc. 17 (1867), p. lxxvi.

[25] Doc. 19 (1865), pp. 41–42.

[26] Doc. 19 (1865), p. 18.

went to provide for such cases." (We read this as alleging that abortions were being performed at Rainsford.) "[T]here is constant danger," the report continued, "that an institution so little visited as this Hospital has been of late years, should be sought by the vicious as a place of concealment.[27]

The Board of Charities demanded "That no more paupers be sent to Rainsford Island, except by consent of the Executive Committee, or some member thereof; to the end that the intent of Chapter seventy-first, Sections twenty-nine and thirty of the General Statutes may be carried out."[28] The island's patient population was expected to drop as a result, and so it did.

Who were Rainsford's "patients" in this period, and how had they ended up there? Frances Hall was 33 years old when she died at Rainsford Island on January 17, 1864. We know some details of her case only because it came out in the press. A lurid story appeared in the *Boston Post* on January 25 under the headline "Death From Abortion":

> A woman named Sarah A. Caswell, alias Sarah A. Watkins, was arrested on Saturday for having performed operations upon one Frances Hall, for the purpose of procuring abortion, from the effects of which she died on the 17th inst. The deceased came to this city from Woodstock, N.B., about three months since, and engaged at housework for Mrs. R. D. Hill, No. 252 Hanover street [sic], She was soon found by Mrs. Hill, to be *enceinte* [pregnant]; and in endeavoring to cover her shame sought the surgical and other services of Mrs. Caswell, at 94 Leverett street [sic], These resulted in a dangerous local inflamation [sic], when she was removed to the Hospital at Rainsford Island where she died. Dr Moore held an inquest on the body, elicited substantially the foregoing facts, and the jury returned a verdict accordingly. The case is not unlike others that occur with more frequency than the public knows of. An examination of the accused will be made in the Police Court to-day.

The timing of this tragedy—in mid-January—presents the terrible picture of Frances Hall, age 33, new to town and friendless, being ferried across to Rainsford Island in the freezing cold to die in agony.

Mrs. Caswell won the day, however; the Grand Jury failed to indict.[29]

---

[27] Doc. 19 (1865), pp. 43–44.

[28] Doc. 19 (1865), xxix.

[29] Death From Abortion," *Boston Post*, Jan 25, 1864; "The Abortion Case," *Boston Post*, Feb 11, 1864.

Soldiers at Rainsford

Toward the end of the Civil War, a new category of patients began to arrive at the island, namely ailing soldiers. Although ostensibly for the benefit of those military men, less noble motives may have been at work. The Annual Report of the Board of State Charities expressed shock at the dumping of soldiers onto the state dole, and the lack of bureaucratic transparency as to how the men got there:

> [I]t may be a matter of surprise that the Inspectors who speak of 'the charity of the public' as an improper support for disabled soldiers, should have taken no pains to save them from the legal consequences of being supported from the pauper appropriation made for the general purposes of the hospital at Rainsford Island. No special appropriation appears to have been asked for, although they were urged to do so by members of your Board, and although the request would probably have been granted by the Legislature. Without such an appropriation the soldiers must necessarily be supported by 'the charity of the public,' in its most repulsive form, —that is, as State paupers . . ..[30]

The author continues, "[N]o pains were taken to follow the law in respect to admission upon certificates, or for contagious and infectious disease, while, by astonishing indifference, those sent were left to become legally paupers. A like indifference was shown as to the class of persons sent. Many, who had a clear right to support from cities and towns under the Military Settlement law, were admitted and long detained there; some whose vices and habits of life made them unfit persons were sent, and, concerning all, no proper records appear to have been kept."[31]

Under Chapter 40 of the Resolves of 1862, the Governor of Massachusetts could send ailing soldiers to any of the State Institutions. Another law passed in 1864 (Chapter 170 of the Acts of 1864, effective April 25 of that year) states: "Soldiers enlisted in the army of the United States, who, while in the Commonwealth, may be sick with any contagious or infectious disease, and needing hospital treatment, may be admitted to Rainsford Island Hospital, upon the certificate of the governor."[32]

---

[30] Third Annual Report of the [Massachusetts] Board of Charities, Public Document No. 17 (Boston: Wright & Potter, 1866) [hereafter Doc. 17 (1866)], pp. 143–44.

[31] Doc. 17 (1866), p. 144.

[32] Doc. 17 (1866), p. 141.

Military barracks were built on the island, which "furnished comfortable quarters for some sixty soldiers who have required hospital treatment," according to the self-flattering Inspector's Report from Rainsford in 1865.[33] A year later, the Inspector's Report reiterated the fine conditions under which soldiers were housed on Rainsford, assured the public that the soldiers got better treatment than "patients directly from the emigrant ships." He decried the Acts of 1866 that sent soldiers back to their communities' charge:

> The improvement of many of these men, from the healthful influences and climate, with little medical treatment, was marked. The rations furnished to these wounded patriots were better than those provided for the ordinary inmates of the hospital. . .. The food of all has been wholesome, well cooked, and sufficient; but certain articles, by the order of the Surgeon-General, were allowed the soldiers, which are not usually found on the diet list of pauper hospitals. This has somewhat increased expenses. . .. [The soldier patients] were removed from the hospital in June. The question of the wisdom of this removal is with those who caused it. By force of chapter 288 of Acts of 1866, they were sent to towns and cities, on whose quotas they had been credited. . .. The result was that many of them were thrown upon the charity of the public. We have seen faces, which had been familiar, every day growing brighter with returning health and healing, piteously asking alms in the crowded streets.[34]

Had there been an urgent need to send overflow soldiers to Rainsford, with appropriate vetting, the Inspector's protestations would have had merit. Instead, new regulations had been exploited to boost the numbers of patients on the island and bring in those extra provisions (possibly alcohol) "by order of the Surgeon General."

The Board of Charities Report flatly contradicted the Inspector's statement:

> It will at once be seen that provision was here made, under proper safeguards, and with proper forethought, for the reception and treatment of disabled soldiers and seamen, no matter what their disease. But it does not appear that any effort has been made to put in force this excellent law, from which it may be inferred that no such emergency as

[33] *Public Documents of Massachusetts Being the Annual Reports of Various Officers and Institutions for the Year 1865*, Public Document No. 26, Twelfth Annual Report of the Inspectors and Superintendent of Rainsford Island Hospital, Boston Harbor (October, 1865), Document No. 28, p. 4.

[34] Annual Reports of Various Officers and Institutions for the Year 1866, Public Document No. 26, Thirteenth Annual Report of the Inspectors and Superintendent of Rainsford Island Hospital, Boston Harbor (October, 1866), pp. 4–5.

therein contemplated has ever arisen, and consequently, that the "urgent necessity" spoken of by the Inspectors of the Rainsford Island Hospital, was only a necessity for additional patients there.[35]

The Board found that no pains were taken to follow the law "in respect to admission upon certificates, or for contagious and infectious disease, while, by an astonishing indifference, those sent were left to become legally paupers." Paperwork and accounting were in chaos:

> According to the statement of Dr. Underwood, most of [the soldier patients'] permits or certificates were destroyed; they were not entered on the hospital books, and the Inspectors, by the statement of one of the Board, did not know their names, or investigate their cases. . .. Such being the general state of confusion and uncertainty in regard to this class of patients, it is, perhaps, no wonder that the Inspectors were led to believe that "many" of those removed in May and June by order of the Governor, have since become beggars on the streets. But since the matter came to my notice, in the Report of the Inspectors, I have carefully investigated it, making use of the full notes of examinations - and removals taken by the General Agent, and I can find little or no proof of the vague statement above cited.[36]

Under pressure from the Board of Charities, the Governor ordered thirty-nine soldiers to be removed from Rainsford on May 19, 1866:

> Twenty-five of these were found or deemed to be cases of settlement or relief under Chapter 230 of the Acts of 1865, known as the Military Settlement Law; namely, nine belonging to Boston, three to Lynn, two to West Roxbury, and one each to Attleborough, Brewster, Georgetown, Gloucester, Marlborough, Medway, Monson, Nahant, North Bridgewater, Roxbury, Saugus and Worcester.[37]

Most became local charity cases, but some were able to work and others were resettled in the Soldiers Home. Two had died on the island.

---

[35] Doc. 17 (1866), pp. 141–43.

[36] Third Annual Report of the [Massachusetts] Board of Charities, Public Document No. 17 (Boston: Wright & Potter, 1866), pp. 144–45.

[37] Third Annual Report of the [Massachusetts] Board of Charities, Public Document No. 17 (Boston: Wright & Potter, 1866), pp. 145–46.

Irregularities at the Pauper Hospital

Record-keeping on the island was consistently slapdash, possibly to obscure traces of graft and sheer incompetence. The City of Boston profited, too, by foisting its poor cases onto the Commonwealth's books. In the spring of 1866, the Board of Charities, having taken a keen interest in affairs on the island, initiated an inquiry into "the manner of admitting patients" to Rainsford Island Hospital. "I discovered that great irregularities were taking place," the Board inspector reported:

> By law the consent of the Board of Charities is necessary before any town or city can send its patients to Rainsford, and, by a vote passed in December, 1863, the city authorities of Boston were directed to send no patients except with permits countersigned by the Executive Committee of your Board. But it appeared that between the 2d of January, 1865, and the 16th of May, 1866, out of 550 persons admitted to the Hospital, only 262 had permits bearing in any form the consent of your Board, while all the rest, or 288, had entered without any legal right to be there. These illegal admissions seemed to have gone on with the knowledge and consent of the Superintendent and Inspectors, and to have been much facilitated by the daily visits of the city steamer, the *Henry Morrison*, to the Island. These trips were made under a contract between the Inspectors and the Board of Directors of Public Institutions of Boston, by virtue of which the State paid $2,250 yearly for a service which Boston was by law required to perform at her own expense. This sum was in addition to the annual cost of maintaining the Island yacht, amounting to upwards of $2,000, so that the Transportation of about one patient daily to Rainsford Island, and of the supplies for the Hospital has cost at the rate of about $10 a day, or enough to support between thirty and forty patients at Tewksbury, the most costly of the State Almshouses.[38]

The costs scandalized the Board investigators: "During the month of November there has been but one patient on the Island, yet the monthly expenses, including the pay of officers, have been nearly $700, or at the rate of more than $8,000 a year. . . [B]y the thriftless management of this Hospital for the past three years, a sum equal to its whole excessive cost for this year has been practically thrown away."[39]

---

[38] Doc. 17 (1866), pp. 146–47.
[39] Doc. 17 (1866), p. 147.

Closure is recommended

The hospital on Rainsford was a failure, and a very expensive one. To justify its existence, and the small but steady stream of patronage jobs and profits from the resale of allocated provisions, it had to keep up its numbers. But despite bending the rules to bring in extra patients, those in charge could not keep the beds filled.

"Much surprise has been expressed that Rainsford is not thronged with patients," the Board of Charities states in the first of its critical reports in 1865. It then cited the reasons therefore:

> The location of the institution.
>
> The want of proper transportation.
>
> The lack of suitable material in its vicinity, after deducting those provided for by the City Hospital and the Massachusetts General Hospital.
>
> The unwillingness of the Overseers of cities and towns to incur the expense and risk of sending thither from a distance those severely sick.
>
> The opposition of the patients and their friends to the removal.
>
> The positive inhumanity of the proceeding under such circumstances.
>
> And finally—
>
> The general decrease of State pauperism since 1861, — the whole number supported in the Almshouses and Rainsford being then 8,886 against 6,148 in 1864, a decrease of 30.8 percent.[40]

Massachusetts was prospering and there simply was no need for an expensive pauper hospital:

> To take a sick man from his bed, transport him to Boston with an attendant, and hire a boat to convey him to the Island, in the absence of the yacht, running the risks of detention, wind and weather, involves an amount of expenditure and inhumanity, which the authorities will not encounter, — especially as they are charged with cruelty in removing those really sick to the comparatively neighboring Almshouse. . . .The true and safe course is to take care of those who are ill with acute diseases in the towns where they

[40] The First Annual Report of the Board of State Charities (1865), Public Document No. 19, pp. xxxv–xxxvii.

may be, except in extraordinary cases. . . . Those suffering from contagious diseases should not be carried through the country in car and coach, scattering poison as they go.[41]

From 1865 to 1867, the Board of State Charities continued to grumble about the inconvenience and expense of caring for a small number of patients on a remote island: "There was no need to carry patients seven miles seaward, when they could be supported more comfortably and cheaply among their friends at home, or to maintain a great establishment for the few that were homeless . . . ."[42]

After expending over $330,000 over the course of a decade, the Commonwealth closed the hospital on December 31, 1866. The remaining patients were relocated to the state almshouses at Tewksbury, Bridgewater, and Monson. A caretaker was hired to remain on the island and look after the buildings.[43] Rainsford could be "held in reserve" in case of urgent need.

A thorough inventory of structures on the island, drawn up at a later date, gives us a good idea of how the Commonwealth's money had been spent. In addition to two wharves, Rainsford counted 7 1/2 acres of productive land, 2 1/2 acres of unproductive land, and 1 1/2 acres of cemetery. The Superintendent had a 2 1/2 story house, and his assistant a 1 1/2 story house. The two wards were segregated by sex, with the men occupying the southwest end (2 story hospital) and the women the northeast (2 story hospital with basement). There were in addition the old mansion house, a bakehouse [sic], a wharf office, a smallpox hospital, a barracks, a carpenter's shop, a dead-house, a storehouse, an ice house, a smattering of barns and sheds, a pumphouse [sic], a "stone shoe-shop," and a boathouse.[44] Thus equipped, the island went into a decade of dormancy.

---

[41] The First Annual Report of the Board of State Charities (1865), Public Document No. 19, p. xxxii.

[42] Third Annual Report of the Board of State Charities. Public Document No. 17 (1867), lxxv–lxxvii.

[43] Third Annual Report of the Board of State Charities, Public Document No. 17 (1868), p. 64.

[44] "Inspectors' of Rainsford Island Hospital, Boston Harbor, Fourteenth Annual Report, October 1867," *Public Documents of Massachusetts, Being the Annual Reports of Various Public Officers and Institutions for the Year 1867*, vol. 4, no. 27 (Boston: State Printers, 1868), pp. 5–6.

Appendix 2.1: Inmate Population as of November 2, 1863

Source: Public Document 19, First Annual Report of the [Massachusetts] Board of State Charities (January 1865), pp. xxix–xxxi.

As of November 2, 1863, inspectors from the Board of State Charities found 135 patients' resident on Rainsford Island. They were 64 males and 71 females; 128 were adults and 7 were boys. Of these, 49 were "well and able to perform more or less labor"; 22 were "feeble, of whom a portion were able to labor, somewhat," for a total of 71. Those unable to work (64 patients) included "convalescing patients and those not necessarily confined to bed" (31) and 33 sick in bed.

Those convalescing or ill were suffering from syphilis and its results (31); paralysis (8); rheumatism (3); pneumonia (2); **phthisis*** (4); and injuries and "surgical diseases" (15).

The 49 employed patients worked as washers and ironers (8); cooks and assistants (5); nurses and watchers (19); house servants (5); sewers (2); lampmen [sic] and firemen (4 each); 1 each of watchman, shoemaker, whitewasher, wood sawyer, and teamster; miscellaneous (4, "three of whom were too feeble to be of much account"), leaving 1 uncategorized.

The inspectors judged that 56 patients could safely be "at large," and that 46 "ought to be transferred to almshouses, as feeble or incompetent to labor." That left 33 sick who could not be moved.

*Phthisis is an archaic name for tuberculosis (TB). Sometimes used instead of consumption.

Appendix 2.2: Rainsford Island Statistics (May 16, 1854 – December 31, 1866)

Year	Admissions	Sentenced Persons Law	Deaths	Births	Weekly Average
1854	569		46	9	168
1855	868	99	73	44	206
1856	820	127	103	47	220
1857	713	62	64	57	250
1858	907	88	91	37	236
1859	415	Repealed	45		171
1860	809		91		169
1861	613		64		165
1862	494		70		155
1863	413		53	16	116
1864	298		67	6	88
1865	394 ([a])		74 ([b])	9 ([c])	68 ([d])
1866	318 ([a])		34 ([b])	17 ([e])	101 ([e])
Total	7,631		875	242 ([f])	

[a] Per Annual Report of the of the Board of State Charities, 1866 & 1867.

[b] Per Records of Boston Deaths.

[c] Public Documents of Massachusetts, Public Document No. 26, Twelfth Annual Report of the Inspectors and Superintendent of Rainsford Island Hospital, Boston Harbor (October 1865); Document No. 28, p. 6.

[d] Public Documents of Massachusetts, Public Document No. 19 (1865), p. 388.

[e] Public Documents of Massachusetts, Public Document No. 26, Thirteenth Annual Report of the Inspectors and Superintendent of Rainsford Island Hospital, Boston Harbor (October 1866), p. 9.

[f] The actual number of births from May 1854 to September 30, 1866 was 305: 160 males; 145 females. Public Documents of Massachusetts, Public Document No. 26, Thirteenth Annual Report of the Inspectors and Superintendent of Rainsford Island Hospital, Boston Harbor (October 1866), p. 17.

Appendix 2.3: Nativity of Admissions

Year	MA	New Eng.	All other States	Brit. Prov.	Great Britain & Ireland	Ger.	Other Countries	Unkn.	Totals
1854	72	19	12	27	381	11	47		569
1855	125	70	31	88	507	15	32		868
1856	134	73	20	64	495	11	23		820
1857	161	28	23	48	417	8	28		713
1858	156	56	39	62	553	7	34		907
1859							*	415	415
1860							*	809	809
1861							*	613	613
1862	92						*	402	494
1863	89			32	209			84	413
1864							*	298	298
1865[a]	97		75	51	137		25	395	395
1866[b]	60		52	26	138		42	318	318

*Records not kept, per The First Annual Report of the Board of State Charities (1865), Public Document No. 19, p. 43.

[a] Public Documents of Massachusetts, Public Document No. 26, Twelfth Annual Report of the Inspectors and Superintendent of Rainsford Island Hospital, Boston Harbor (October 1865); Document No. 28, p. 6.

[b] Public Documents of Massachusetts, Public Document No. 26, Thirteenth Annual Report of the Inspectors and Superintendent of Rainsford Island Hospital, Boston Harbor (October 1866), p. 9.

Appendix 2.4: Age at Death on Rainsford (May 16, 1854–December 31, 1866)

Age at Death		Men 525		Women 344
<1		34		24
1---10		17		15
11--20		39		50
21- 30		157		121
31- 40		136		66
41- 50		77		34
51- 60		39		16
61- 70		22		10
71- 80		4		7
Age- 82		0		1

Appendix 2.5: Causes of Death at Rainsford (May 16, 1854–December 31, 1866)

Cause of Death		Men 525		Women 344
Small Pox		99		34
Consumption		68		51
Phthisis		47		30
Other		39		26
Diarrhea & Dysentery		36		21
Lung Disease		21		10
Typhus		20		15
Alcoholism, Delirium Tremens		17		11
Heart Disease		16		15
Marasmus & Inanition		16		7
Paralysis		14		6
Pneumonia & Pleurisy		12		6
Syphilis		12		21
Brain Disease		11		5
Ship Fever		11		9
Cancer		9		12
Spinal Diseases		9		10
Apoplexy		8		3
Bright's & Kidney Disease		8		3
Liver Disease		8		5
Dropsy		5		10
Epilepsy		5		1
Bladder		4		1
Debility		4		2
Gastrointestinal		4		4
Gangrene		3		2
Old Age		3		0
Scrofula		3		4
Amputation		2		0
Bronchitis		2		3
Burns		2		4
Cholera		2		1
Exhaustion		1		4
Peritonitis		1		5
Stillborn		1		0
Suicide		1		0
Wounded in Battle		1		0
Criminal Abortion		0		1
Homicide		0		1
Premature birth		0		1

Appendix 2.6: Places of Birth for Deceased at Rainsford (May 16, 1854–December 31, 1866)

Place of Birth		Men 525		Women 344
Ireland		204		179
Other States		102		41
Canada		44		29
Boston		31		32
England		30		15
Rainsford Island		27		18
Other MA Towns		19		14
Not Noted		13		5
Sweden		12		0
Scotland		9		3
Germany		8		4
Azores		8		1
France		3		1
Italy		3		1
Cape Verde		2		0
Spain		2		0
Norway		2		0
Haiti		1		0
Chile		1		0
Antiqua		1		0
Belgium		1		0
Deer Island		1		0
Netherlands		1		0
House of Ind.-5 mos.		0		1

Appendix 2.7: Deaths of African-Americans on Rainsford (1854-1866)

Age at Death		Men 35		Women 11
Age 10		0		1
11 - 20		8		1
21- 30		10		5
31- 40		7		0
41- 50		5		4
51- 60		5		0

Chapter 3: The Men's Era, 1872–89

An Empty Island

The passage of the Sick Law of 1865 by the Massachusetts State Legislature led to the closure of Rainsford Island at the end of 1866. The purpose of the law, as later reported, was to move the Commonwealth "in the direction of allowing or requiring the towns to do more for the relief of the class now considered state paupers." The "sick poor" were to be examined by a doctor and sent either to local medical treatment or to the local almshouse—in any case removing them from the responsibility of the Commonwealth.[45] How this change affected the cities and towns was of little concern to the State House.[46]

Apparently, the Governor was pleased: expenditures for Rainsford dropped from $25,000 per annum to about $1,500. With no patients on the island, expenses stayed low in the following years—in the range of $2–3,000 per year—with just $1,000 paid to the caretaker who lived on the island, a few hundred for inspectors, and miscellaneous sums for repairs to the extant structures.[47]

By 1869, the Commonwealth determined to rid itself of a useless island. A Resolve was passed on April 27, 1869, permitting the Governor to put Rainsford up for sale "and pay the proceeds of the sale into the state treasury." The yacht *Thatcher* was to be sold as well, and anything else of value was to be distributed to charitable institutions on shore.[48]

Nothing much happened for the next year and a half. The caretaker remained on the island with his family, earning his modest salary. Finally, in 1871, Boston stirred:

> Rainsford Island with the buildings thereon was, under authority given to the Executive by Resolve 39 of 1869, sold at public auction on October 7, 1871. The City of Boston was the purchaser, paying $40,000.[49]

The care of its sick poor had been foisted upon the City of Boston by the changes in state law. It is perhaps not surprising that with the peak immigration years coming on, the city should

[45] Seventh Annual Report of the Board of State Charities, Public Document No. 17 (1871), pp. lxxii–lxxiii.
[46] Fourth Annual Report of the Board of State Charities, Public Document No. 17 (1868), p. 86.
[47] Fifth Annual Report of the Board of State Charities, Public Document No. 17 (1869), p. 128.
[48] Sixth Annual Report of the Board of State Charities, Public Document No. 17 (1870), p. xxiv.
[49] Eighth Annual Report of the Board of State Charities, Public Document No. 17 (1872), p. 142.

have looked around desperately for a place to put its indigent patients. A new chapter in the use and abuse of Rainsford Island began.

A City in Crisis

Between 1860 and 1870, Boston's population rose from 177,840 to 250,526, an increase of almost 40 percent. Growth in the following decade was even stronger: by 1880, the population had reached 362,839—a 44 percent increase over a decade. This dramatic growth was in part due to the annexation of formerly independent cities such as Roxbury (1868), Dorchester (1870), Roslindale (1873), and later Brighton and Charlestown (1874). In addition, Boston's frantic program of drainage and filling in the decade after the Civil War added tens of thousands of acres of land, which was then opened to development. But the population growth also reflected the influx of European immigrants, primarily from Ireland. (The Italians would arrive in the 1880s.)

The city fathers, mostly the descendants of Puritan stock, were faced with the problem of housing, feeding, and nursing the newcomers, most of whom were very poor, while trying to hold on to political power. It did not always go well. The middle-class moved out of marginal neighborhoods such as the North End and Fort Hill, and the poor moved in. As immigrant historian Oscar Handlin wrote, "enterprising land-owners utilized unremunerative [sic] yards, gardens, and courts to yield the maximum number of hovels that might pass as homes. . .. Every vacant spot, behind, beside, or within an old structure, yielded room for still another."[50] In the crowded conditions of these repurposed neighborhoods, tuberculosis was nearly universal, and epidemics of smallpox, infantile cholera, and influenza found fertile ground for propagation.

By the 1870s, the system of caring for the poor was in crisis. The acquisition of Rainsford Island offered the potential for extra bed space to take the spill-over from other pauper warehouses, such as Deer Island and Long Island. In 1873, a City report recalled:

> In 1870, the inmates of the several institutions at Deer Island numbered 1,004. . .. In his report for 1870 the Superintendent stated that the almshouse department, the hospitals, and the dormitories, were crowded to such an extent as to interfere seriously with the health and comfort of the inmates.

---

[50] Oscar Handlin, *Boston's Immigrants* (Cambridge, MA: Harvard/Belknap, 1941; rev. ed. 1991), p. 105.

The superintendent's plea for a new almshouse and funds to improve the existing ones fell on deaf ears. And so it went, year after year, as Rainsford Island took in more and more inmates.[51]

Our information about Rainsford in the men's era comes almost entirely from the annual reports on public institutions published among the official documents of the City of Boston. Journalists never, as far as we can determine, ventured out to the island to see what was going on. The City reports do express several points of view. The Superintendent (not necessarily domiciled on the island) defends his institution while pleading for more money. The resident physician sometimes reports, blaming the high mortality of the residents on their poverty, chronic illnesses, and moral turpitude, while also pleading for more money. The City inspectors from the Board of Public Institutions weigh in and their reports are usually the most candid. The State Board of Charities occasionally looks in as well. All these reports are long on generalities and short on specifics and anecdotes that might help us get a more nuanced picture of life on the island.

The Men's Era

The patient population at Rainsford was no longer as general as before. Women and children were housed at other institutions, and only "adult pauper males" were admitted to Rainsford, though a number of women "inmates" were employed there.[52]

The annual City reports document the increasing population and a gradually rising death rate as well. After noting overcrowding at the other institutions for the poor, the charities report for 1875–76 states:

> The same difficulty has been experienced at Rainsford Island. At one time, during the winter, 282 inmates were literally packed into the same space that was crowded the year before with 242 inmates. The largest number at one time at Rainsford Island was

[51] Documents of the City of Boston for the Year 1873, Vol. 4, City Document No. 108, Reports of Committee on Public Institutions on a Site for Home for the Poor, pp. 3–4.

[52] Documents of the City of Boston for the Year 1876, Vol 3, City Document No. 77, Report of the Committee of Prisons, p. 8.

296, but of these fourteen were provided with bunks in the attic of the bakery previously unoccupied.[53]

The complaints were reiterated the next year, with greater urgency:

> At Rainsford Island the buildings have been crowded far beyond their comfortable capacity. It is recommended that the southerly wing of the brick building be extended to give us more dining-room and dormitory accommodations, and also a chapel. At present there is no chapel. The dining room is so small that the tables have to be set three times for each meal.[54]

Finally, in 1877 funds were allocated for building on Rainsford, and the charities report took on a more optimistic tone:

> This difficulty [overcrowding] will, however, in a great measure, be obviated by the erection of an extension to the south wing, whereby a dining-room, chapel and dormitories will be obtained. The City Council have appropriated the sum of $16,000 for this purpose, and the work of building will be commenced immediately.[55]

A new boat-house and a wooden annex to the main building were built in 1876, and in 1877 a new barn and a coal shed were added.[56] One bright spot was that chapel services could now be held in the dining room:

> We are indebted to Dr. Wallace, Port Physician, for the frequent use of the Quarantine Steamer, "Samuel Little," in carrying the Chaplain and inmates of the pauper girls' and girls' reform schools to Rainsford Island for chapel services, which have been held in the dining-room of the main brick building, - a room not large enough to accommodate one-half of all the inmates, but the best that could be used with the present accommodations.[57]

---

[53] Documents of the City of Boston for the Year 1876, Vol 3, City Document No. 73, Report on Almshouses, p. 3.

[54] Documents of the City of Boston for the Year 1877, Vol. 2, City Document No. 49, Report on Public Institutions, pp. 25–26.

[55] Documents of the City of Boston for the Year 1877, Vol. 2, City Document No. 49, Report on Public Institutions, p. 18.

[56] Documents of the City of Boston for the Year 1878, Vol. 2, City Document No. 53, Report on Public Institutions, p. 23.

[57] Documents of the City of Boston for the Year 1877, Vol. 2, City Document No. 49, Report on Public Institutions, pp. 25–26.

It had been hoped that the crowding would abate with the new construction. Instead, more men than ever were assigned to the island: "Three hundred and twelve adult male paupers were . . . crowded into quarters none too ample for two hundred and twenty-five," it was reported in 1877.

The population pressure was just one of many problems that plagued Rainsford. Another was water. Other than rain, there is no source of fresh water on the island, for drinking, washing, or laundering, all attempts at digging wells having met with failure. In times past, a steam water-boat had plied the harbor multiple times a day, at great expense, to provide drinking water. As of 1877, a two-inch pipe was laid between the steamboat wharf and a system of cisterns on the island, so that adequate water could inexpensively be pumped into them.[58]

Putting the Men to Work

The men were required to work if they were able, and the island administration fretted about how to "provide labor"—that is, assign work—for the large number of men under its care. The Rainsford inmates were used, among other things, to prepare the Austin Farm in West Roxbury for "the reception of the adult female paupers who have heretofore been domiciled at Deer Island," and later to tend the fields there.[59] The farm products sold were added to the profits column in subsequent years.[60]

In 1878, stone yard labor began on the island.[61] Those who were not disabled by illness were now required to spend their days breaking rocks: "A shed for stone-cutting purposes has been erected here, and 16 men are now employed in this work."[62] Sale of the paving blocks, edge-stone, and catch-basins that the men hammered out, and the leased labor of prisoners, netted the City $10,755.20 in 1879.[63]

---

[58] Documents of the City of Boston for the Year 1877, Vol. 2, City Document No. 49, Report on Public Institutions, pp. 25–26. Documents of the City of Boston for the Year 1879, Vol 2, City Document No. 66, p 7.

[59] Documents of the City of Boston for the Year 1877, Vol. 2, City Document No. 49, Report on Public Institutions, p. 20.

[60] Documents of the City of Boston for the Year 1880, Vol. 2, City Document No. 66, Report on Public Institutions, p 69.

[61] Documents of the City of Boston for the Year 1878, Vol. 1, City Document No. 36, Report on Treatment of the Poor, p. 21.

[62] Documents of the City of Boston for the Year 1878, Vol 2, City Document No. 53, Report on Public Institutions, p. 23.

[63] Documents of the City of Boston for the Year 1879, Vol. 2, City Document No. 66, p. 15.

The introduction of stone-labor had an immediate impact on the numbers of paupers on the island. The Superintendent of Deer and Rainsford Islands fairly gloated over this development:

> Stone-cutting was introduced there a year ago. It is a kind of labor not eagerly sought after by the able-bodied pauper, hence the decreased numbers. Some of the regular winter inmates have taken care of themselves outside of an institution, others have availed themselves of the benefits of "U. S. Soldiers' Homes" to which they were entitled. It is safe to state that in consequence of having stone-cutting for able-bodied paupers to labor at, there has been an average of seventy-five less inmates during the past winter, than would have been, had there been no regular employment. Those who have left and have been kept away in consequence of being put to regular work, are not the deserving poor, but men who are lazy, shiftless and determined to have a living without labor.[64]

Though the total number of paupers on the island may have dropped, the death rate jumped dramatically in the year stone-breaking was introduced. In 1877, there were 25 deaths among 239 men (10.4%); in 1878, with 240 men, there were 45 deaths (18.6%). By the following year, the numbers were back down at the earlier level. Perhaps tubercular men realized that stone-breaking was a death sentence and stayed away from the island, taking their chances on land.[65]

A patronizing, Anglocentric tone is clearly legible in the City reports, which discuss the poor in moralistic and contemptuous language. The 1879 report outdoes its predecessors in this respect, as Chairman Thomas C. Amory opines:

> Large cities attract tramps, who would live upon other men, and also the honest and enterprising seeking employment. . .. Without means, and not all of them scrupulous, they prey upon the industrious and unwary, a danger and a detriment, and whether they obtain work or charity, it is a disadvantage to those better entitled — *our own resident poor*. . .. Itinerancy, degenerating into vagabondage, endangering property and menacing the unprotected, proved as objectionable in country villages as in larger places. Some of

---

[64] Documents of the City of Boston for the Year 1879, Vol. 2, City Document No. 66, p. 39.

[65] Documents of the City of Boston for the Year 1879, Vol. 2, City Document No. 66, pp. 48, 65.

the States adopted repressive measures almost as stern as those of the Tudors after the Reformation, when the dissolution of the monasteries inundated *our motherland* with mendicants. (Emphasis added.)[66]

A later City report expresses regret that more of the paupers are not working in the stone shed:

There is always a large number of inmates physically incompetent to perform hard labor, who would be far better off if some light kind of work was introduced. This class now have nothing to do but idle their time away, and no matter how well they are cared for, and kindly treated, many of such are continually inventing excuses for fault finding and grumbling.[67]

The City's 1885 report refers to the "Loafer's Hall" at Rainsford as much improved by rebuilding and enlargement.[68]

In 1887, the management established a shoe-shop at Rainsford, employing a few more inmates and avoiding the expense of shipping worn shoes off-island for repair. [69]

The men were not entirely without diversion. According to the 1884 City Report:

At Rainsford Island three entertainments have been given: the first by Prof. Ryerson, and Mr. Felch; the second by the McCullough Dramatic Club; and the third by Messrs. Bascombe, Kiernan, and O'Brien, and Misses Parker and Simonton. For the last two entertainments we are indebted to Mr. Bascombe, through whose influence and exertion the gentlemen and ladies were induced to favor us. All of the performances were very much enjoyed by those who were privileged to hear and see.[70]

---

[66] Documents of the City of Boston for the Year 1879, Vol. 2, City Document No. 73, p. 12.

[67] Documents of the City of Boston for the Year 1882, Vol. 1, City Document No. 66, Report on Public Institutions, pp. 47–48.

[68] Documents of the City of Boston for the Year 1885, Vol 2, City Document No. 63, Report on Public Institutions, p. 40.

[69] Documents of the City of Boston for the Year 1887, Vol 1, City Document No. 13, Report on Public Institutions, p. 40.

[70] Documents of the City of Boston for the Year 1884, Vol 2, City Document No. 70, Report on Public Institutions, p. 44.

Overcrowded Once More

By 1885, even the threat of rock-breaking was not enough to deter the poor from seeking shelter on Rainsford Island. As of May 1, that year, there were 263 men in care on the island, but at year's end there were 375.[71] A note of alarm begins to appear in the annual reports:

> The capacity of Rainsford Island as an almshouse for adult males has been tested this year as never before. Nearly one hundred more men than were ever previously reported have found a home there, and the wards have been so much overcrowded that the chapel has been used as a dormitory during the winter. If, in the consolidation of the almshouses at Long Island, this island shall continue to be used for its present purpose, additional accommodations will be required.[72]

The hospital building had seen a number of improvements, including flush toilets to replace the old "earth-closets" and hot water on tap.[73] But hospital space sufficient for forty patients had somehow to be made to accommodate twice that number. The hospital building, now more than forty years old and showing its age, was in desperate need of enlargement or replacement, neither of which the City would fund. J. H. O'Neil, President of the Board of Directors for Public Institutions, did not hesitate to call the whole island "an eyesore" and "no credit to Boston."[74]

Yet more men kept coming. The end of December 1887 found 419 men in residence, a 12 percent increase from the year before.[75] The resident physician on Deer Island, E. M. Schwab, who also oversaw the care at Rainsford, pleaded for relief:

> It may seem unnecessary to again refer to the condition of the hospital at Rainsford Island, this being a subject of annual comment in the reports of your medical officers for these many years past. I desire, however, to respectfully urge the advisability of taking some step for the IMMEDIATE relief of the crowded condition existing here. During the

[71] Documents of the City of Boston for the Year 1885, Vol 2, City Document No. 63, Report on Public Institutions, p. 43; Documents of the City of Boston for the Year 1886, Vol 1, City Document No. 16, 29th Annual Report on Public Institutions, pp. 32–33.

[72] Documents of the City of Boston for the Year 1885, Vol. 2, City Document No. 63, Report on Public Institutions, p. 32.

[73] Documents of the City of Boston for the Year 1885, Vol. 2, City Document No. 63, Report on Public Institutions, p. 74.

[74] Documents of the City of Boston for the Year 1886, Vol. 1, City Document No. 9, Report on Public Institutions, p. 31.

[75] Documents of the City of Boston for the Year 1886, Vol. 1, City Document No. 9, Report on Public Institutions, p. 41.

winter months, which are now upon us, the usual increase in the number of acute cases will occur, and their chances of recovery will be materially affected by the crowding to which they will be subjected.[76]

The roof was leaking when loaded with snow and the building was "fast becoming absolutely uninhabitable."[77]

Nonetheless, the population rose remorselessly. At the end of 1888, there were 489 men on the island—double the number housed a decade before.[78] The next year it was up to 537: "The institution building is filled to its capacity, and the chapel is used at times for dormitory purposes," the reporter complained.[79] A telephone to communicate with the shore was begged for: "Occasions are frequent when time and expense could be saved this department, and friends of inmates who may be ill, if telephonic connection existed, and the Board will again request the City Council to appropriate money for this purpose."[80]

With the higher population came an increase in the number of deaths. Despite some repairs in 1888 to the attic, "so much dreaded by the men as a sleeping-room," the number of those "discharged by death" at Rainsford Island rose to 67: "Never before has there been such a large number of inmates on that island, and never before have we felt such a want of room and proper accommodations for the sick."[81]

The Swap

The year 1889 closed out the men's era at Rainsford: "male paupers were transferred from Rainsford to Long Island, and the female paupers from Long Island to Rainsford on November 7th." Long Island, it was observed, comprised 200 acres of mostly arable land, whereas Rainsford was a mere 11 "barren and rocky" acres. One acre was taken up by the cemetery which, as always, was located next to the 1832 hospital building. The men could more

---

[76] Documents of the City of Boston for the Year 1886, Vol 1, City Document No. 9, Report on Public Institutions, p. 72.

[77] Documents of the City of Boston for the Year 1887, Vol 1, City Document No. 13, Report on Public Institutions, pp. 174–75.

[78] Documents of the City of Boston for the Year 1888, Vol 1, Appendix, p. 67.

[79] Documents of the City of Boston for the Year 1888, Vol 1, City Document No. 17, Report on Public Institutions, pp. 33–34 [hereafter Doc. 17 (1888)].

[80] Doc. 17 (1888), pp. 35–36.

[81] Doc. 17 (1888), pp. 171–72.

profitably be put to work on Long Island than they could on Rainsford. A “considerable” number of repairs were undertaken “for the reception of the females . . . principally for new plumbing, steam-heating apparatus, and for the renovation of the hospital building, as well as for new drains.”[82] But evidently it was considered worth the expense: “A large proportion of the male paupers are able to perform more or less work upon the land, and it is the intention of the Board to utilize their labor, both for economic reasons and as a discouragement to idleness.”[83]

The gender of the inmates on Rainsford changed, but the overcrowding and deterioration of conditions did not, as we will see in the following chapter. At the end of 1889, 461 females were counted on Rainsford Island; between their arrival on November 7 and the end of the year, no fewer than 14 had already been “discharged by death.”[84]

Appendix 3.1: Age at Death, Men’s Era (December 9, 1872–November 7, 1889)

Age at Death		Men 771
< 1		2
age 1		1
11--20		16
21--30		74
31--40		117
41--50		105
51--60		130
61--70		170
71--80		122
81--90		28
91 - 97		5

[82] Documents of the City of Boston for the Year 1889, Vol. 1, Appendix, pp. 77–78.

[83] Documents of the City of Boston for the Year 1889, Vol I, City Document No.25, Report on Public Institutions, pgs. 34–35.

[84] Documents of the City of Boston for the Year 1889, Vol. I, City Document No. 25, Report on Public Institutions, pp. 144–45.

Appendix 3.2: Place of Birth, Men's Era (December 9, 1872–November 7, 1889)

Place of Birth		Men 771
Ireland		291
Boston		231
Other States		122
Other MA Towns		44
Canada		19
England		14
Germany		14
Scotland		10
Not Noted		5
Cape Verde		2
Italy		2
Sweden		2
Wales		2
Long Island Hospital		2
Bermuda		1
Austria		1
Azores		1
China		1
Deer Island		1
East Indies		1
France		1
Isle of Malta		1
Russia		1
Norway		1
Spain		1

Appendix 3.3: Cause of Death, Men's Era (December 9, 1872–November 7, 1889)

Cause of Death		Men 771
Phthisis		171
Heart Disease		79
Bronchitis		43
Insanity & Senility		42
Pneumonia & Pleurisy		40
Old Age		38
Other		35
Paralysis		35
Debility		34
Bright's & Kidney Disease		26
Diarrhea & Dysentery		26
Rheumatism		22
Alcoholism, Intemperance, Delirium Tremens		20
Consumption		18
Brain Disease		16
Dementia		14
Epilepsy		14
Syphilis		13
Tuberculosis		12
Cancer		10
Gastrointestinal		10
Apoplexy		8
Liver Disease		8
Asthma		7
Bladder		6
Diabetes		3
Spinal Diseases		3
Typhus		3
Cholera		2
Drowning		2
Exhaustion		2
Gangrene		2
Scrofula		2
Suicide		2
Dropsy		1
Marasmus & Inanition		1
Peritonitis		1

Chapter 4: The Women's Era, 1889–95

Mr. Chairman, I am here in the interest of humanity, and I hope I may be heard.

Alice North Towne Lincoln[85]

The State Board of Lunacy and Charity of Massachusetts took a skeptical view of Boston's plan to place the women on Rainsford and the men on Long Island. There was some effort to improve the facilities at Rainsford to receive the women and children— "the bath rooms and closets in almshouse are in much better condition than has been case previously"— but "The buildings on Rainsford Island are in rather poor repair, the hospital being especially so."[86]

Citizen oversight of the pauper islands, such as it was, changed at this juncture as well. The new supervisors of public welfare were the Commissioners of Public Institutions for the City of Boston, and they were not uncritical of condition on Rainsford. They wrote in their first annual report:

> Although the hospital has been thoroughly renovated, there still remains the fact that it is entirely inadequate to the demands upon it. In previous annual reports I have made earnest appeals to remedy existing conditions, and have shown the necessity of a new hospital. It is remarkable that a building which was a small-pox hospital fifty-seven years ago, and which since then has undergone no material improvement, should up to the present time be the only hospital connected with our pauper institutions.[87]

Dr. Thomas L. Jenks, Chairman of the Commissioners of Public Institutions, approved of the exchange of women for men, however. He told the *Boston Globe*:

> We have about 200 acres of land at Long [Island] and can there employ the paupers who are able to work at weeding and on the farm. Rainsford Island is substantially a ledge, and gives nothing for them to do. Under the old system men were at

[85] Documents of the City of Boston for the Year 1894, vol. 4, Document 211 (1895) [hereafter Doc. 211 (1895)], p. 5.

[86] Eleventh Annual Report of the State Board of Lunacy and Charity of Massachusetts, January 1890, Public Document No. 17, p. 67.

[87] Documents of the City of Boston for the Year 1894, Document 25, Report on Public Institutions, p. 159.

Rainsford Island, where there nothing for them to do, but now they are at Long Island we can use all of them who are able to work.[88]

Dr. Jenks was very used to having his way in all matters regarding the management of public institutions.

The Birth of an Activist

It is at this juncture, when the women paupers had been moved into the dilapidated hospital building at Rainsford Island that we first hear from Alice Towne Lincoln. Because she plays a vital role in the next decade of the island's history, it is worth finding out who she was.

Alice North Towne was born in Philadelphia into a family with deep roots in New England. Her aunt Ann (Sophia) Towne Darrah (1819–1881) was a successful painter of New England landscapes, and perhaps provided Alice with a local foothold when she moved to Boston as a young woman. Early on, Alice's interests were directed toward social welfare and she attended "the School for Social Workers," an institution we have not succeeded in identifying with any certainty.[89] She married Roland Crocker Lincoln (1843–1926), an attorney, in 1880 and lived with him at 269 Beacon Street in the Back Bay of Boston and later at "Stoneleigh" in Jamaica Plain.[90] They also maintained a summer house in Manchester-by-the-Sea. They had no children, and as Alice's husband died within a month of her, no one was left to write her very interesting life story.

She began her career as a manager for the New England Hospital for Children, and later for the Burnap Free Home for Aged Women, which was founded in 1878 for "aged, friendless, and indigent women."[91] She became a director of the Boston Co-operative Building Co., which was incorporated in 1871 to "hold and improve real estate in said city (Boston), as homes for

---

[88] Boston Globe, December 8, 1889, p. 6.

[89] S.v. "LINCOLN Alice North," *Who's Who in New England*, ed. Albert Nelson Marquis, 2nd ed. (Chicago: A. N. Marquis & Co.), 1916.

[90] "On July 10, 1890, 269 Beacon was purchased from George Cotton by Roland Crocker Lincoln, He and his wife, Alice North (Towne) Lincoln, made it their home. They previously had lived in Manchester, where they continued to maintain a home. Roland Lincoln was an attorney in Boston. Alice Lincoln was active in public welfare issues, and served as manager of the New England Hospital for Women and Children and of the Burnap Free Home for the Aged. On November 23, 1898, he transferred the property into his wife's name. They continued to live at 269 Beacon during the 1907-1908 winter season, but moved thereafter to Jamaica Plain." https://backbayhouses.org/269-beacon/

[91] "Benevolent Institutions," U.S. Bureau of the Census (Washington: USGPO, 1904), p. 234.

working people, at moderate cost."[92] One of their efforts, begun in 1879, was to rent an entire 27-unit tenement building in Boston's North End for $1,000 a month. The building was notorious for its filth and its unruly immigrant inhabitants. Her fellow crusader Rev. Louis Albert Banks (1855–1933) described it in his muck-raking book *White Slaves, Or, the Oppression of the Worthy Poor*: "Its entries and corridors were blackened with smoke, and dingy and uninviting. The sinks were in dark corners, and were foul and disease-breeding. The stairways were innocent of water and broom...."[93]

Keeping careful track of expenditures and rental income, however, the partners demonstrated that a vigilant landlord could still make a profit while improving sanitation, fixing peeling paint and plumbing, and treating tenants like sentient human beings. The building became known as "Good Luck House," every room of which was filled. She reported her findings at a general conference of the Associated Charities of Boston on November 23, 1883.[94] Of this project she later wrote: "We did not attempt too much at once. We expected to improve the character of the inmates as we did that of the house, gradually. It has been my experience that tenants of this class often need only the stimulus which interest and sympathy give to enable them to do better."[95]

Animals as well as humans received the benefit of Alice Lincoln's philanthropy. She established a medal for valor given annually by the Animal Rescue League, for people who risked their lives to save animals.[96] It was in a sense the repayment of a debt: in 1909, her home caught fire, and the alarm given by her dog Dixie saved the lives of Alice, Roland, and their four servants.[97]

Lincoln also helped to spearhead a vital act of historic preservation when the Park Street Church (now St. Paul's Church), built in 1809, was sold to a developer and slated for demolition. Lincoln was one of 18 outraged Boston citizens who demanded the preservation of

---

[92] http://beatleyweb.simmons.edu/collectionguides/CharitiesCollection/CC022.html

[93] Rev. Louis Albert Banks, D. D., *White Slaves, Or, The Oppression of the Worthy Poor* (Boston: Lee and Shepard Publishers, 1892), 204.

[94] Alice North Lincoln, "Three Years' Experience in Managing a Tenement-House," Century Illustrated Monthly Magazine, vol. 28 (1883), pp. 145–47.

[95] Marcus T. Reynolds, "The Housing of the Poor in American Cities," *Publications of the American Economic Association*, Vol. 8, nos. 2–3 (1893), pp. 65–66.

[96] Boston Globe, February 4, 1942, p. 7.

[97] Boston Globe, March 11, 1909, p. 10.

this landmark church, from whose pulpit William Lloyd Garrison had spoken out against slavery in 1829; they raised hundreds of thousands of dollars and saved the church.

Lincoln implemented kindness in her personal life as well. She and her husband, having no children of their own, "adopted" a fatherless girl named Mary Ellen Kay. Later known as Edith K. Lincoln, she became the Lincolns' principal heir.[98] Edith Lincoln went to China in 1910 to work as a secretary to the bishop in the Episcopal Mission at Hankow, and remained there for many years.[99]

Alice Lincoln was an early and zealous proponent of cremation at a time when it was illegal in most states and looked upon with horror by most Americans. In 1893, she addressed the New England Cremation Society, describing a cremation she had witnessed: "We stood in silence, watching the rosy glow which played over the white surface of the retort, a feeling came over us of awe, certainly, but also of peace and rest. There was something so spiritual, so elevating, in the absolute purity of the intense heat that it seems to all of us who stood there far less appalling than the blackness of the open grave. . . ."[100]

Interviewed by the Boston *Sunday Post* in 1903, Lincoln was asked about her home life: "'I really have none,' she said. 'I am quite busy—so busy that I could hardly enumerate the details of my daily life, and I have no social life.'"[101] Many Bostonians had reason to be grateful that she didn't.

---

[98] Birth records for the City of Boston (May 4, 1885) list Mary Ellen Kay, with father unknown, mother Alma of unknown address, a native of New Brunswick. Alma Kay later married Christian P. Christiansen, a piano-maker of Boston, in 1888 (Boston Marriage Record, December 19, 1888). The Lincolns' wills: Mass Trial Court Record Centers, File # 154605, Location NEW2, 094-004-0004-0002, Box # 153244, Essex Probate File Papers, Wills of Alice & Roland Lincoln, date November 10, 1919.

[99] *The American Church Almanac and Year Book* (New York: Edwin S. Gorham, 1915). In 1915, Edith came back to Boston for six months and returned to Hankow to work in the American Consulate. Except for a three-month visit home in late 1921, she remained in Hankow until 1924. When Alice and Roland died in early 1926, Edith was working at the American Consulate, where she was still employed in 1930.

[100] "Paper Read by Mrs. Alice N. Lincoln at the Annual Meeting of the New England Cremation Society, December 19, 1893," *Transactions of the New England Cremation Society*, no. 2 (1894), 43.

[101] "A Woman Who Helps To Rule Boston: Advice of Mrs. Alice N. Lincoln Is Sought by Men High in Power: Her Notable Achievements," *Boston Sunday Post* (July 5, 1903), p. 1.

Lincoln v. Rainsford

In the course of Lincoln's work with immigrant tenants, she had occasion to see some of them consigned to city institutions for indigents such as Rainsford and Long Islands and the notorious Austin Farm in Mattapan, when they became too poor or ill to keep themselves even in low-cost housing. In 1887, one of her tenants, Margaret Mulhearn— "a worthy and tenderhearted woman" in Lincoln's words, whose disreputable nephew stole every penny she came by—could no longer pay her rent, and Lincoln offered to take her to the Austin Farm. They went there together on August 11, and Mulhearn was taken in by a surly attendant with "not one recognition of the step that was made that day from independence to pauperism."[102] When next Lincoln saw Mulhearn, she had been sent to Long Island, the Austin Farm building having closed:

> She was very unhappy there. Her clothes had been taken by other inmates and worn before her eyes. One of my letters to her had been opened and read to the whole ward; the food was poor, the life miserable, and worst of all, she was thrown with depraved and degraded companions, with whom, naturally, she had nothing in common. She said the life was killing her, and it soon did.[103]

Mulhearn died in April 1889.

Alice recalled that event, in a speech called "Individualism in Charity" given on April 11, 1895, to the State Federation of Women's Clubs. The encounter with the Austin Farm attendant appears to have been the catalyst for her involvement at Rainsford and Long Islands. She warned her audience of a vice she called "officialism":

> I think some of us have a pretty clear idea of what that means, even though the word is not to be found in the dictionary. We are all of us in danger of falling into it, when for a time we are clothed with a little brief authority; and it should be our daily aim to remember that there are really no such things as classes in the world; that it is made up of individuals, and that its progress is largely dependent upon individual work. . .. I cannot leave the subject of officialism without begging you all to fight it wherever it may

[102] Doc. 211 (1895), pp. 12–13.
[103] Doc. 211 (1895), p. 13.

be found. It has nothing to do with law and order—*those* we all believe in. It might be described as duty performed in a perfunctory manner, and not from the highest conception of duty as the fulfilment of God's law.

> I think my first introduction to officialism was when I took an old woman to the poorhouse, and the matron, seeing two figures standing in the doorway, glanced at us carelessly, and said, "What, are there *two* of them?" Yes, there were two, one a poor unhappy woman, reduced to seek the refuge of the almshouse in her last extremity, the other a woman resolved from that day to proclaim the wrongs and abuses which such innocent sufferers as her companion are compelled to endure under the regime of indifferent officials. It is for ourselves and for our own actions that we are judged; we are not simply "two of them" here or hereafter; and we ought to be willing to accord to our fellow-beings that intelligent consideration as individuals which we claim for ourselves. In no other way can we comprehend their difficulties.[104]

In 1887, another of Lincoln's tenants, Mary Abbott, was afflicted by breast cancer and needed hospital care. Lincoln took her to Boston City Hospital, but they would not take her because she had an infant with her. Instead, she and the child were sent to Rainsford Island Hospital. Abbott soon communicated to Lincoln the miserable conditions on the island and their lethal consequences.

As Lincoln later testified:

> [Mary Abbott] complained first of having to strip in the presence of others, no screen or curtain being provided as a shelter when the bath, which is the first step in the entrance to an institution, was taken, and that during her stay of three weeks she had no towel given her and only one clean sheet was furnished her. She was expected to cook all her own food and all the food, for her baby, and to make and clean her own bed, although she was partly incapacitated by the lump in her breast, which affected one arm. . .. Her

[104] Alice N. Lincoln, "Individualism in Charity," in *Lend A Hand: A Record of Progress*, ed. Edward E. Hale, vol. 14 (1895), p. 414.

baby fell ill on a Wednesday, and she could obtain no medicine for it until Sunday, although she asked for it repeatedly, and on Monday the baby died.[105]

Lincoln came out to have a look for herself. She was horrified.

In addition to the crowding, the evidence of bedbugs, and the miserable food, Lincoln found that the patients, mostly elderly and ill, were required to get out of bed at 5:30 a.m., after which they had only hard chairs to sit on— "chairs without any rest for the head." She "thought it was a hardship for them to be obliged to sit in those chairs." The patients were not allowed to lie down during the day without permission.[106] Lincoln made her first appeals to the Commissioners of Public Institutions in 1890, citing the issue of chairs as well as woeful hygiene, food quality, and fire safety.

A *Globe* reporter, possibly alerted by Lincoln, visited Rainsford in September 1890, and called it "a disgrace to the city of Boston": "[The hospital] building would be condemned as a place to keep pigs. The rooms are small, low-studded [i.e., low-ceilinged] and as a consequence badly ventilated." In the garret, built to dry clothes but now put to use as a sick ward, "29 women were penned like a lot of cattle . . .. The flies were frightfully thick but no preventative is known."[107] Despite this bad publicity, nothing changed.

It would later become evident that the chief obstacle to progress was Dr. Jenks, the chairman of the Commissioners of Public Institutions. His work was supposed to be supported by three board members, but in practice he rarely consulted them; if he did, he bullied the elderly member, Dr. Riley, into compliance, while the other two—Mr. Prescott and Mr. LaBorde—remained powerless. The chairman was wont to speak with "much emphasis," probably a euphemism yelling and cursing.[108] Prescott later testified that as a board member "[He] soon learned that unless the chairman of the board favored a measure it was useless to bring the measure to formal vote before the board and was simply putting yourself in an

---

[105] Doc. 211 (1895), vol. 1, p. 113.

[106] Doc. 211 (1895), vol. 1, p. 106.

[107] Boston *Globe*, September 26, 1890, 13; for the dimensions and earlier uses of the hospital spaces, see Commonwealth of Massachusetts, House of Representatives, "Resolve for Defraying Expense of protecting Rainsford Island from the ravages of the Sea," of Jan. 28, 1835, p. 8.

[108] Doc. 211 (1895), vol. 2, p. 1725. The career of Dr. Jenks deserves much more scrutiny than we have space for here. In addition to being chairman of Public Institutions, he was a druggist, the director of the East Boston ferries (which were accused in 1885 of defrauding the city), and president of the North End Savings Bank.

unpleasant position as a sort of obstructionist."[109] At one point, in July 1890, Jenks replaced the physician in charge of Long and Rainsford Islands without informing, much less consulting, the members of his board. The island superintendent, Mr. Galvin, complained to Prescott of the appointed physician, a Dr. Holmes, as "being of intemperate habits, as an opium eater, and as having improper company in his room"; despite such reports, "the board didn't do anything."[110]

In August 1891, the Boston clergy renewed its attack on the system. Reverend Banks gave a blistering sermon from the pulpit of the First Methodist Episcopal Church of Boston on the city's public charitable institutions. "It is a shame and a disgrace," he wrote, "that Boston, which less than five years ago could spend more than $20,000 in feasting and wining a Hawaiian woman who visited us, spending $4000 for flowers alone, cannot afford to furnish a little butter to spread on the bread of the helpless old women on Rainsford island who are unable to work." The sermon was reprinted in the *Boston Post* on August 24, 1891.[111] A week later, in an article of five-columns in the *Boston Herald*, Banks made a mathematical comparison of what was spent on criminal inmates versus those housed as paupers. Expenditures for everything from subsistence and bedding to fuel and lighting were often twice as generous for criminals as for the dependent poor. The *Herald* concluded, "the criticisms which have been made public do not give an adequate idea of the disgraceful condition in which the institutions are at present, nor the treatment which the paupers receive and under which they exist rather than live."[112]

The Rev. Frederick B. Allen endorsed Banks's recommendation that the advisory boards of charities start including "three or four level-headed and humane women, [who] would work the revolution that is needed in the treatment of 'our brothers and sisters, the Boston paupers.'"[113] Despite the cry from press and clergy, conditions on Rainsford and Long Islands

---

[109] Doc. 211 (1895), vol. 2, p. 1731.

[110] Doc. 211 (1895), vol. 2, p. 1736. We believe this doctor to be William Dennison Holmes (1860–1903), a Harvard Medical School graduate who died at the River Crest Sanitorium on Long Island of "acute nephritis" at age 42. See "Return of a Death" report, Commonwealth of Massachusetts, filed May 22, 1903. River Crest was for "the treatment of drug and alcohol habitués": Henry M. Hurd et al., *The Institutional Care of the Insane in the United States and Canada*, vol. 3 (Baltimore: Johns Hopkins University Press, 1916), p. 276.

[111] "Four Thousand Paupers: Our Brothers and Sisters; The Boston Paupers, Says Dr. Banks: He Criticizes the System on Managing Public Charitable Institutions," *Boston Post* (August 24, 1891), p. 8.

[112] Boston Sunday Herald (August 30, 1891), reprinted as "The Gold Gods of Society" in Banks, *White Slaves*, p. 291.

[113] Boston Herald (August 31, 1891), reprinted in Banks, *White Slaves*, p. 301.

did not improve in 1891 and 1892. The women were not even afforded better chairs, much less cleaner bedding or decent food.

In early 1893, a tragedy took place in Dover, N.H., that galvanized the Boston reformers. There an old, overcrowded insane asylum burned during a snowstorm, killing 41 inmates: "Tongues of flame leaped about the skulls and bones of the cremated insane," the *Dover Enquirer* reported.[114] Citing the tragedy in New Hampshire, the Rev. Banks preached in Grace Church that same month:

> Because of the shameful neglect of somebody who should look after the needs of that institution, 41 lives went out in that fire. Absolutely no provision for the escape of the inmates in case of conflagration was made.
>
> The only hospital upon Rainsford Island is an old building which was condemned over a quarter century ago by the city, and was pronounced as a place unfit for the housing of people in poor health.
>
> The room for confinement cases is about 17 by 12 feet. In that small space tonight, there are several women suffering untold pain and misery.
>
> You will not find a fire escape upon any building at Rainsford Island.
>
> What should be done? The whole thing should be lifted out of politics and an advisory board of benevolent and Christian citizens should be formed who would see to it that something like justice and humanity was introduced into the treatment given these poor unfortunates, and that something that could be called business was introduced into the management of the institution for the poor and unfortunates of our city.[115]

Alice Lincoln decided to force the issue. She organized a drive to purchase enough rocking chairs that every inmate at the island might have one. In less than two weeks, she had a consignment of eight dozen rocking chairs delivered to the wharf. But Chairman Jenks declared that he had no authority to accept them, and furthermore that with many women confined to bed, there was no need for any more chairs. The chairs sat in a warehouse for another month as

---

[114] The reporting of this event, which echoed around the country, hews suspiciously to the contemporary stereotypes of the mentally ill, but the description from the local newspaper a week after the event is convincing. "Cremated; Forty Crazed People burned to Death; Insane Asylum at the County Farm Burned to Ground," Dover Enquirer, February 17, 1893, p. 1.

[115] Boston Globe, February 20, 1893, p. 5.

Lincoln fed the newspapers proof upon proof of the indifference and incompetence of the commissioners in charge of charitable institutions. "There was a lively discussion at the meeting of the Board of Aldermen yesterday over the Common Council order authorizing and requesting the commissioner of public institutions to accept a number of rocking chairs given by Mrs. Alice N. Lincoln for the aged women at Rainsford Island," the *Globe* reported on March 28. The city council passed the buck, referring the rocking chair matter back to the Committee on Public Institutions.[116] The commissioners parried, producing some specious mathematics "proving" that not only were no more rocking chairs needed but that everything on Rainsford was in fine order: "Permitted to carry out our plans," Commissioner Pillsbury told the *Globe*, "I believe Boston will be second to none and in fact first among the cities of the country in its care of paupers and insane, both in appointments and conveniences."[117] But, confronted with headlines like "Boston Paupers Not Allowed to Rock the Rocking Chairs" and berated by the clergy, the mayor of Boston intervened, ordering the commissioners to accept the rocking chairs as "a gratuity."[118] This was finally done in mid-April, 1893.[119] Matters were hastily adjusted on the island as well. When Boston reporters went out to have a look around Rainsford Island, the inmate numbers had abruptly dropped: "There are now but 140 women in the institution and 21 men . . .. The attics are closed and the main brick building on the island is shut up."[120] The Rainsford Hospital patients had been transferred to Long Island Hospital, with the intention of renovating the hospital buildings. Only the pauper women were left on Rainsford.

It was the rocking-chair incident, we believe, that set Mrs. Lincoln on the path to war. In retrospect, the city no doubt wished it had ferried the chairs out to Rainsford when first asked.

Demanding a Hearing

In 1894, Lincoln at last found the means of airing the abuse, formerly going on at Rainsford and continuing to go on at Long Island, to which the paupers had been transferred.

[116] Boston *Globe*, March 28, 1893, p. 9.
[117] Boston *Globe*, April 12, 1893, p. 9
[118] Boston *Globe*, March 31, 1893, p. 2; Boston Globe, April 1, 1893, p. 1; see also Doc. 211 (1895), vol. 1, p. 122.
[119] Boston *Globe*, April 14, 1893, p. 5.
[120] Boston Globe, April 14, 1893, p. 4.

With the young Louis D. Brandeis as her legal counsel, she set about making the City of Boston Board of Aldermen listen to the litany of complaints and criticisms that the Board of Visitors and the press had for years pointed out to the Commissioners of Public Institutions, and which the commissioners had done nothing to address.

It is not clear when Lincoln met Brandeis, but she is described by Brandeis biographer Melvin I. Urofsky as a "longtime friend" at the time of the hearings. Brandeis had been active with his alma mater, Harvard Law School, since graduating as valedictorian there in 1875; he may have met Alice through her husband Roland Lincoln, who was also involved in Harvard affairs. Brandeis's friend and law partner, Samuel Warren, Jr., would have traveled in the same social circles as the Lincolns. "Brandeis never went looking for reform work;" writes Urofsky, "causes seemed to find him." In this case, Lincoln invited him out to have a look at the pauper institution on Long Island: "Brandeis later called his visit there 'the most depressing & distressful experience' of his life and said that as he walked through the syphilitic ward, he had a 'sense on uncleanness.'"[121] When Lincoln asked him to represent her at hearings before the city, he agreed.

A series of fifty-eight hearings began in March 1894 and strung over nine months; they are transcribed for posterity in City of Boston Document 211. Brandeis elicited testimony from Mrs. Lincoln but also from former employees at Long and Rainsford Islands, who seemed eager to illuminate the greed, corruption, and incompetence of their bosses. Their aim, said Brandeis, was "to throw what light we can upon a very dark spot in Boston."[122] In her opening statement, Lincoln recalled her long struggle to get a hearing: "I appealed to the Commissioners, asking that the young should be separated from the old, the vicious [vice-ridden] from the good, the sick from the well. In other words, that the inmates of the Almshouses should be *classified* and *occupied*. Gentlemen, this was in 1889, and I have been asking the same things ever since."[123] Appendix 4.1 gives a complete list of Lincoln's complaints.

George McCaffrey, former deputy superintendent at Long Island, testified to institutional indifference, to employee drunkenness, self-dealing, and corruption. The

[121] Melvin I. Urofsky, *Louis D. Brandeis: A Life* (New York: Pantheon, 2009), pp. 89–90, n90 (p. 776). The quotation is from a letter to Felix Frankfurter, February 26, 1927.

[122] Doc. 211 (1895), vol. 1, p. 11.

[123] Doc. 211 (1895), vol. 1, p. 13.

superintendent at the time, Dr. Cogswell, McCaffrey testified, boasted that "within six weeks of this time I propose to have this island so that it will run itself, and I will have nothing to do but sit here and draw my salary." Asked if Dr. Cogswell ever treated patients, McCaffrey replied, "Never."[124] Dr. Cogswell lived well doing nothing, skimming milk and meat off the official allocation for personal use or resale, while patients including infants went without.

In addition to bad medical care, poor diet, and lax supervision of staff, patients lay in peril from fire. The Board of Visitors had notified the Commissioners that patients were warehoused in the attic of the old wooden hospital, where kerosene lamps and candles provided the only light at night.[125] The stairs to the lower floors were narrow, and no provision for fire escape had been made. Hoses that might be used to put out a fire were rotted. The island authorities had politely tolerated the visits of Mrs. Lincoln and her cohort, but it is evident they resented the intrusion into what had become both a sinecure and a patronage opportunity. The Commissioners, but especially Jenks, resented any criticism of the way in which they were running the public institutions. Charles J. Prescott, one of the commissioners, testified that the chairman of the board, Dr. Jenks, had turned on him after Mrs. Lincoln had pleaded the case for closing the Rainsford Island Hospital, saying, "Mr. Prescott, have you got any more of your damned old-woman cranks to bring before me? If you have, you can trot them in now."[126] In response to the complaints by Mrs. Lincoln and Mr. Prescott, "the board did nothing."[127]

Testimony piled up day after day, and the transcript, Document 211, had to be published in two thick volumes to contain it all. City officials grilled Lincoln on the stand, no doubt hoping that she would become discouraged and go away. "Mrs. Lincoln," said one, "do you think it is fair for you to make a comparison between these two institutions if you do not know how many are in one of the institutions?" To which Lincoln replied: "I think so."[128]

The point was not simply that Rainsford or Long Island or the Austin Farm was poorly run and seething with bedbugs: it was that the entire management structure was faulty,

[124] Doc. 211 (1895), vol. 1, p. 139.
[125] Doc. 211 (1895), vol. 2, p. 1724.
[126] Doc. 211 (1895), vol. 2, p. 1724.
[127] Doc. 211 (1895), vol. 2, p. 1725.
[128] Doc. 211 (1895), vol. 1, p. 80.

permitting graft and patronage to flourish while the poor were humiliated and neglected. It was this *system* that Lincoln sought to overthrow.

Lincoln won the day. At the end of 1894, Rainsford Island was closed as a hospital and pauper-storage facility. The City documents for 1894–95 report that "The pauper women are now being removed from Rainsford Island to Long Island, and when their removal is completed, it is intended to remodel the buildings for the reception of the inmates of the House of Reformation."[129] One woman, with her allies, had succeeded in shutting down a place of infamy. Regrettably, another would open in its place.

The closure came too late for twenty-eight-year-old Mary A. Smith. Per the City of Boston's Records of Deaths, on January 10th, 1895, she died at Rainsford Island. Mary, an unmarried domestic worker, was 28 years old when she died from phthisis. She is not buried on the island as her body was claimed.

Alice North Towne Lincoln rests, with her husband Roland Crocker Lincoln, in Lot 817, Snowdrop Path, at Mount Auburn Cemetery. In 1926, they died three weeks apart at their mansion, Stoneleigh, located on South Street, Forest Hills, Boston.

---

[129] *Commissioners of Public Institutions of the City of Boston, For The Year Ending, January 31, 1895*, City Document No. 29, p. 21.

Appendix 4.1. Alice N. Lincoln's List of Complaints

I myself have seen —

1. That the protection against fire at both Long and Rainsford Islands is utterly inadequate, not even an alarm gong being furnished in any of the institutions.

2. That when the water supply is stopped, as it has been many times during the past year, the condition of the plumbing in the hospital and institution on Long Island is indescribably filthy and unsanitary.

3. That the standard of cleanliness in the hospital at Long Island in regard to bed linen, clothing, and floors is far below what it ought to be.

4. That personal cleanliness in the care of hospital patients is not enforced.

5. That the quality of the food is not what it should be for the sick, and that too little care is taken in the preparation of the food for the well.

6. That sufficient paid assistance is not employed in the hospital, and that the grade of nursing is not so high as in similar institutions in this and in other States, where less dependence is placed on help furnished by inmates.

7. That women and children are kept in an institution for men.

8. That there is no telephone connection between Long Island and the city of Boston.

9. That no attempt at classification is made.

From these facts I draw the following deductions:

First. That as the existing evils are largely those of mismanagement, an improvement could be made in the condition of Boston's paupers.

Second. That to bring about this desirable result and to fix the responsibility where it properly belongs, a radical change in the present method of administration of the public institutions is absolutely necessary.[130]

See page 115- Appendix 4.2. Inventory of Rainsford Island, 1890

---

130 "Care and Management of the Public Institutions," Documents of the City of Boston for the Year 1894, vol. 4 (Boston: Rockwell and Churchill, 1895), Document 211 (vol. 1), pp. 16–17.

Appendix 4.3. Age at Death, Women's Era (November 7, 1889–January 31, 1895)

Age at Death		Women 166	Children 16
< 1		0	15
Age -- 1		0	1
11 -- 20		2	0
21 -- 30		6	0
31 -- 40		14	0
41 -- 50		23	0
51 -- 60		22	0
61 --70		51	0
71 -- 80		37	0
81 - 90		10	0
Age -- 99		1	0

Appendix 4.4. Causes of Death, Women's Era (November 7, 1889–January 31, 1895)

Cause of Death		Women 166		Children 16
Insanity & Senility		31		0
Heart Disease		18		0
Diarrhea & Dysentery		14		1
Pneumonia & Pleurisy		14		1
Phthisis		12		0
Other causes		9		3
Bright's & Kidney Disease		11		0
Bronchitis		10		1
Brain Disease		9		0
Gastrointestinal		4		2
Paralysis		6		0
Unknown		6		0
Cancer		4		0
Debility		4		0
Marasmus & Inanition		2		3
Syphilis		0		4
Rheumatism		3		0
Tuberculosis		2		0
Alcoholism, Intemperance, Delirium tremens		1		0
Asthma		1		0
Cholera		0		1
Drowning		1		0
Epilepsy		1		0
Gangrene		1		0
Peritonitis		1		0
Suicide		1		0

Appendix 4.5. Place of Birth, Women's Era (November 7, 1889–January 31, 1895)

Place of Birth		Women 166		Children 16
Ireland		101		0
Boston		19		4
Canada		11		0
Rainsford Island		0		11
Other States		9		0
England		8		0
Germany		4		0
Scotland		4		0
Not listed		4		0
Other MA towns		2		1
France		1		0
Italy		1		0
Norway		1		0
Sweden		1		0

Appendix 4.6. Women Remaining as of December 31, 1889 -1894,

Year		Remaining at Year End	Largest Number During The Year	Data Merged With Long Island
1889		461		
1890			483	
1891				Not Available
1892				Not Available
1893			421	
1894		272		

City of Boston's Annual Reports on Public Institutions Numbers One to Five, 1889-1894

Chapter 5: The Infants' Summer Hospital, 1894-1898

Starting in the summer of 1894 and in subsequent years up until 1898, Rainsford Island was the home of the Infants' Summer Hospital. It was located on the west side of the island in the old Grecian style building that was constructed in 1832, about which so many complaints had been lodged over the years. But the authorities appear to have taken some lessons from the scandals of the Women's era on the island. In the fifteen months after the evacuation of the women in April 1893, substantial repairs were made. According to the *Boston Globe, (*August 8 1894, p.8.) "The finishing touches have all been put on the walls of the old gray stone fortress are now a shiny white, both inside and out... Every room has been scraped, scrubbed and painted; steam heating apparatus has been put in throughout, and the second floor is filled with a row of cribs and cots covered with snow white linen." In addition, the number of patients was kept quite low. Unlike in prior uses of the Rainsford Hospital, when patients were packed in by the hundreds, only 50-70 infants were taken at a time.

The mortality rate among these small children-nearly 30 percent in the last 3 years of operation-was very high, as the mortality charts show (Appendix 5.1). But this should not necessarily be held against the institution. The Children sent to the island were very ill, and the age of sulfa drugs and antibiotics was still decades away. In fact, the treatments given these children were often life-saving: innovative methods developed there, and on the contemporary Floating Hospital, discussed below, would save thousands of lives in the ensuing decades.

Unlike the Women's era (Chapter 4), this interval at Rainsford was carefully supervised by competent, well-meaning professionals. As such, it constitutes perhaps the happiest chapter in Rainsford's history of occupation.

The Summer Complaint

Despite progress in obstetrics and pediatrics, infant mortality remained shockingly high in the late nineteenth century. At the time, of which we write, nearly 17 percent of babies born alive in urban environments did not survive infancy.[131]

Physicians had long known that child deaths spiked in the summertime: infants died in great numbers from the "summer complaint"—also called summer or infantile cholera and today called gastroenteritis. It is not the same as cholera proper, which is caused by the bacterium *Vibrio cholerae* and spreads through fecal matter in unsanitary water systems.[132] Summer cholera, in contrast, was caused by a variety of bacteria, including *E. coli* (or Escherichia coli, named after its discoverer, Theodor Escherich), which during hot weather propagated in food, especially unpasteurized milk. The bacteria caused serious, often unstoppable diarrhea and vomiting in children.[133]

The Summer Hospital concept was devised to reduce infant mortality by extricating children from their contaminated environments, dosing them with sanitary food and fluids, and watching them carefully as they tried to recover. The children were examined and weighed upon admission, and their food and fluid intake were tracked.

Rehydration efforts sometimes involved "gavage," the administration of nutrients through a rubber nasal tube. The necessity for this treatment was explained by Dr. John W. Bartol, who oversaw cases at the Summer Hospital on Rainsford Island:

> [T]he infant . . . often has in its morbid conditions of body or mind a positive distaste for nourishment of any kind; but, unlike the adult [so afflicted], is not able to call to its aid the power of will so often essential for the obedient execution of the physician's mandates. It is obviously our duty, then, in appropriate cases to feed him if need be directly against his will. . .. [T]he method not only offers the advantage of administering food of fixed amount and definite proportions at appropriately regulated intervals, but

---

[131] Marcella Alsan and Claudia Goldin, "Watersheds in Infant Mortality: The Role of Effective Water and Sewerage Infrastructure, 1880 to 1920," NBER Working Paper 21263 (June 2015; rev. May 2018). https://www.nber.org/papers/w21263

[132] Boston saw its last true cholera epidemic in 1849, when the disease killed over 600 victims, mostly in the crowded North End. "Course of Cholera in Boston," Map, Boston Committee on Internal Health (J.H. Bufford lith., ca. 1866). Boston was unaffected by the epidemic of 1873, the last in the United States: see *The Cholera Epidemic of 1873 in the United States*, H.R. Doc. No. 95 (Washington: D.C.: USGPO, 1875).

[133] The *Journal of the American Medical Association* provides a lengthy description of the symptoms in its publication of May 7, 1892; XVIII (19): 578–83.

also furnishes a ready means of exhibiting [i.e., administering], at the same time, such medicine as may be desirable. [134]

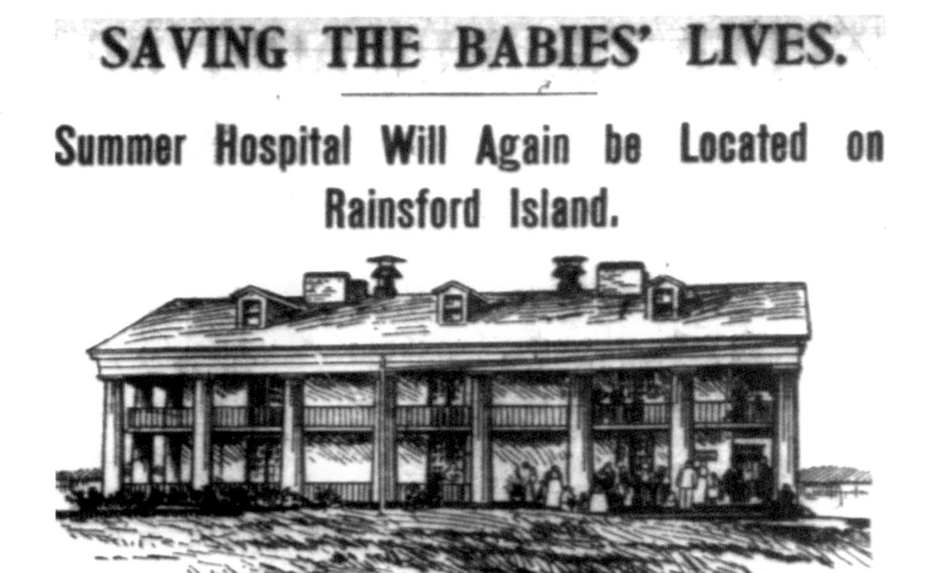

Fig. 5.1. The Hospital Building, as depicted in the Boston Globe, (May 5, 1896, p. 6)

A Private Effort, 1894–95

The Summer Hospital was first organized by Dr. H. C. Ernst, a bacteriologist at Harvard Medical School. Summer heat turned the hospital wards into conduits of infectious disease, as patients packed the airless wards and spread bacteria among themselves. An article in the *Boston Medical and Surgical Journal* in 1896 explained that "[a]s experience has shown that it is not wise to keep the wards at 37 Blossom Street [the pediatric hospital] open in the summer, the directors of the Infants' Hospital have decided to close the wards, but to keep the hospital open for outpatients, seven to eight thousand [sic] of whom are treated annually."[135] In July 1894, Ernst persuaded the board of directors of Public Institutions to spruce up the hospital building on Rainsford Island for the care of sick children. Nursing was provided by members of

[134] John W. Bartol, "Gavage in Infants," *Boston Medical and Surgical Journal*, vol. 136 (May 27, 1897), pp. 513–14.

[135] "The Summer Hospital for Infants," Boston Medical and Surgical Journal, vol. 134, no. 21 (May 21, 1896), p. 520.

the Sisterhood of St. Margaret Hospital.[136] The hospital opened its doors on August 8, 1894. The *Globe* reported, "…when 75 or more tots from Boston arrive there, a place fit for their every comfort will await them."[137] A doctor from Children's Hospital named Paige was the resident physician, with Dr. Ernst visiting several times a week.

The hospital opened without proper funding, and Ernst was obliged to appeal to the public for charity. A *Globe* article published on the hospital's opening day contained a plea:

> Dr. Ernst still in need of funds sufficient to do all that has been intended. The best time to save life is at its budding. The baby hospital has been supplied with a pair of scales with which to weigh the little ones on their arrival and departure, and those who desire to see them make a good record are at liberty to donate anything, from a rattle box to a merry-go-round.[138]

Unlike the Floating Hospital, which was established in the same year, the Summer Hospital offered inpatient care and accommodation for family members as well. As the *Globe* reported later:

> The admissions to the hospital were made as easy as possible and blank forms were sent to all of the large medical charities, as well as to any reputable physicians who cared to apply for them. Any but infectious cases were received, and while the babies were the patients especially desired, any sick child of the surrounding towns was accepted…. It was open from Aug 8 to Sept 12 for the reception of patients, and was closed Sept 15. In this time there were received 250 mothers and children, of which number 129 entered as patients. Of these patients seven died in the hospital. This mortality is considered exceedingly low. For the time it was opened there was an average household of about 60, and the time being 38 days the entire cost of each person was a fraction over 34 cents. Mothers and children were fed upon the best milk, meat, and vegetables procurable.[139]

Funds continued to be short, despite the appeals in the press. The following June, Dr. John W. Pratt of the Massachusetts General Hospital warned that the Summer Hospital would

---

[136] *The Medical Register for New England*, Vol. 2 (1895), p. 202.
[137] Boston *Globe* (August 8, 1894) p. 8.
[138] Boston *Globe* (August 8, 1894) p. 8.
[139] Boston *Globe*, May 6, 1895, p. 6.

not be able to open unless more money was found. Less than $500 of the needed $3,000 had been raised, he warned, which was "wholly inadequate for the purpose in hand." "It is hardly necessary," Pratt added, "to speak of the amount of suffering that can be alleviated if this charity is supported."[140] Midway through that second season, Pratt made another appeal, informing the public that "this is the only hospital receiving babies under 2 years of age; that patients are taken from any place and with any disease but infectious, and that not infrequently an entire family is taken in order to reach one sick child, would seem to furnish a sufficient reason for carrying on the work."[141]

The Floating Hospital, established in 1894 and still going (though now on dry land, part of Tufts Medical Center), offered the Summer Hospital some competition, but its mission was quite different. It was essentially a shipboard clinic rather than a hospital, offering mothers and children a "day's outing on Boston Harbor," with a physical examination and care by volunteer nurses and doctors. It was the brainchild of Rev. Rufus B. Tobey, who "was concerned about the plight of ill, impoverished children," and shared the Victorian view of the healing properties of "beneficial harbor breezes."[142] The Floating Hospital was notable for furthering pediatrics and the science of nutrition in this period through careful experimentation. But, as the *Boston Post* noted in a long article about the Floating Hospital: "The cases which are too far gone for this treatment are sent to the Seaside Hospital on Rainsford Island, which is really an outcome of this charity."[143]

The Commissioners of Public Institutions, in their year-end report for 1894, reproduced a letter from Charles A. Dever, M.D., which sang the praises of the Summer Hospital:

> As a health resort for children during the summer months, I think, Rainsford has no equal in this section of the country; this has been fully demonstrated by results obtained at the summer hospital last season. An institution of this kind, supported by the

[140] Letter to the Editor, Boston *Post*, June 13, 1895, p. 4.

[141] Letter to the Editor, Boston *Post*, August 10, 1895, p. 2.

[142] "History of Floating Hospital for Children," https://www.floatinghospital.org/About-Us/History (accessed 16 Jan 2019). The belief in the therapeutic value of fresh air was a holdover from the miasmatic theory, which held that bad odors were the source of disease. The value of sunshine as an antidote to rickets and Vitamin D deficiency was not discovered until the twentieth century.

[143] Boston *Post*, July 21, 1895, p. 1.

city and under the control of the Commissioners of Public Institutions, would supply a want which is greatly needed.[144]

The City Takes Over, 1896–98

In 1896, the City of Boston's Department of Public Institutions took control of Summer Hospital. The reasons for this change may simply have been financial: Dr. Ernst and his cohort may have been unable to raise sufficient funds to keep the Rainsford hospital going. But it is conspicuous also that a complete change of personnel occurred. Dr. Ernst was out, as was Dr. Paige. So were the nurses from St. Margaret's. In their places were a new supervisor, Dr. Dwight, a new medical director, Dr. T. M. Rotch, and nurses from the "West End nursery [and] infant hospital." In May 1896, the Globe reported:

> This addition to the institution's department has been decided upon [by] the Commissioner of Health, and it will go into effect this summer on a permanent basis. Work is going on at the island under the supervision of Dr. Dwight. The old hospital building being thoroughly cleaned and painted, and rooms being prepared for 50 babies. Detached from the hospital buildings will be booths for cooking and laundry purposes, also one for the resident physician and others for stores and servant sleeping quarters.[145]

The City was effusive in praising Dr. Ernst, now that he was no longer in charge:

> At the time when Dr. Ernst brought up this question there was no place in or about Boston where proper care could be given the large number of children and infants under two years old, suffering from the ordinary summer complaints. Dr. Ernst has successfully demonstrated the importance and necessity of such an institution, and it is entirely due to his efforts that it has been carried on for these years so satisfactorily and successfully.[146]

---

[144] Commissioners of Public Institutions of the City of Boston for the Year Ending January 31, 1895, City Document No. 29, p. 148.

[145] Boston Globe, May 8, 1896, p. 8.

[146] Annual Report of the Executive Department of the City of Boston (1895), Part 1, Document No. 14, p. 23.

The *Boston Medical and Surgical Journal* noted that this "important addition to the Institutions Department" had been made at the behest of one Dr. Heath, the Institutions Commissioner:

> [T]he Infants' Hospital, having the same director as the summer hospital, can be a center to which physicians from all parts of the city can telephone for information as to the admission of patients to the summer hospital, and thus coöperate [sic] with the city in rendering the management of its hospital more efficient, while still remaining a separate institution and a private corporation.

Patients would be met at the wharf every day, and a nurse would travel with them on the boat ride to the island.[147]

The first summer of city control did not go as smoothly as hoped. It was almost forced to close on August 12, when scarlet fever, a highly contagious and deadly disease, came with one of the children to the island. A somewhat overwrought article in the *Boston Globe* described this single case as an epidemic.

> On Sunday physicians in charge of the institution discovered suspicious symptoms in one of the infant patients, and later on the case proved to be one of scarlet fever. . .. Since then, the building has been thoroughly fumigated and disinfected, and all possible precaution has been taken to prevent the spreading of the disease. Commissioner Heath yesterday said everything possible has been done and hoped that it would not be necessary to close the hospital. As soon as the fever was discovered, he gave orders that no more babies should be received, and this order will be in effect for the last two weeks, whether or not other cases develop.[148]

In fact, of the forty infant deaths that occurred on the island that summer—the highest number since the opening of the Summer Hospital in 1894—only one was caused by scarlet fever, and that was on August 9. The final death of the 1896 summer term occurred on September 18.

---

[147] "The Summer Hospital for Infants," *Boston Medical and Surgical Journal*, vol. 134, no. 21 (May 21, 1896), p. 520.

[148] "Epidemic in Hospital: Scarlet Fever May Close Babies' Asylum at Rainsford Island," Boston *Globe* (August 12, 1896).

In its end-of-year report for 1896, Boston officials boasted that: "The Summer Hospital on [Rainsford Island] has performed a very useful work for the community, and it is proposed to continue the same general plan as was pursued last year in its management."[149] The same system and management went forward in 1897, running from June 11 to September 30, with 124 cases admitted and 35 deaths (28 percent mortality).[150] This represented a substantial decrease in the mortality rate relative to the previous year. As the *New England Journal of Medicine* noted, "in consideration of the serious condition of many at entrance [this] is regarded as a low percentage." The use of trainee nurses helped curb costs."[151]

CHILDREN'S HOSPITAL, RAINSFORD ISLAND.

Fig. 5.2. *New England Magazine: An Illustrated Monthly*, Vol. 17 (Sept. 1, 1897–Feb. 1, 1898), p. 332.

The End of the Summer Hospital

The year 1898 proved to be the final year of the Summer Hospital. New doctors were in charge—Dr. Joshua Hubbard at the Hospital on Rainsford and Dr. Joseph B. Howland at the Boston wharf evaluating patients. Administration was provided by Miss C. V. Cayford and Miss H. W. Aubin. Their work was lauded as "great and very satisfactory." The morbidity and mortality statistics for the final summer were in line with previous years. Between June 9 and September 24, 1898, there were: "Admitted 152; Discharged Well 41; Much improved 24; Improved 18; Not improved 10; To other institutions 1; Against advice 18; Dead 45; Total

[149] Annual Report of the Executive Department, City of Boston (1896), vol. 1, Doc. 14, p. 13.
[150] Fifteenth Annual Report of the West End Nursery and Infants' Hospital (1898), p. 12.
[151] *New England Journal of Medicine*, vol. 137 (December 23, 1897), p. 663.

number of days stay in Hospital 3,157; Average number of days stay 20; Longest stay in Hospital 100 days; Shortest stay 2 hours; Mortality 29 per cent."[152]

Despite these laudable statistics, the Rainsford Summer Hospital did not reopen in 1899. It is not easy to discover why. It may be that the new use to which the island was being put in early 1895—as a boys' reform school (see Chapter 6)—did not mesh well with the presence of an infants' hospital. It is evident also that Floating Hospital expanded and took over the treatment of the summer ailment in Boston. This is in part because it mastered the art of fundraising. Through emotional appeals, it drew money, sometimes pennies at a time, from well-wishers all over New England.[153]

The *Boston Medical and Surgical Journal* wrote in July 1899:

> The Boston Floating Hospital which for several years has done an excellent work in caring for infants during the hot summer months will this year fill a more important place than ever before owing to the lack of accommodation for sick infants in other institutions. The West End Nursery and Infants Hospital has closed its doors for the summer to house patients and the hospital on Rainsford's Island which for a number of years has been a refuge for many babies will not be opened this year. It is a perfectly well-recognized fact that the mortality among infants during the summer in large cities is very great, even if they have the care which a hospital affords. It therefore becomes imperatively necessary that provision should be made for their treatment outside the confines of the crowded portions of the city.[154]

[152] Documents of the City of Boston for the Year 1899 (1900), Vol. 1, Doc. 6, p. 67.

[153] Florence Hunt, "The Floating Hospital," *New England Kitchen Magazine*, vol. 1, no. 5 (September 1894), p. 267.

[154] "The Floating Hospital," *Boston Medical and Surgical Journal*, vol. 141, no. 2 (July 13, 1899), p. 48.

Appendix 5.1. Mortality at the Summer Hospital.

The following charts indicate the ages and cases of death of the 138 infants who died during the five summers that the hospital operated.

Age at Death		Infants 138
< 1 Month		4
1 Month		10
2 Months		18
3 Months		16
4 Months		16
5 Months		12
6 Months		9
7 Months		14
8 Months		6
9 Months		7
10 Months		6
11 Months		3
12 Month		14
2 Years		3

City of Boston, Records of Deaths, 1894–1898

Causes of Death – Infants' Summer Hospital

Cause of Death		Infants 138
Diarrhea		48
Infantile Atrophy		23
Pneumonia		12
Cholera Infantum		7
Malnutrition & Inanition		10
Gastro Intestinal		5
Marasmus		4
Tuberculosis		4
Ileocolitis		3
Meningitis		3
Milk Infection		3
Cerebral Congestion		2
Eclampsia		2
Improper Feeding		2
Phthisis		2
Abscess Dropsy		1
Anemia		1
Asphyxia		1
Eczema		1
Heart Disease Congenital		1
Nephritis		1
Scarlet Fever		1
Vomiting		1

City of Boston, Records of Deaths, 1894–1898

Chapter 6: The House of Reformation, 1895–1920

The Summer Infants' Hospital was not the sole tenant on Rainsford Island after 1895. The babies and their relatives occupied the old hospital building on the west side of the island. After March 1, 1895, the east end hosted the "House of Reformation," a facility for wayward boys that had previously been located on Deer Island, along with the House of Industry, the Truant School for Boys, and the Truant School for Girls. It occupied a hodgepodge of buildings and workshops on the island, none particularly well-suited to human habitation or public scrutiny.

The narrative of this period follows the pattern that is now familiar. First, the City authorities find a use for an isolating island. Second, it sends a vulnerable population there, without adequate resources. Third, warnings and complaints roll in, to which the City is unable or unwilling to respond. Fourth, after many unnecessary deaths, there is closure. But the harm inflicted on those isolated and neglected on the island, especially the young, no doubt left permanent scars.

The House of Reformation lasted for nearly twenty-five years, which is a scandal in itself. All one can say in its favor was that it was that last period of abuse on Rainsford. The next phase—excepting a few flurries of activity that will be dealt with in the Epilogue —was abandonment.

Mass Incarceration and the Problems of Deer Island

While the Summer Infants' Hospital continued the public-health role of Rainsford Island, the House of Reformation called up a new use: that of prison.

Islands have long been used as places of isolation and punishment. Citizens of the Roman Empire who ran afoul of authority were commonly stripped of their property and sent to distant places, including the Mediterranean islands of Ponza (where Emperor Nero was sent) and Ventotene (Agrippina the Elder); the modern Italian state also used the islands for political dissidents. The continent of Australia served as an island prison on a vast scale for the British Empire in the eighteenth and nineteenth centuries. And the United States has maintained prison islands in California (Alcatraz), New York (Riker's Island), and elsewhere. Islands make escape (and visiting) difficult—though not impossible, as we will see.

New prison space, for young and old, was considered necessary at the end of the nineteenth century because of the mass arrest and incarceration of the underclass in Boston, which at the time was predominantly Irish and Italian in ethnicity. Deer Island, where city prisons were located, was over capacity due to new laws aimed at curbing drunkenness, both private and public.[155] A previous drunk law, which went into effect on July 1, 1891, abolished the five-dollar fine for drunkenness and instead gave judges a choice between dismissing the charges and sending the accused to jail for a few weeks or months. The law was criticized in a city report a year later as ineffectual. "[I]n but 41 cases, out of the whole 8,866 commitments for all offences, was a sentence of one year imposed": hardly enough time, the reporter felt, to break habitual drunkards of their bad habits.[156] A new drunk law that came into force on June 29, 1893, apparently corrected this deficit: the *Boston Globe* snidely assured the public that "Although the number of people enjoying summer board down the harbor at the expense of the city has increased considerably during the past couple of months, there is no fear that any deserving person cannot find room if the city of Boston or the judges of the municipal court consider that they ought to be accommodated."[157] With so many adults being jailed for drunkenness, there was no longer room on Deer Island for the younger inmates, who it was feared would be "contaminated" by exposure to "depraved men and women."

Within the custodial system there always existed a highly inappropriate mixture of genders and ages; physical and mental illness; petty criminals and murderers; those sober and those with severe addictions. The lack of classification and segregation allowed for close contact between many of the inmates. Syphilis and other venereal diseases were common in Boston. This confinement system provided a human petri dish for many whose only affliction was poverty and abandonment. It was unlikely that any one who did not die while in custody was improved from that experience.

---

[155] The Massachusetts laws were part of a nationwide push for temperance legislation, which in a few decades would result in Prohibition. The war on alcohol, like the later wars on marijuana and crack cocaine, was fueled by larger racial, ethnic, gender, and religious conflicts in society. See Daniel Okrent, *Last Call: The Rise and Fall of Prohibition* (New York: Scribner, 2010) and Lisa McGirr, *The War of Alcohol: Prohibition and the Rise of the American State* (New York: Norton, 2015).

[156] "Report of the Special Committee . . . to Inspect the Public Institutions of Boston," Documents of the City of Boston for the Year 1892, vol. 4, Doc. 122, pp. 15–16.

[157] "Drunk Law Being Enforced," Boston *Daily Globe* (August 12, 1893), p. 1.

We can get some idea of the Deer Island population from a city report: on December 31, 1891, the following groups of inmates were housed at Deer Island:

House of Industry:

Prisoners	1,202
Children of sentenced mothers (including infants)	11
Paupers	18

"The House of Industry is a prison to which persons of both sexes are sentenced for such offences as drunkenness, assault and battery, vagrancy, etc. On Jan. 1, 1892, it contained 1,205 prisoners, 868 men and 337 women . . .. [A new drunk law having gone into effect] about 80 per cent of the commitments were for drunkenness . . .. [T]he courts were given discretionary power to sentence a person convicted of being drunk for a term not exceeding one year."

House of Reformation:

Boys — 8 to 19 years old	68

"As regards general influences, it is evident that in the presence of an army of depraved men and women, some serving their twentieth, their fiftieth, their eightieth sentence, it is hard to expect reformation of anyone. The moral atmosphere of the whole place is so inexpressibly depressing that it is not surprising that the officers from the superintendent down have learned to abate something of their hopes for those young in crime, and they frankly confess sometimes in the presence of the boys themselves that what they call the Reformation side is largely a recruiting ground for the House of Industry and other prisons . . .."

Truant School for Boys

Ages 7 to 15	95

Truant School for Girls	1

"Quarters for a School for Truant Girls adjoin the Boys Truant School at Deer Island. But the rooms stand vacant for lack of pupils, only one having been committed last year, in part because truant officers and judges prefer to let them roam the streets rather than send them to Deer Island. This means that many girls who might easily be checked in the first steps of a downward career are left in temptation until they become bad enough to be sent to a reform school or to prison."[158]

It says something profound that even truant officers were not hard enough to send girls to the Deer Island Truant School.

When the efforts of Alice Lincoln were beginning to be felt in 1894, and the scramble was on to re-house the pauper women in more humane quarters, the Commissioners of Public Institutions hit upon the idea of relocating the House of Reformation from Deer Island to Rainsford Island:

> We recommend that upon the removal of the female paupers from Rainsford to Long Island, the House of Reformation be transferred to Rainsford, where with little expense the buildings can be remodeled for its use, and provision made for training in the various trades, in addition to the regular school work, and thus the boys be freed from contamination with adult criminals, from which they now suffer.[159]

With this idea in mind, one of the island's large buildings was fitted for the boys. This multi-floor brick structure had first been built in 1855, in conjunction with the Rainsford's new usage for housing paupers. It was called the "new" female hospital.[160]

The brick building was expanded in 1877–78 by 3,460 square feet. The extra space accommodated bout 200 beds; 50 additional feet of much-needed space in the dining room on the first floor; a chapel to seat 300; a new boiler room; and a storeroom. A large commodious iron staircase was added, used commonly by the new and old parts of the building: a proper means of emergency egress had been seriously lacking in the old structure.[161]

Few images of this building remain, but it and the "Rainsford Island Boys" are pictured in a laudatory article published in the *Bay State Monthly* in January 1898. There we see a three-story brick building, with dormer windows piercing the roof; elsewhere groups of teenagers,

---

[158] "Report of the Special Committee . . . to Inspect the Public Institutions of Boston," Documents of the City of Boston for the Year 1892, vol. 4, Doc. 122, pp. 12–30.

[159] Fifth Annual Report of the Commissioners of Public Institutions of the City of Boston, for the Year Ending January 31, 1894, Vol. 2, Doc. 29, pp. 13–14.

[160] First Annual Report of the Board of State Charities (1865), Public Document No. 19, pp. 11–13.

[161] Auditor of Accounts, Annual Report of the Expenditures of the City of Boston and the County of Suffolk, State of Massachusetts, For the Fiscal year 1877–78, p. 29.

black and white, gaze joylessly at the camera. In this article on "Children's Institutions of Boston," William I. Cole writes:

> [T]he House of Reformation receives such as have been sentenced by the courts for all offences except truancy, and aims so to mould [sic] them that they will become law-abiding children and worthy members of society. . .. In 1896, at Rainsford, 75 boys were received and 58 discharged. The largest number in the institution at one time during the year was 127; the smallest, 111. Of those committed last year, 46 were born in Boston, 4 in Massachusetts outside of Boston, 4 in other states of the Union, 3 in Ireland, 3 in Russia, 3 in Newfoundland, 4 in England, 2 each in Italy, Scotland and Nova Scotia, and one each in Germany and Norway. Offences for commitment were chiefly larceny, stubborn child, and assault and battery. One boy was sent to the island for drunkenness, one for being idle and disorderly, and three for 'playing ball on the Lord's day.'[162]

Boys under the age of eight were sent to the Marcella Street Home rather than to Rainsford, which means that boys as young as eight could be exiled to Rainsford. Cole describes a daily routine than began at 5:40 a.m., "summer and winter alike." Fifteen minutes was allotted for more than one hundred boys to complete their "morning ablutions" in the lavatory, including use of their numbered toothbrushes. Physical drill began at 6:15, with the boys organized along military lines into three companies. Breakfast at 6:30 consisted of oatmeal, bread, sugar, and "cereal coffee." At 7:30 the boys were put to work in industrial classes conforming to the Sloyd system,[163] making shoes and wooden articles and doing print jobs "not only for the island, but for other institutions as well." They also performed "domestic duties." In addition to their work, the boys had four hours of school instruction and half an hour for play, before supper and bed at 7:30 p.m.[164] Visitors were permitted on the second and fourth Wednesdays of the month (not the most convenient day of the week for a working parent).

---

[162] William I. Cole, "Children's Institutions of Boston," *The Bay State Monthly* (January 1, 1898), pp. 327–41. Building photo on p. 332; teenagers on p. 334. The Superintendent's home, looking very comfortable and well-tended, appears on p. 333.

[163] Sloyd was a system of craft-based education developed in Finland in 1865: see Richard Aldrich, "The Impact and Legacy of Educational Sloyd: Head and Hands in the Harness," *History of Education*, vol. 44, no. 3 (2015), pp. 391–93. The system is still in use in certain craft schools, such as the North Bennett Street School in Boston.

[164] Cole, "Children's Institutions," pp. 336–37.

The boys' sentences were open-ended and subject to the whims of discipline. Cole writes, "Boys are sent to Rainsford for an indeterminate time during minority. The actual length of their stay depends largely upon their conduct." A point-based merit system required boys to maintain perfect behavior and academic performance for months at a time: "The more merits a boy accumulates, the shorter is his stay in the institution *likely* to be [emphasis added]. A boy is expected, however, to remain not less than two years."[165] Many boys were there because they could not pay fines they had incurred.[166]

A later report written after the school had changed its name from the House of Reformation to the Suffolk School for Boys, noted:

> To this institution are sent the boys of the city whom the police find to be too irregular to be kept in the community. Often a boy is committed to the institution technically for a certain offence, when in fact, if complained of for such an offence, he would not be sent to an institution by the court unless it were thought impossible to keep him in good order at home by probationary and other methods.
>
> These boys, technically called delinquents, come to the School between eight and sixteen years of age and remain on the average about a year in the institution. They are then placed on probation subject to visitation until they are twenty-one.[167]

A negative assessment of living conditions on Rainsford appeared in the Annual Report of Boston's Executive Department:

> The improvement in the appearance, work, and spirit of the boys since the transfer from Deer Island, in May (1st) last, is highly gratifying. . .. The old buildings, formerly occupied by paupers, are now used by the boys, and are in many ways entirely unfitted for this purpose. These buildings, could, however, be utilized to good advantage as workshops, which are much needed, and will be still more, as the development of trade schools goes on.
>
> Proper dormitory, hospital, heating, power, lighting, and kitchen facilities should be provided before another winter, if possible. . ..

---

165 Cole, "Children's Institutions," pp. 338.

166 Annual Report of the Executive Department of the City of Boston for the Year 1895, Vol. 1, Doc. 14, p. 135.

Documents of the City of Boston for the Year 1911, vol. 1, Report on Childrens' Institutions Department, Doc. 9, p. 6.

The credit system has been introduced, and each boy is now expected to settle by his own exertions the length of his stay in the institution. It is not intended in the future to interfere with the good results of this system by exercising the power of release, granted to the commissioner under chapter 449, section IG, Acts of 1895. . .. Corporal punishment has practically been abolished, and it is being demonstrated that mental suasion has at least as good an effect as the older method.[168]

Indenture

The system had many critics. Early on, misgivings about the House of Reformation system were expressed, even by those in charge. "Boys of this class need the influences of a good home in some respectable family more than the discipline of a reform school," a city bureaucrat wrote. He added, hopefully, "Children boarded out could be placed out of state."[169] "Boarding out" of these problematic children would both lessen the city's financial burden and keep the young people from idleness, a vice that people in that era seemed to regard with horror.

In fact, boys and girls in that time could be put out for indenture, a practice of involuntary, unpaid labor most of us associate with the founding years of the American colonies. With much use of words like "wholesome" and "moral" to describe the hoped-for work environments, the Commonwealth had in 1882 written into law a means to acquire unpaid child labor (see Appendix 6.1). It must have been very difficult to find "wholesome" placements for the Rainsford boys: the total number of children indentured over the twenty-five-year history of the Suffolk School was only 12 (see Appendix 6.2).

One success story touted in 1909 by the Rainsford staff was of a boy who had been committed for stealing a horse. When "[i]t was found that Daniel was very fond of horses," he was placed on a farm where he thrived.[170] Employers interested in this free labor were not always interested in the boys' welfare, however. Mary Boyle O'Reilly told a *Boston Post*

[168] Annual Report of the Executive Department of the City of Boston for the Year 1895, Part 1, Doc. 14, pp. 17–18.

[169] Annual Report of the Executive Department of the City of Boston for the Year 1895, Part 1, Doc. 14, p. 162–64.

[170] "Disciplining Boys on Rainsford Island," Boston Daily Globe, July 4, 1909, p. 23.

reporter in 1909: "[A] man came to us wanting to take as many of our boys as we would give. He said he would take them to God's own country—those were his own words—and care for them well. He wanted them for cutters in his glass factory in Sandwich. The average age life of cutters is 28 years. That man is now in jail at Charlestown."[171] It is to their credit that the Rainsford officials did not supply the boys asked for.

Fire and Escape

Almost as soon as the House of Reformation was transferred to Rainsford Island, the young inmates began to express their unhappiness. The boys have left no written records of their time on the island, except for one issue of a newspaper, *The Leader*, that appeared in the last year of the school's operation. But it is clear from their actions that many were extremely unhappy to be there and desperate to leave. Over the twenty-five-year history of the institution, boys set fire to buildings on numerous occasions, and stole or concocted boats in which to escape. Others washed up on shore, either suicides, failed escapees, or murder or accident victims.

When the first blaze occurred, it was possible to chalk it up to accident. On August 17, 1899, the *Globe* reported an outbreak of fire in the attic of the main dormitory on Rainsford: "The cause was attributed to spontaneous combustion."[172] When another, much bigger blaze started two nights later, arson was immediately suspected. That fire was clearly set in order to cover an attempted escape. As flames spread in the dormitory building, which was described as a "fire trap," half a dozen boys seized a yacht and tried to get away. Others launched themselves on improvised rafts:

> A quick investigation revealed that, amongst the older boys, there was a large plot to escape. A large amount of shavings and oil were ignited in the guard's sleeping room in the attic.
>
> Of the 136 boys that were present when the fire began, 10 remained missing, 45 were transferred to Deer Island. 56 of the older boys were placed back in the damaged

[171] Boston Post, October 4, 1909, p. 6.
[172] Boston Globe, August 17, 1899, p. 3.

dormitory complex and 25 of the younger boys were sent to cottages at the extreme edge of the island (Smallpox Point).[173]

On September 1, 1899, the Boston Globe noted that the Trustees of Children's Institutions estimated that $35,683 was required to repair the fire damage.[174] The buildings were repaired by the end of September, and the boys returned to Rainsford.[175] The ringleader, a "clever pickpocket" named Harry Bernstein, but also called Joseph Myers and Abraham Romanofsky, was only reeled in by police in September.[176] That was a month after their arson and escape. Many of the boys caught and sentenced for their part in the fire were returned to Rainsford, to remain there until they turned age 21.

The inmates set another fire just six months later. This one, on March 20, 1900, raged for close to an hour. It killed several horses and nearly devastated the entire island, which was apparently the aim. The *Boston Post* reported that "Many of the boys were hysterical, others danced in evident glee and shouted like demons." Under the cover of steam and smoke, some of the boys flung stones through the windows.[177] James McNulty, age 13, was one of five boys arrested for setting this fire; McNulty later set a barn on fire at the Lyman School in Westboro (a state reform school, established in 1886), to which he was sent in the aftermath of the Rainsford fire.[178] His co-conspirators on Rainsford—George Eiffler (age 18) and Joseph Cox (age 17)—had also been associated with the previous fire on the island in September, and were charged in the "vicious beating" of an island employee who found them hiding at the dock.[179] The boys in that case had taken the precaution of cutting the telephone wires so that help would be delayed in coming. The *Boston Globe* cited the cost of repairs this time at $10,000.[180]

---

173 "Sent to Deer Island," Boston *Globe*, August 22, 1899, p. 1.
174 Boston Globe, September 1, 1899, p. 12.
175 "Absolute Order at Rainsford," Boston Globe, September 14, 1899, p.7.
176 "Police Capture Incendiary Subject," Boston *Post*, September 15, 1899, p. 8.
177 "Boys Set Fire to Buildings on Rainsford," Boston Post, March 21, 1900, p. 1.
178 Boston Globe, August 27, 1900, p. 7.
179 Boston Post, March 21, 1900, p. 1.
180 Boston Globe, March 23, 1900, p. 42.

In 1905, a twelve-year-old named Domenico Palmarello "was sentenced to Rainsford Island for setting a fire at a building resulting in damages of $6,000. He told the Judge that he 'liked the excitement of a good fire.'"[181]

The buildings were showing their age. The final two fires, occurring on December 21, 1916, and February 13, 1919, were ascribed to faulty wiring. The first of these burned the shoe factory in which the boys toiled and the warehouse, with damages of $15,000; the second burned the sewing and locker room, with damages of $38,000.[182] No one was hurt, and the boys in both cases were credited with helping to douse the fires, but the damage plus the destruction of the moneymaking end of the Rainsford operation must have been a bad blow to the balance sheets.

During the first decade of its operation, the House of Reformation/Suffolk School for boys experienced a number of non-arson related successful and unsuccessful escapes. The earliest reported escapes occurred during the first week of November 1896. Seven boys left the island in three separate groups, deploying a lifeboat and landing at Quincy Point.[183] One of the boys, Thomas Harrington (age 16), made his way to Charlestown to his brother's house, but before long he alienated his brother's affections by stealing $15 from him; the brother then turned him over to the police. He was returned to Rainsford "to complete his education."[184]

Several attempts ended in injury or death. In the dead of a winter's night in 1897, four boys ranging in age from 12 to 14 took a life boat from the wharf. They attempted to row, using three oars, but were soon overwhelmed by "the strong flood tide and head wind." Their boat washed up on the shore ice, and the three older boys were able to walk to a nearby farmhouse at first light. The twelve-year-old, Henry Butler, was too frozen to leave the beached boat, and was found later with serious frost damage to his feet and hands.[185] A boy who escaped later that year was not so fortunate. The body of thirteen-year-old James Leahy, who had escaped from Rainsford in March, was found "at Atlantic" (today called Wollaston Beach) in early May.[186]

---

181 "Reform School for Boy Firebug," Boston Post, July 28, 1905, p. 7.

182 "Boys Fight $15,000 Fire," Boston Globe, December 22, 1916, p. 1; "Fully Engulfed," Boston Globe, February 14, 1919, p. 1.

183 "Three Sets of Boys Disappear," Boston Globe, November 8, 1896, p. 12.

184 "Must Go Back Now," Boston *Globe*, December 21, 1896, p. 10.

185 "Fugitives from Rainsford in Custody," Boston Globe, February 3, 1897, p. 4.

186 "Body of James Leahy Found," Boston Globe, May 3, 1897, p. 9.

Other breaks for freedom occurred in April, August, October, and December 1898, and in September 1899.[187] One clever youth got as far as the mainland concealed in a laundry basket.[188] Others made their escape during the particularly cold winter of 1918 in which much of Boston Harbor was frozen; they were immediately caught and sent back.[189]

The drowning of four boys in two escape attempts in 1913 resulted in the dismissal of the Suffolk School supervisor, Richard C. Soule. It is one of the few instances in which anyone in a top position was disciplined for the death of children under his charge.[190]

Incompetence, Corruption, and Abuse: "A Form of Inquisition"

Reasons for attempted escape must have been various, and there was some speculation in the newspapers about what these reasons might be. Certainly, the leadership at the reformatory was not always competent. The early superintendent of the House of Reform, Lorenzo Perkins, declined to punish boys who attempted to escape, though after the break in February 1897, he pleaded for an additional night watchman. Perkins announced that he would resign his post as of January 1899, after a string of escapes.[191] The boys responded to the gap in leadership by staging a strike at Christmastime, flouting their instructors: "The teachers expostulated and wept, and threatened that Santa Claus wouldn't come if the young rebels weren't good. The infants replied 'Aw rats' and other . . . rude things." The *Boston Post* deduced that "the teachers and officials dwelt together on terms of anything but harmony," and that the unpaid overseers board, as in the women's era, was managing to do nothing about accumulating issues.[192]

There are many indications that politics played a part in both confining boys for trivial offences and releasing them prematurely. The *Globe*, reporting on a speech by Mary Boyle O'Reilly, then serving on the Prison Commission, wrote:

---

[187] "Went Sailing in a Box," Boston Globe, April 15, 1898, p. 7, "Got Away From Rainsford's," Boston Globe, August 3, 1898, p. 7; "Boys Returned to Rainsford Island," Boston Globe, October 24, 1898, p. 12; Boston Globe, December 7, 1898, p. 4; "Escaped from Rainsford," Boston Globe, September 30, 1899, p. 1.

[188] "Basket Was Heavy," Boston Globe, January 31, 1906, p. 6.

[189] "Rainsford Island Boys Caught After Flight," *Boston Post*, February 12, 1918, p. 2.

[190] "Discharged School Head Fights for Job," *Lowell Sun*, July 11, 1913, p. 13.

[191] Boston Globe, December 7, 1898, p. 4.

[192] "Boys on Strike," Boston Post, December 25, 1898, p. 2.

[A] youthful lawyer just entering the game of politics allowed a boy, who had been found guilty of stealing 5 cents and who was sentenced to the Suffolk School, to be returned to jail on appeal. Miss O'Reilly found the boy sharing a cell in jail with one of the worst crooks this side of New York, the result, she said, of the lawyer's desire to appeal to a higher court.

In another case, a politician had, against the advice of the trustees and a physician, secured the release of a boy who died three days later of heart failure. O'Reilly called Rainsford "a most unfit plant for which we have to thank the era of economy in Boston."[193]

Once enrolled in the reformatory's system of behavioral incentives, it could be almost impossible to get out. And the offences for which boys were thrown into the system ranged from the truly scary to the absurdly trivial. How was it wise to put a child arrested for pickpocketing ten cents in the same dormitory with murderers?[194] A later city report confessed:

> It was surprising to learn that children were incarcerated for non-payment of fines. A report for the period September 27, 1895 to July 7, 1900, noted that 126 boys were sentenced for non-payment of fines. Sixty-four were released when their fines were made. Sixty-two did not pay their fines and did their entire sentences. For the majority of that time, the sentences were as follows: $10 or less, thirty days; over $10 and less than $20, forty days; over $20, ninety days.[195]

Boys incarcerated indefinitely for being poor might be inclined to resent it. An exasperated citizen, trying in 1906 to secure the liberty of a boy named Edward Nolan, who had been 21 months on the island for lifting a quart of milk from a peddler's cart, declared that "Superintendent Seavey of the Rainsford institution enforces a system of merits and demerits and because of boyish pranks and minor acts of a trivial nature the Nolan boy has been held prisoner . . .. The system that they refer to is outrageous and a form of inquisition insulting to an intelligent community."[196]

Evidence was put forward over the years of physical and psychological abuse of the boys. (Likely there was sexual abuse as well, but that was not a topic anyone was willing to

---

[193] Place is Unfit for Children: Miss O'Reilly Scores Economy at Rainsford Island," Boston Post, October 4, 1909, p. 6.

[194] "Boy Pickpocket Sent to Rainsford Island," Poston Post, January 3, 1903, p. 8; "Confine 3 Boys in Case of Death," Boston Globe, January 19, 1913

[195] Documents of the City of Boston for the Year 1921, vol. 5, Doc. 128, pp. 2–5.

[196] "Boy Held 21 Months Because He Took Milk," Boston Post, December 22, 1906, p. 1.

discuss in that era.) As early as 1899, an unannounced inspection of the Suffolk School by members of the Boston City Council turned up some ugly facts. Councilman Frank J. Linehan, who led the expedition, reported that "there were dark cells in the basement, where boys were put" for three or four days at a time. The dormitory was noted as a fire trap.[197] "Corporal punishment, [Linehan] says, is very common at the institution, and he claims it is so severe that the boys bear the marks of the treatment long after it is inflicted." He also charged that there were a great many idle people on the payroll, who were "friends of the trustees."[198] The Trustees of Children's Institutions denied all the charges, though during a follow-up visit attended by reporters, Mr. Anthony, the man in charge, "admitted that the boys had been handcuffed to beds."[199] One of the boys—Frank Novak, age 15—reported that Anthony had "struck him on the head with a billy [i.e., club], so heavily as to knock him down."[200]

A grand jury was convened to hear these complaints and others. There were reports that members of the staff, including one of the woman teachers, ordered beer to be delivered by local lobstermen.[201] Witnesses noted that medical service to the island was capricious, "depending upon a signal system to Long Island to call a physician when a boy was sick."[202] The grand jury recommended removing the reformatory from Rainsford to the mainland, and the city's investigating committee "denounce[d] Mayor Quincy's Methods and the management of the reformatory," charging "criminal negligence," as well as "financial recklessness."[203]

The Committee's report, published in the city documents, detailed the costs of patronage hiring: "The so-called athletic instructor, who does not instruct in athletics, but whose duty appears to consist in abusing and beating the boys, receives $40 a month for doing work which was formerly performed by House Officer Leighton at a salary of $35 per month. He is assisted by the so-called baker, who does not bake . . . ."[204] Children waited weeks for treatment of injuries and ailments. The educational program was "seriously injured by the fads, theories and

---

[197] "Rainsford Home for Boys," Boston Globe, March 10, 1899, p. 4.

[198] "Charges of Mr. Linnehan," Boston Globe, April 14, 1899, p. 5.

[199] "At Rainsford's," Boston Globe, April 26, 1899, p. 12.

[200] Boston Post, April 26, 1899, p. 2.

[201] "Got Beer off Lobstermen," Boston Globe, June 16, 1899, p. 4.

[202] "150 Boys at Rainsford Island: No Daily Medical Service," Boston Globe, June 19, 1899, p. 1.

[203] "Grand Jury Report," Boston Globe, June 22, 1899, p. 14; "Councilmen on the Rainsford Island Investigating Committee," Boston Post, July 14, 1899, p. 1.

[204] Documents of the City of Boston for the Year 1899, vol. 4, Doc. 113, "Report of Joint Special Committee Investigation of Rainsford Island," p. 5.

favoritism which are used in the management of the schools." The teachers managed between vacations and leaves of absence to be out of the classroom for thirty weeks a year. The funds lavished on no-work jobs left little money for legitimate employees:

> Your committee found the conditions under which a number of employees were obliged to perform work at pauper salaries or for nothing so absolutely filthy as to be a serious menace to the health of every one on the Island. We brought to the attention of the superintendent and trustees an open water tank, into which articles of old clothing and food refuse were thrown, from time to time, and allowed to remain there indefinitely, the water from which was drunk daily, at morning and evening, by the boys in two of the dormitories, and which in all probability was the mysterious source of fevers and other troubles which made their appearance in the Institution.[205]

In the wake of this embarrassing report, a number of trustees resigned, and staffing on the island was thrown into confusion.[206] But the fuss blew over, and the grand jury's recommendation to move the reformatory to the mainland was ignored. By September 1889, many of the teachers who had been fired or who had resigned were back at their jobs.[207] A superintendent was recruited from the prison system.[208] Certain improvements were made: an electric generator was donated by the Pauper Institutions Department in 1900, and indoor toilets and "shower baths with hot and cold water" replaced unheated fixtures at the school.[209] But the fires and escapes continued, and the physical plant continued to degrade.

A city report published a decade later, in 1908, noted: "It is the plain, solemn truth that, relatively, the pigs [on Rainsford Island] are better housed than the boys and officers."[210] But rather than suggesting closure of the island reformatory, it envisioned a healthy transformation. Fill could be brought out to expand the available acreage; the old cemetery "should be transferred with all due reverence to Long Island as other cemeteries on islands in the harbor

---

[205] Documents of the City of Boston for the Year 1899, vol. 4, Doc. 113, "Report of Joint Special Committee Investigation of Rainsford Island," p. 3.

[206] "Trustees Helpless: Demoralization at Rainsford Island," Boston Post, September 21, 1899, p. 2.

[207] "Going Back to Rainsford Island," Boston Globe, September 27, 1899, p. 3.

[208] "Supt. Sumner Seavey," Boston Globe, October 2, 1899, p. 3.

[209] "Expenditures—Institutions," City of Boston Statistics Department, Special Publications no. 9, Receipt s and Expenditures of Ordinary Revenue, 1898–1903 (Boston: Municipal Printing Office, 1903), p. 93.

[210] Documents of the City of Boston for the Year 1908, vol. 4, "Report on the Special Committee of the Common Council Appointed to Investigate and Report Upon the Abandonment by the City of the Suffolk School for Boys and the Transfer of the Boys there Detained to the Lyman School for Boys at Westborough, Doc. 151, p. 3.

have been." New buildings were envisioned: "Plain, substantial structures, well lighted and well ventilated. . .. [I]f the material is judiciously selected, the cost will not be appalling."[211]

No such buildings were erected on the island. The situation went on as usual and was even occasionally reported in the press. But it took another decade to finally close the reformatory on Rainsford Island.

Closure

Whereas the women's era of Rainsford Island ended when Alice Lincoln and her confederates exposed the abuses there, the boys' reform school era went on and on, despite grand jury recommendations, pleas from mayors, and minority reports from investigating committees. It is hard to say why, except perhaps that no one was willing to fund an alternative.

The Trustees for Children condemned Rainsford Island repeatedly in reports of 1898, 1899, and 1900 (see Appendix 6.3). Mayor Josiah Quincy VI (in office 1896–1900) called for its closure in 1899: "The experience of another year has further emphasized the importance of removing the house of reformation from Rainsford Island to some point upon the mainland."[212]

The Special Committee convened in 1908 was equally clear: "[T]hese views call for the abandonment of Rainsford Island and the transfer of the boys to the care of the State at the Lyman School for Boys at Westborough. The reasons given are that the island is wholly inadequate for the purposes of a reform school, and that the cost per boy, per year, per week is too great. . . ."[213]

In 1910, three of the Trustees for Children whose terms were expiring—Charles P. Putnam, Lee M. Friedman, and Caroline S. Atherton—lodged a protest against Rainsford in a minority report: "It must be only a question of time when the city abandons this waste of money and of youths. We recommend that it be now, and that the Legislature of 1910 be asked for authority to transfer to the Lyman and Shirley Schools the boys now at Rainsford and that the

---

[211] Documents of the City of Boston for the Year 1908, vol. 4, "Report on the Special Committee of the Common Council Appointed to Investigate and Report Upon the Abandonment by the City of the Suffolk School for Boys and the Transfer of the Boys there Detained to the Lyman School for Boys at Westborough, Doc. 151, pp. 4–5.

[212] "Call to Remove Children from Rainsford Island," Boston Globe, January 2, 1899, p. 7.

[213] Documents of the City of Boston for the Year 1908, vol. 4, "Report on the Special Committee of the Common Council Appointed to Investigate and Report Upon the Abandonment by the City of the Suffolk School for Boys and the Transfer of the Boys there Detained to the Lyman School for Boys at Westborough, Doc. 151, p.2.

Suffolk School be abandoned."[214] The new mayor of Boston in 1911, John F. "Honey Fitz" Fitzgerald, (whose grandson was the 35th President of the United States, John Fitzgerald Kennedy) made the same argument:

> Boston is paying approximately 40 per cent of the expense of these schools [Lyman and Shirley] and has equal privilege with the rest of the state to have its boys taken care of in these institutions. Yet Boston insists on duplicating these expenses to run its own local school as a survival of an old system [that] has long since disappeared from the rest of the state. There is not a single argument to justify this, yet it remains a monument to inertia that handicaps the city's development when the calls [come in] for cutting salaried places from the city payroll.[215]

Despite these perceptive words, the inertia continued under his administration. It continued after 1914 under that of his successor, James Michael Curley, despite the fact that Curley had campaigned on a platform that included closure of Rainsford.[216]

The Finance Committee of the City of Boston used the now-familiar arguments in 1916 in calling upon the city to close Rainsford.[217] Curley cited this report and tried to convince the Commonwealth to take over the Suffolk School; he also tried to get rid of truant schools altogether, arguing, "There are never any children of wealthy parents in the truant schools."[218]

Damaging fires in 1916 and 1917 brought the cost of necessary repairs for the facility to an untenable level. Facing a bill of nearly $140,000, the Trustees of the Children's Department finally stepped up and, with a single vote, did what no other board had managed to do:

> Under the authority vested in it by chapter 182, Acts of 1826, the Board of Trustees of the Children's Institutions Department voted, in February, 1920, to restrict commitments to the Suffolk School for Boys and notified the judges of the several courts of the county that no further commitments were to be made without the assent of the Board of Trustees. By thus restricting commitments and by the parole of deserving cases,

---

[214] "Additional (Minority) Report on the Suffolk School," Documents of the City of Boston for the Year 1910 (1911), Vol. 1, p. 9.

[215] Boston *City Record*, February 2, 1911, pp. 59–60.

[216] Boston Globe, November 27, 1913, p. 2; Mayor Curley reiterated the pledge in his inaugural address, see Lowell Sun, February 3, 1914.

[217] The Finance Commission of the City of Boston, Reports and Communications, Vol. 11 (1916), pp. 201–206.

[218] "Offers Rainsford Island at a Bargain," Boston Post, February 3, 1917, p. 8.

the number was so reduced that on December 1, 1920, but 50 inmates remained, who, before Christmas were paroled to go to their homes and the school closed.[219]

Not every child had a home to go to. The newspapers reported on the last forlorn case on Rainsford Island. A nine-year-old named Jackie ate Christmas dinner in 1920 alone with the skeleton staff on the island because "Jackie's mother never could properly care for him. He has no home." He was ultimately transferred to a state institution, along with two others who could not be left at large in the community. In parting, the caretakers "gave their 'favorite' a wonderful day with: a new suit, a real turkey dinner, a box of candy, a toy boat, Santa arriving on the ferry; being taken to Long Island to see a movie."[220]

It is significant that in their closing reports, the newspapers abandoned the euphemistic language of reform and frankly called Jackie "Rainsford Island's Lone Prisoner."

Appendix 6.1: Laws of Indenture, 1882

Source: Public Documents of Massachusetts: Being the Annual Reports of Various Public Officers and Institutions for the Year 1882 (Boston: Wright & Potter, 1883), vol. 4, "Manual for the Use of the Boards of Health and Overseers of the Poor of Massachusetts: Industrial and Reform Schools and Juvenile Offenders" (June 1882), p. 133.

Sect. 38. The trustees may bind out as an apprentice or servant any girl committed to their charge until she is eighteen years of age, and any boy until he is twenty-one years of age, or for any less term; and the trustees, master or mistress, apprentice or servant, shall respectively have all the rights and privileges and be subject to all the duties set forth in chapter one hundred and forty-nine, in the same manner as if such binding or apprenticing were made by overseers of the poor. In binding out girls and boys, the trustees shall have scrupulous regard to the religious and moral character of those to whom they are to be bound, that they may secure to the girls and boys the benefit of a good example and wholesome instruction, and the best means of improvement in virtue and knowledge, and thus the opportunity of becoming intelligent, moral, useful and happy.

[219] Documents of the City of Boston for the Year 1921 (1922), Vol. 2, Doc. 14, p. 4.

[220] "Jack of the Winsome Smile To Dine Alone," Boston Post, December 24, 1920, p. 6: "Own Boss Though an Inmate: Rainsford Island's Lone Prisoner Has Real Holiday," Boston Globe, December 26, 1920, p. 6.

Appendix 6.2. Final Statistics for the House of Reformation, 1895–1921.

Status on January 31, 1921, of 2,826, boys admitted to the Suffolk School for Boys since May 1, 1895. A partial account of the discharges notes:

Entered Military Service	**302**
Released to their home	**319**
Indentured*	**12**
Released out of state	**107**
Committed to Mass Reformatory	**253**
Lost track of	**22**
Committed to State Prison	**5**
Committed to Industrial School Shirley	**28**
Discharged to parents as unfit subjects	**2**
Discharged to other State schools	**8**
Discharged to Insane Hospital	**3**
Discharged to School for Feeble Minded	**10**
Discharged as wrongfully committed	**3**
Discharged on or of the Trustees	**385**
Discharged on payment of fines or credit for time served	**199**
Discharged on arriving at age 21	**495**
Died	**47**
Names occurring more than once	**542**
Readmitted	**49**

Source: Documents of the City of Boston for the Year 1921, Vol. 2, Document 14, p. 32.

Appendix 6.3: Financial Summary of the Rainsford Island Reformatory, 1916.

Source: The Finance Commission of the City of Boston, Reports and Communications, Volume 11 (1916), pp. 200–205.

"…Recently an order has been introduced in the City Council calling upon the Mayor to introduce an order for an appropriation or for the transfer of an unnamed sum of money to the Children's Institutions Department, to be expended on the Suffolk School, for the purpose of separating the younger from the older boys.

In view of the above facts the Finance Commission believes that now is the time to take remedial action on the condition of the Suffolk School for Boys at Rainsford Island and in furtherance of that object reports as follows:

The school before 1901 was called the House of Employment and Reformation of Juvenile Offenders. It had been removed May 1, 1895 from Deer Island to its present location Rainsford Island because of the close proximity of the school at that time to the prison for adult offenders.

Rainsford Island has an area of about eleven acres of which nearly one acre is occupied by the old national cemetery. It occupies the buildings left vacant because they were not suitable by the removal of the pauper women to Long Island. The buildings in question consist of a main building between sixty-five and seventy years old and minor frame buildings some of which are old voting booths and none of which have been built for the present purposes.

The main building referred to contains crowded dormitories a printing office a chapel schoolrooms officers' rooms dining rooms kitchens pantries sanitaries [sic] and bathrooms and a heating and power plant. The dormitories are very crowded and one of them has such a low ceiling that its ventilation is bad. The danger from fire is very much heightened by the construction of the buildings the youth of the occupants and the isolated situation of Rainsford Island.

Boys of Suffolk County under the age of fifteen years may be committed to the Suffolk School during their minority. The average daily population is 125 and the average stay of boys in the institution released or discharged last year was 16.74 months. The class of boys in the school is made up of those who have been brought up under circumstances that lead to idleness, dissipation and crime of boys from good homes who have not responded to the ordinary discipline of the community of those who have been given a chance on parole and have been returned to the school for further discipline and a limited number who have not been benefited by the efforts made by the school in their behalf who cannot be reformed and will eventually enter the prisons of this or other states.

The diverse elements in the Suffolk School have a tendency to level down since the younger learn evil. That the more advanced are able to teach them. The problem to be worked out by a boys' disciplinary school is complicated in the extreme namely to teach a willful youth habits of obedience to inculcate standards of good community life and at the same time to protect him from those who can teach him evil faster than he can learn good. The problem to be solved at the Suffolk School is especially difficult because of the fact that the children committed to it during the last five years or returned from parole have ranged from the age of nine to sixteen.

In disciplinary schools like that of the Suffolk School, the cottage system of dormitory living is much more effective than the method of grouping the children of all ages together. The physical situation on Rainsford Island is such that a proper classification such as is called for in the cottage system is difficult if not impossible.

A cottage known as the Point Cottage used for a number of years for the younger boys last year fell into utter disrepair but has been remodeled and made habitable at considerable expense for the twenty-three young boys now at the island. Its location gives some separation for those that dwell there but there is no play or farm space near it. The play space of the institution which must be used in common by the young and older boys lies in a hollow which has recently been partially filled in and drained in winter it is flooded for skating but when so flooded and not frozen as often happens in this climate it becomes a small lake and then no sensible and harmless play is possible. The piece of farm land lies on a hillside and in spite of its location small area and poor soil good use has been made of it.

The health of the institution because of its situation is good in many respects yet boys with weak lungs have suffered and a few deaths have resulted because of the exposed location.

It is claimed on one hand that the islands in the harbor are favorable for disciplinary institutions because of the difficulties presented to its inmates for running away. On the other hand, it is said that this advantage is overestimated. Four deaths from drowning of runaways from the Suffolk School during the past two years more than offset the possibly larger number of runaways that might occur at a disciplinary school on the mainland. It is to be remarked that the isolation of the school and its distance from the city tends to lessen the interest of the citizens in the school and the needs of its inhabitants.

The boys are brought to Rainsford Island on the boats of the City of Boston which ply between the mainland and the houses of correction on Deer Island and the hospital and almshouse on Long Island. On the wharf waiting for the boat the boy is confined in the same room with the adult offenders destined for Deer Island.

The Trustees for Children in the past have done their full duty in bringing the condition of affairs to the public In the report of the first year of the department's existence January 31, 1898, pages 7 and 8, and in their reports of 1899 and 1900, and every year thereafter up to 1911, they have condemned the conditions on Rainsford Island and have said, Is it not time that the city cease to spend its money upon buildings unsuited to their use and to furnish proper location and buildings for its reform school for boys. The trustees of these earlier years earnestly recommended that the school be removed to a situation upon the mainland with sufficient land for farming purposes. Again, and again have former boards with more or less detail repeated this recommendation stating that it must be only a question of time when the city abandons this waste of money and of youths.

In 1901 the trustees appealed to the Legislature and succeeded in having passed Ch. 359 of the acts of that year which changed the name of the institution from House of Employment and Reformation of Juvenile Offenders to the Suffolk School for Boys and authorized the department to select a suitable site on the mainland within or without the County of Suffolk This latter authority carried with it a mandatory direction to the City Treasurer to issue bonds for $300,000 upon the acceptance of the act by a two thirds vote of the City Council.

These bonds were to be issued within the debt limit but the mandatory provision of the act left no option to the city officials to refuse to issue the bonds after it had been accepted by the City Council. The act however has never been accepted although in the past the trustees of the department have strongly urged such action.

A tabulation of the expenditures for repairs and improvements from 1897 to 1915 shows that the large sum of $131,799.39 has been spent at Rainsford Island for repairs and improvements.

In the reports of the last three years the trustees have not expressed any discontent with the location and equipment of the Suffolk School although these later reports urge that cottages be built upon Rainsford Island.

The commission believes that the portion of the island to be used for cottages is so small that it would be necessary to place them so near together as to lose the full advantage of a cottage system.

It has been proposed in past years to transfer the Suffolk School to the Commonwealth because the latter maintains similar disciplinary schools like those of the Lyman School and the Shirley School for Boys for which Boston pays its proportional share of the cost. Such action would have represented the annual saving of the cost of the institution $50,000 to the city. The proposed changes have not been favorably received.

The Finance Commission believes:

1. In the principle of separating the younger from the older boys.

2. That in a school like the Suffolk School the cottage system of dormitory living is much more effective than the method of grouping the children of all ages together and in that way the separation of the young and older offenders can be best accomplished.

3. That the portion of Rainsford Island which could be used for cottages is too small to place them sufficiently far apart in order to obtain the full advantage of a cottage system.

4. That Boston should expend no more money than is absolutely essential for the maintenance of the plant at Rainsford Island until a new site can be obtained.

5. That while the protection against boys running away is a recommendation in favor of Rainsford Island yet the benefits that the many may receive in a more favorable location far outweigh in importance the fact that a few boys run away each year for as a rule they are soon found and returned.

6. That Rainsford Island is unsuited for the Suffolk School for Boys both because of location and the fact that so small a portion of it can be used.

7. That if the City of Boston desires to maintain this school and not transfer it to the state it should do its full duty by the juvenile offenders and should at least give them opportunities equal to those the Commonwealth is ready to provide.

8. That the conditions surrounding the Suffolk School on Rainsford Island are of such a nature that drastic action should be immediately taken for their improvement.

The Finance Commission recommends.

1. That the Suffolk School on Rainsford Island be abandoned….

2. That the school be transferred to the mainland and located on a site which would allow the use of the cottage system and provide ample opportunities for farming."

Chapter 7: The Dead of Rainsford Island

If you visit Rainsford Island today, you find no indication that anyone is buried there. Even allowing for the choppy history of the island and its legacy of poor or nonexistent record-keeping, this is surprising for a quarantine island: some sort of cemetery would be expected. But the dead are indeed there, and in numbers far greater than sources led us to expect. An exhaustive search of burial records from the City of Boston from 1800 to 1896 leads us to conclude that over 1,777 people, including numerous Veterans, are interred there in an unmarked burial ground.[221]

The site of the Rainsford Island cemetery was sufficiently melancholy to draw poetic regret from Moses Sweetser, the author of *King's Handbook of Boston*. In 1888, he wrote:

> Boston families sent members with dangerous infectious diseases: they were certain never to return; unfortunates rest within sight of the spires of their home town; isolated on this dreary strand; allowed to drift down into the darkness of death uncomforted by their neighboring friends and relatives.[222]

Who are the dead of Rainsford Island and how did they come to be buried there?

The Cemetery

The Rainsford Island Cemetery is today simply a clearing on an otherwise overgrown harbor island. According to Boston city documents from a century ago, it covers an area of 43,560 square feet on the West Head of the island.[223]

A reconstruction of the island buildings shows that the cemetery is located a very short distance from the hospital built in 1832 and from Smallpox Point, and also close to the piggery built in 1878 (Fig. 7.1). A row of lilacs was planted on the side of the cemetery nearest to the hospital and survives to this day. The conjecture is that the lilacs were there to buffer the

---

[221] Bill McEvoy conducted the records search and created a database recording all persons who died at Rainsford Island, including vital statistics where available, and all persons buried at Rainsford Island Cemetery rather than elsewhere. Data before 1800 is so spotty as to be useless for our purposes.

[222] Moses Foster Sweetser, *King's Handbook of Boston Harbor*, 3rd ed. (Boston: Moses King Corp., 1888), p. 203.

[223] Documents of the City of Boston for the Year 1919, Vol. 3, No. 37, Municipal Register of the City Government (Boston: City of Boston Printing Department), Cemetery Department, p. 45.

hospital from the foul odors emanating from the cemetery, though that could only have been a seasonal reprieve. The Superintendent's house, by contrast, was located at the highest elevation on the opposite side of the island, as far as possible from the dead.

During the period when the Commonwealth was still in charge of the island, some attempts had been made to regularize the care of the dead. In May 1855, the Governor approved a resolve in aid of the State Hospital at Rainsford Island to build a number of structures on the island, including a "tomb":

> Resolved: That there be allowed and paid, out of the treasury of the Commonwealth, for the enlargement of the female hospital, the erection of a workshop, a wash-room and laundry, the construction of a tomb, and for other necessary improvements at the State Hospital, on Rainsford Island, the sum of twenty thousand dollars to be expended by the inspectors of the hospital, and that the governor be authorized to draw his warrant for the same, accordingly.[224]

Of what this "tomb" consisted can only be guessed at.

The Rainsford cemetery administration was not entirely devoid of records. Although we have not found any centralized record of burials, a Rainsford Island cemetery, a burial book, for the period from late 1887 to 1896, was discovered at Mount Hope Cemetery by Joseph Bagley, the City of Boston's archeologist. It appears that it was begun when Long Island Hospital began accepting residents (September 1887). That book has its shortcomings but notes all interments at Rainsford Island of Long Island's unclaimed bodies from September 1887 until June 23, 1893. During that period, the bodies of 240 unclaimed people who died at Long Island were transferred to Rainsford Island and buried there. Six of those were Civil War Veterans.

After June 23, 1893, the bodies of men and women who died at Long Island that were not claimed for private burial, remained and were buried at Long Island.[225] The burial book also notes the burials of unclaimed bodies who died at Rainsford Island from late 1887 to 1896.

---

[224] *Acts and Resolves Passed by the General Court of Massachusetts in the Year 1855* (Boston: William White, 1855), Chap. 76, p. 971.

[225] Reports of the Committee of the Whole Board of Alderman of the Care and Management of the Public Institutions with an Appendix Giving Testimony Submitted at the Investigation, Vol. 3 (1894), p. 2888.

"Carted Down to the Graveyard"

Care of the dead at Rainsford Island appears to have been just as casual as care of the living. The problems became more apparent after September 1887, when the unclaimed bodies of those who died at Long Island Hospital were transported for burial at Rainsford Island. The first interment at Rainsford Island of a death at Long Island was Ellen Hennessey, age 64, who died on September 15, 1887.[226]

The process did not go smoothly. In December 1891, the *Boston Globe* printed a letter from Richard J. Geary, Deputy Superintendent of Long Island Hospital:

> About a week before Thanksgiving, . . . I . . . wrote a letter to Dr. Newell, one of the commissioners, calling attention to the fact that dead bodies were left from 10 to 14 days on Long Island before burial [on Rainsford Island] . . .. Dr. Newell went down to the island the same day and found two bodies there, as I had stated, and soon Dr. Harkins, the resident physician, made an order that all dead bodies should be interred after three days . . ..[227]

Apparently, little was done to correct the procedures, as we learn in Alice Lincoln's fifty-eight hearings in 1894 (see Chapter 4). During those hearings, conditions at Rainsford Island, as well as at other public institutions, were discussed at length, including the circumstances of death and burial on the island.

Louis D. Brandeis, acting as counsel to Alice N. Lincoln in her challenge to conditions at Rainsford and Long Islands, summed up the treatment of the deceased as of June 23, 1893. He spoke of Long Island, but we have no reason to believe the situation on Rainsford was any better. "The dead," Brandeis asserted, "were as ill provided as the living." Despite deaths occurring "every other day on average":

> Shrouds were not ready, coffins were not ready, and when the dead were put in their coffins, they were not treated with that respect which the meanest of mankind pays to the dead. These corpses, stored first in the slaughter-house, then in a blacksmith shop, were, when they got ready to bury them, carted down to the graveyard and dropped into

---

[226] City of Boston Death Records, 1887.
[227] Boston Globe, December 4, 1891, p. 4.

the open grave—not a grave dug for that occasion, but dug, as it were, by the wholesale, in order that they might be a warning and a preparation to the inhabitants of that island of what was in store for them.

...[T]here was not even the care taken to cover up these bodies which were put so carelessly into the ground. For days they remained uncovered, and as late even as after this investigation began that flagrant disregard of the most common instincts of man found a place in this institution of which the city of Boston is called upon by some to be proud. When they found their place there, unaccompanied by any service, unaccompanied by a word or sign of respect, treated as none of you gentlemen would treat a dog, that was the end, that was the comedy of the unfortunate poor of the city of Boston who found at Long Island a pauper's grave.[228]

Dr. Otis K. Newell, a member of the Board of Commissioners of Public Institutions who was cited in the *Boston Globe* article in 1891, testified at the hearings. Responding to questions from a Boston citizen, Thomas Riley, on May 17, 1894, he gave a graphic description of how the dead were treated:

Q. [Mr. Riley] . . . Now, what do you know in regard to the treatment of dead bodies at Long Island?

A. [Dr. Newell] Well, I know that the treatment of dead bodies at Long Island was something improper almost beyond belief.

Q. Describe it.

A. I have gone down there and found dead bodies—in the first place, they were kept a good part of the time in a shed or building where hogs were dressed or slaughtered; and they were piled in there indiscriminately. On one occasion I knew of two bodies being there, one of which had been there six days, and the other twelve days; and on one occasion in August, there was one there nineteen days. It was putrid, and was running out from the receptacle. [. . .]

Q. Were the bodies in coffins?

A. Yes, sir, in a coffin.

---

[228] Documents of the City of Boston for the Year 1894, Vol. 4, *Report on the Management of Public Institutions, Appendix*, Third Hearing (March 27, 1894), p. 132.

Q. Now, why were they kept there?

A. Well, they were kept in the sheds and in this other old building that I don't know what the exact name was—I think it used to be an old ice-house—because they had no proper receptacle for them.

Q. Well, having ascertained that condition of things, why didn't you, as a member of the Board, have it remedied?

A. Well, I did propose to have it remedied.

Q. Did you bring it to the attention of the Board?

A. Yes, sir.

The witness went on to describe the inaction of the Board and the indifference of Dr. Jenks, the superintendent.[229]

Possibly as a result of the unflattering spotlight cast upon Rainsford Island's administration, modest efforts were made to regularize the Rainsford cemetery. In 1899 it was enclosed by a new fence, neatly painted.[230] By 1914, the cemetery was under the "direct charge" of the general superintendent of cemeteries, Leonard W. Ross.[231] However, the city documents warn that "on account of the conditions, we cannot expect perpetual care funds to be received for the Warren and Rainsford Island Cemeteries."[232]

---

[229] Documents of the City of Boston for the Year 1894, Vol. 5, *Report on the Management of Public Institutions, Appendix*, Evening Session (May 17, 1894), pp. 1080–82.

[230] City of Boston, Statistics Department, Special Publications No. II, Extraordinary Receipts and Expenditures, 1898-1902 (1910), p. 95.

[231] Documents of the City of Boston for the Year 1920, Vol. 1, Document No. 7, Cemetery Department, p. 2.

[232] Documents of the City of Boston for the Year 1914, Vol. 1, Document No. 7, Cemetery Department, p. 16.

Google Earth

Civil War Soldiers and Veterans

During the Civil War, soldiers, sick with any contagious or infectious disease, were allowed admission to the Rainsford Island Hospital, upon approval of the Governor (see Chapter 3).[233] The isolation of these men dismayed many who heard of it, and the issue was raised with the governor's office. On May 19, 1866, the governor ordered all Veterans still remaining at Rainsford to be removed and given over to the responsibility of their home districts. They were to be placed by the Overseers of the Poor at the cities or towns that were responsible for them, in accordance with the Military Resettlement Law of 1865.[234]

In the relatively short interval when Civil War Veterans were placed in care at Rainsford Island, nine of them died. From 1863 to 1866, eight soldiers and one sailor died and were buried at Rainsford. Four died from smallpox, and one each from edema, pneumonia, diarrhea, phthisis, and heart disease. One of those soldiers was a member of the 5th Massachusetts Calvary, Colored. On February 15, 1866, a Veteran sailor died of heart failure and is also buried

233 Third Annual Report of State Charities of Massachusetts, Public Document No. 17 (1867), pp. 141–45.
234 Third Annual Report of State Charities of Massachusetts, Public Document No. 17 (1867), pp. 141–45.

at Rainsford.[235] These were neither the only nor the last Veterans to be interred at Rainsford, however (see Appendix 7.1).

The database of those buried at Rainsford was cross-checked to male names noted on *U.S. Civil War Soldier Records and Profiles, 1861–1865* on Ancestry.com. By noting the year and place of birth, as well as occupation, many Veterans were identified. In addition, we reviewed over one thousand Boston newspaper articles that referred to Rainsford Island. The final total of Veterans buried at Rainsford was determined to be 119. That number includes one sailor from the War of 1812 who died in active service. Fourteen were African American.

The City of Boston purchased Rainsford from the Commonwealth in 1871.[236] By the time the City reopened Rainsford in the fall of 1872, the buildings and the cemetery had been left to the elements for almost six years. Between 1873 and 1893, a further 108 Veterans were buried at Rainsford, and their graves left to the mercies of the appointed bureaucrats and patients of the City-run hospital island. The residents at the beginning of that era were described by the *Boston Globe* in unflattering terms:

> [O]ne third are people with broken lives; victims of circumstance, sickness; disabling injury, accident; poor by loss or swindle; one third are criminals released from institutions or inebriants; one third are subjects of ingrained and incorrigible vagabondism; lack of enterprise has preserved them from crime; drifted to almshouses naturally as bottle corks thrown into the river and float downstream.[237]

It stands to reason that conditions at the cemetery improved little during the following twenty-three years.

Our search revealed that periodic attempts had been made to acknowledge the deceased Veterans and to mark their graves at Rainsford. After 1879, the U.S. government provided Civil War burial markers for twenty-eight Veterans' graves.[238] And private Veterans associations stepped in. Newspapers repeatedly mentioned Memorial Day commemorations at Rainsford by the Robert A. Bell Post No. 134, G.A.R. (Grand Army of the Republic), which was located at

---

[235] City of Boston, Records of Death, 1866.
[236] Boston *Post*, October 9, 1871, p. 3.
[237] Boston *Globe*, December 30, 1872.
[238] Ancestry.com, "Headstones Provided for Deceased Union Civil War Veterans, 1861–1904."

the old Smith Schoolhouse, 46 Joy Street, now occupied by the Museum of African American History. Members of this G.A.R. Post included Veterans of the legendary 54th Massachusetts Regiment, whose intrepid service under Col. Robert Gould Shaw proved the mettle of African-American troops in the Civil War. With the exception of a single mention in 1902 that alluded to 280 graves,[239] the most consistent numbers stated each Memorial Day were 100 to 120.

The May 31, 1885, edition of the *Globe* noted Memorial Day exercises involving 32 members of the Bell Post travelling by boat to Rainsford and decorating 75 Veterans' graves. Two years later, the *Globe* reported that the Bell Post Veterans were escorted on their island excursion by the "Shaw Guards" (the 14th Unattached Company of the Massachusetts Volunteer Militia, an African American squad).[240] One 1888 article reports that they were joined by the "Carney Camp 82, Sons of Veterans" in decorating 100 graves.

Dignitaries were invited to speak at the decoration ceremonies. In 1892, Pauline Elizabeth Hopkins, writer and civil rights activist, was the post-decoration speaker. Her step-father was a member of the Bell Post.[241] Robert T. Teamoh, an African American member of the Massachusetts General Court, was the speaker at the Rainsford visit in 1894.[242] Sgt. William Carney, a member of the Bell Post and a Medal of Honor recipient, was the speaker in 1907. He died the following year.[243] The Bell Post's women's auxiliary, the Women's Relief Corps Post 67, attended many of the ceremonies.[244]

---

[239] Boston *Globe*, May 31, 1902, p. 4.

[240] Boston *Globe*, May 30, 1887, p. 2; For the Shaw Guards, see Alan I. Johnson, "In Search of Freedom: African Americans and Massachusetts' Militia from 1852–1917," M.A. Thesis, Brandeis University (May 2107).

[241] Boston *Globe*, May 31, 1892, p. 3.

[242] Boston *Globe*, May 31, 1894, p. 10.

[243] Boston *Post*, May 31, 1907, p. 5.

[244] To date, we have been unable to locate any records or photographs of either organization. We welcome any information as to their location.

The Relocation of Bodies

There is conflicting information regarding the removal of burials at Rainsford and reinternment on the grounds of the nearby Long Island Hospital. Many times, authorities were urged to remove the dead from Rainsford Island, but we found no hard evidence that anyone did so.

The suggestion to relocate the Rainsford graves appeared in the *Boston Globe* on December 24, 1908, thirteen years after the hospital had closed and the island was put to use as the House of Reformation (see Chapter 6). The City of Boston Common Council, in reporting (yet again) the woeful conditions at Rainsford Island, called attention to the neglected dead who dwelt on the island alongside the neglected children: "There is an old cemetery on the island [that] should be transferred to Long Island, as other cemeteries on islands in the harbor have been. . .. We recommend that the Trustees take immediate steps for removal of the cemetery. . . ."[245]

Closure was brought up again in the *Globe* in 1912:

> On Rainsford Island is an old cemetery in which are buried quite a number of paupers, also soldiers of the United States Army, who died at various forts in the harbor. It is proposed to abolish the cemetery, and it will be necessary to transfer the bodies elsewhere. The Mayor ['Honey Fitz' Fitzgerald] will ask the City Council to make an appropriation to remove the bodies of the paupers to Mount Hope Cemetery, and the Department will be asked to make an estimate of the cost. The National Government is willing to stand the cost of removing the bodies of soldiers to the grounds at the Soldiers' Home in Chelsea, but first wants to know the names, rank, and service of the men who are to be removed. The question is can they be obtained.[246]

The city council, however, pushed back. A month later, the *Globe* reported:

> Mayor Fitzgerald's plan for the removal of the bodies buried at Rainsford Island, in order that the land might be used for the Suffolk School for Boys, was opposed by Chairman Phillips of the Cemetery Board yesterday on the ground that the disinterment

[245] Boston *Globe*, December 4, 1908.

[246] "National Government and City to Transfer the Soldiers and Paupers Buried on Ransford Island," Boston *Globe*, August 31, 1912, p. 4.

might be dangerous. For 50 years the island was used as a quarantine station, and other contagious disease are buried there. Mr. Phillips suggested that the cemetery be grassedover [sic] and fenced in, to prevent the boys on the island from playing there.[247]

Once again, no bodies were removed. But in transferring oversight of the Rainsford burial ground to the Cemetery Department, the city did provide a useful summary of its use:

> This island was used as a quarantine station as early as 1737, and continued under the jurisdiction of the state until 1866. It was purchased by the City of Boston for an almshouse in 1871, and in 1895 its present use as a house of reformation for boys was inaugurated. It is unquestionable that burials were made from the earliest occupancy of the island, and *several thousand persons* [emphasis added] must have been interred in this small cemetery. The earliest stone standing at the present time is dated 1749. Between 1871 and 1882 indigent Veterans were sent to Rainsford Island, and those who died were buried in the cemetery there. An agitation started in 1912 and finally taken up with the United States government has resulted in the preparation of plans for the erection of a monument in this cemetery to the Veterans buried therein. Pending the final action of the government relative to the erection of the monument, this department has delayed carrying out plans to place the cemetery in good condition.[248]

Delays, evasions, and outright lies continued, even as vandals and the elements eroded what remained of the grave markers and fences.

That condition was noted again in the Boston Globe on December 17, 1933. Page A1 announced the commencement of various Civil Works projects in Boston. All of the old structures at Rainsford Island were to be razed. Only the pier was to be repaired. The cemetery was described as a Potter's Field for those who lacked the means to buy a grave. A few wooden markers and crosses were noted. The Emergency Relief Fund was to be used to build a wrought-iron fence around "the lonesome, God's Little Acre".

Again in 1946, after the passage of two world wars, the *Globe* took up the issue:

---

247 "Disinterment Opposed: Chairman Phillips Urges Danger in Proposed Action at Rainsford Island Cemetery," Boston *Globe*, September 26, 1912, p. 15.

248 Documents of the City of Boston for the Year 1914, Vol. 1, Cemetery Department, Document No. 7, p. 20.

The graves of 200 Civil War and 50 Spanish War soldiers have been neglected and desecrated on Rainsford Island in Boston Harbor, a Sons of Union Veterans spokesman disclosed last night. "This is only one example," said George W. Kimball, S. U. V. [Sons of Union Veterans] department commander. "In this case, the city of Boston, is responsible. The situation is so bad on that island you can't tell the graves from the beach." He charged "almost all of the gravestones have been pulled around and knocked apart like rocks. There has been absolutely no care given to those who died to keep our Union intact." A year ago, he said, Col. Frederick G. Bauer of Boston S. U. V. department counsel, obtained the promise of Boston officials to rectify the situation, "but nothing has been done. Today, you can't even tell where the graves were!" [249]

In fact, no Veterans of the Spanish War were ever buried at Rainsford as the cemetery became inactive before the beginning of that War, and the number of 200 Civil War Veterans interred at Rainsford cannot be substantiated. As noted above, previous newspaper articles, beginning in 1882, placed the Veterans graves at about 100 to 120.

The *Globe* story elicited a reaction from City Hall. In April 1947, six months after the neglect of Veterans' graves was publicized, the paper reported that "Bodies [Were] to Be Removed from Rainsford Island":

The remains of 350, including 79 Civil War Veterans, will be removed from Rainsford Island to Long Island, where they will be safe from desecration by vandals and picnickers, Mayor [James Michael] Curley said last night. The action was taken following a protest lodged by officials of the Sons of Union Veterans, who said markers had been burned for firewood and the burial area ruined by vandals. Many of the Veterans died from Small Pox, when the city maintained an institution on the harbor island.[250]

This article was printed shortly before Mayor Curley began serving a sentence for mail fraud at the Federal Prison at Danbury, Connecticut. (He was released by Thanksgiving of that year, having been pardoned by President Harry S Truman.) What directives, if any, the mayor

[249] "Boston Assailed for Neglect of Veterans' Graves," Boston *Globe*, November 12, 1946, p. 5.
[250] "Bodies to Be Removed From Rainsford Island," Boston *Globe*, April 18, 1947, p. 13.

put in train before heading to prison are unclear, but certainly some effort was made to convince the public that bodies had been removed from Rainsford Island and reinterred at Long Island. A handsome plaque was commissioned for Long Island to honor the 79 Civil War Veterans "who are buried here and whose names are inscribed here."

The *Boston Herald* reported the plaque's dedication in September 1948:

> Constitution Day will be observed in Boston today with the dedication of a plaque of Civil War heroes at their Long Island graves and a dinner meeting of patriotic organizations at 6:30 P.M. in the Women's Republican Club. In co-operation with the Bay State camp of the Sons of Union Veterans, the city will unveil the plaque to Veterans originally buried on Rainsford Island and reburied, after a fire….[251]

Fig. 7.2. Plaque in memory of reburied Civil War Veterans, Long Island, 1948.

[251] "Civil War Heroes Plaque Will Be Dedicated Today," Boston *Herald*, September 19, 1948, p. 5. The fire mentioned may relate to the 1947 article above, noting that markers were used for firewood.

Fig. 7.3. Plaque at Long Island- August 26, 2019. Island is closed to the public. W. A. McEvoy

Expenditure for the plaque appears in the City of Boston Records: the 1948 City of Boston's Annual Report of the Art Department notes that the department "has approved the monument and bronze tablet to Civil War Veterans, by John Francis Paramino and Tito Cascieri, placed, with the help of the Public Institutions Department, at a site on Long Island."[252] Paramino (1888–1956), a graduate of the North Bennet Street School, was a resident of Wellesley, MA, who sculpted many bronze memorials in Boston. His works include memorials to Commodore John Barry, Marquis de La Fayette, The Founders, and The Declaration of Independence, all on the Boston Common; and the World War II Memorial on the Fenway.[253] He completed the Long Island plaque while he was sculpting figures for the WW II and John Barry monuments.

---

[252] City of Boston's Annual Report of the Art Department for the Year Ending December 31, 1948.

[253] Mr. Paramino appears to have been a favorite of James Michael Curley's. Among his many commissions for the mayor was a Commemorative Coin designed in 1936, memorializing Curley's service as a member of the Boston Common Council (1900–1901); the Massachusetts House of Representatives (1902–1903); the Boston Board of Aldermen (1904–1909); U.S. Congress (1911–15); Mayor of Boston (1914–17, 1922–25, 1930–33); and Governor of Massachusetts (1935–36). After the coin with struck, Curley served again in Congress (1943–47) and as Mayor of Boston (1946–50).

What we cannot locate is any documentation of funds expended for the removal and reburial project, which would have been substantially more involved and expensive than ordering a plaque. Assessing and surveying the cemetery, digging up the dead (assuming they could be accurately located), rehousing and transporting the remains of 79 individuals out of the hundreds buried at Rainsford would have been the work of a team for weeks if not months, and nowhere do we find funds disbursed for such an effort. The City of Boston's records of deaths were not amended to note any transfer of bodies to Long Island Hospital. The Rainsford Island Cemetery was under the care of the City of Boston Park Department until December 1949; no expenses were listed for at least four years prior to that date.[254]

Furthermore, the names on the plaque do not align particularly well with the names of the dead known to be buried on Rainsford. The plaque lists 79 names of Civil War Veterans who were purported to have been removed from Rainsford in 1947 or 1949. A review of all burials at Rainsford Island indicates that the names of 45 Civil War Veterans who were certainly buried at Rainsford do not appear on the Long Island memorial plaque.[255] Seven of those missing names were African Americans. One was Stephen Ennis of Company D, 54th Regiment MVI, mentioned in the Preface; he died at Rainsford on August 14, 1882, of phthisis. We believe that he and many others still lie in unmarked graves in the unmarked cemetery.

Of the 28 names on U.S. Government Civil War headstones that were delivered to Rainsford Island in 1879, noted above, only one name also appears on the Long Island memorial plaque.

By 1946, no stones were identifiable on Rainsford Island. To check whether either bodies or headstones had been transferred to someplace other than Long Island, visits were made to all of the City of Boston cemeteries, Fort Devens, and the Chelsea Soldiers Home plots at Woodlawn Cemetery in Everett. Not one of the 28 headstones was located, nor were their names inscribed on any monuments to Civil War Veterans. The management of the City of

---

[254] *Annual Report of the Park Department for the Year Ending December 31, 1949*, Document 19-1950, pp. 13 & 26.

[255] Their names appear in Civil War service records.

Boston's cemeteries shows no record of those 28 individuals being buried at any of their locations.

There are 7 names on the Long Island Memorial that do not match anyone who was buried at Rainsford Island; nor could they be matched with certainty to Civil War service records. They were not even identifiable as deceased persons who were of age to have served in the Civil War. Five Civil War Veterans listed on the plaque at Long Island died on that island before June 23, 1893, before the cemetery there began to accept burials.[256] Therefore, those Veterans, as well as all other deaths at Long Island during that period, were buried at Rainsford Island's cemetery and almost certainly remain there.

We conclude that *all* of 1,777 known individuals, as well as others unknown, who were buried at Rainsford are still there, without commemoration of any kind.[257]

See Appendix 7.1, page 121: Known burials at Rainsford Island

[256] Boston Globe, August 22, 1965, p. A-88.
[257] We welcome any hard evidence to the contrary to correct the record.

Appendix 7.2: Soldiers, Sailors, & Veterans Buried at Rainsford Island, 1812–1893

Year of Death		Non-African Americans 105		African Americans 14
1812		1		0
1863		1		0
1864		2		1
1865		3		0
1866		2		1
1873		4		1
1874		4		0
1875		4		1
1876		4		1
1877		9		0
1878		9		0
1879		3		0
1880		7		0
1881		5		2
1882		4		0
1883		4		0
1884		7		3
1885		8		0
1886		6		1
1887		5		0
1888		6		0
1889		3		1
1890		2		0
1891		1		2
1893		1		0

Epilogue

The Suffolk School for Boys was closed just after Christmas in 1920, as noted in Chapter 6. Shortly thereafter, the island was once more put to use as a quarantine station. In mid-February 1921, the *Boston Globe* reported that for twelve days the Boston Harbor islands would be utilized to isolate and delouse 1,213 steerage passengers arriving from Danzig on the ship *Manchuria*. Of these, 800 were to be held at the abandoned school buildings at Rainsford Island with the rest lodged at Long Island.[258] In March 1921, the *Globe* noted the arrival of three more passenger ships from Eastern Europe carrying several thousand immigrants, mostly riding in steerage class.

The arrivals in Boston reflected the inability of New York's Ellis Island to keep up with the waves of immigrants fleeing Eastern Europe in the chaotic years after World War I and the Russian Revolution. Private donors stepped in to help the government cope with the influx: The *Globe* edition cited above reported donations totaling $2 million from the Rockefeller Foundation and the Laura Spellman Rockefeller Memorial Fund to the American Relief Administration to "safeguard the health of 3,500,000 European children in both Allied and former enemy countries." John D. Rockefeller Jr. had recently donated $1 million to the same cause.

This unplanned use of the Boston Harbor Islands quickly resulted in a crisis of overtaxed resources. The cost to process the *Manchuria* was $26,000, which triggered an impromptu meeting of steamship operators and government officials at Boston on March 19.[259] After the arrival and ad-hoc processing of several more passenger ships at Gallops and Rainsford Islands in April, the Port of New York came to the rescue: it acquired land at Rockaway Park and was thenceforth able to process all new arrivals. The *Globe* noted that Rainsford Island "would not be needed unless there was an emergency, which is not likely to arise."[260]

Rainsford Island ceased processing and delousing immigrants by the middle of April 1921, subsiding into a quieter pattern of activity. What use the island got in the following years was more benign and augured its future while harking back to the days of the Summer Hospital.

[258] Boston Globe, February 18, 1921, p. 8.
[259] Boston Post, March 20, 1921, p. 18.
[260] Boston Globe, April 5, 1921, p. 11.

Summer Outings

Less than five months after the closure of the School for Boys, the City of Boston was trying out a new use for it. A philanthropist named George L. Randidge (1820–1890) had left $50,000 to the city "for children's excursions in the months of July and August."[261] With Rainsford Island empty, the Globe reported: "Facilities are being arranged for the entertainment of 15,000 Boston Children as Randidge Fund excursionists at Rainsford Island, the Institutions Department announces. Formerly the children went to Long Island on these daily outings. The recent abandonment of the Suffolk School for Boys at Rainsford leaves these buildings available for use in connection with the Randidge trips." Daily outings would begin on July 1, 1921: "The trips will be made aboard the little steamer Monitor. As usual outdoor sports will be enjoyed. On rainy days, the children will be entertained with a movie show in one of the buildings at Rainsford."[262]

Adult groups of private and governmental organizations also ventured out to Rainsford. On June 24, 1921, 500 "neophytes," members of the Order of Alhambra—a Catholic Fraternal Order—convened at Rainsford Island.[263] Later that summer, groups of 1,500–1,600 members of the Knights of Columbus went with their families, transported by the "largest Nantasket excursion steamer."[264] The sheer number of people ferried out for these gatherings is astonishing, given the relatively small size of the island.

The number of outings appears to have declined with the onset of the Great Depression. After 1931, no further articles appeared in the Boston newspapers noting outings at Rainsford Island. In the 1940s, only a few such excursions were noted by the *Globe*, though yachting races apparently attracted some visitors.

A City Albatross

Although no one had resided on the island since 1921, the costs of maintaining it continued. The *Boston Globe* reported in April 1927 that since its closing, $14,000 had been expended to guard "second-rate" buildings with no end of that expense in sight. It was

---

[261] "City Trusts," https://www.cityofboston.gov/images_documents/City%20Trusts%20-%20Purpose_tcm3-53149.pdf

[262] "Randidge Excursions to Rainsford Island," Boston Globe, May 22, 1921, p. 10. Earlier Randidge excursions had taken an astonishing 13,540 children to Long Island: Boston Globe, January 2, 1899, p. 7.

[263] Boston Globe, June 4, 1921, p. 10.

[264] Boston Globe, July 17, 1921, p. 8.

anticipated that $1,100 was to be spent for each of the two guards; $2,000 for repairs, coal and the telephone; and $1,000 for furniture for the watchmen's dormitory.[265]

The City Council, having perhaps forgotten the good reasons for closing the Reform School on Rainsford, unanimously voted in 1923 to use the island as a summer haven for tenement boys and girls. Mayor James Michael Curley, who may have had a longer memory, stated that he was going to veto the measure.[266] A few years later, the City Council recommended that Rainsford Island be sold. It was appraised for $145,300, but no further action was taken.[267] A proposal to establish a Junior Naval Cadets Corps at Rainsford Island, consisting of 200 boys, may or may not have come to fruition.[268]

On June 22, 1932, the three-story brick administration building at Rainsford Island was destroyed by fire. The blaze coincided with the presence of thirty unauthorized picnickers from the South Boston Grocers Association. The building was burned to embers, with only the brick walls remaining; the wooden building and shed were also destroyed. At that time, a number of lobstermen had been squatting on the island.[269] Only the old Grecian style Hospital, built in 1832, was still standing. The Boston Port Authority had to clear the burned remains and clean up the island, though the Boston Sea Scouts continued to use it.[270]

Depression-era work programs contributed something to the maintenance of the island. Federally funded Civil Works Projects helped clear the rubble at Rainsford, and "a plain wrought iron fence" was to be erected around the cemetery.[271] The National Park Service enlisted the Civilian Conservations Corps to reforest various Boston Harbor Islands, including Rainsford.[272]

Still, the island was regarded as a useless drain on very limited resources during the Depression. In 1933, Mayor Curley proposed defunding it.[273] The coup de grace was a fire that started one night in August 1934. Flames so high they could be seen from Cohasset, on the

---

[265] Boston Globe, April 27, 1927, p. 8.
[266] Boston Globe, June 26, 1923, p. 20.
[267] Boston Globe, July 22, 1927, p. 25.
[268] Boston Globe, June 5, 1930, p. 29.
[269] Boston Globe, June 23, 1932, p. 12.
[270] Boston Globe, March 26, 1933, p. A21; Boston Globe, October 2, 1932, p A62..
[271] Boston Globe, December 13, 1933, p. A1.
[272] Boston Globe, November 5, 1933.
[273] Boston Globe, April 13, 1933, p. 10.

mainland, destroyed the coal shed (apparently still full of coal) and the pier.[274] Unloading the island took a long time, though. The City Finance Commission recommended in 1936 that Rainsford Island be sold, but only in 1948 was it finally put up for sale.[275]

Civil War Decoration Day Honors

Amid all the chaos of Rainsford's long career as a public waystation, one consistent occurrence was the faithful journey, made by members of the Robert A. Bell, Post 134, G.A.R. and their Women's Relief Corps, Post 67, each Decoration Day to honor the 119 Veterans buried in the island cemetery (see Chapter 7). Those two organizations, comprised of African Americans, travelled to Rainsford Island every year after participating in the decoration of the Memorial to Robert Gould Shaw and the Massachusetts Fifty-Fourth Regiment on Boston Common.

It is sad to see the dwindling number of members, due either to by infirmity or death, who were able to participate each year. Travel to the Rainsford Island Cemetery ended after the 1933 services. By Decoration Day 1935, only three members of Post 134 were alive. That year, only William Jackson was able to render honors at the Memorial to Robert Gould Shaw and the Massachusetts Fifty-Fourth Regiment, closing out a half century of devotion to his comrades' memory.[276] In 1939, the *Globe* reported:

> Reverend E. George Biddle, 94, the last member of the Robert A. Bell Post 134, G.A.R., and dean of the clergy at the African Episcopal Zion Church of Columbus av(sic), was the guest of honor at impressive exercises in honor of the 54th Massachusetts Infantry, (colored regiment) held yesterday at the Robert Gould Shaw Memorial in front of the State House. The ceremonies were sponsored by Civil War Veterans organizations and shared in by two colored American Legion posts from Roxbury.[277]

Reverend Biddle died in 1940 and was laid to rest with full-military honors at Mount Hope Cemetery in Boston.[278]

---

[274] Boston Globe, August 27, 1934, p. 1.

[275] Boston Globe, December 18, 1936, p. 30; October 30, 1948, p. 5.

[276] Boston Globe, May 31, 1935, p. 2.

[277] Boston Globe, May 31, 1939, p. 1.

[278] Boston Globe, April 12, 1940, p. 30. The authors are keenly interested in locating records of the Bell Post and the Women's Relief Corps.

A Call to Action

The people who lived and suffered on Rainsford Island *matter*; those buried there *matter*. It is our great hope that the publication of this book will inspire interest in demarcating the cemetery with a fence, as well as listing the names of those buried there. The cemetery should be given a name that reflects the struggles of all that lay there. That name should also reflect there having been cast-out by the government and society. A memorial should be dedicated to the 119 Veterans known to be buried at what was described as "the now-lonesome God's acre."[279] As the *Globe*, the persistent chronicler of the island's failings, put it: "Those buried there had not at death the wherewithal to buy themselves a corner of earth in which to sleep forever."[280]

Edward Rainsford died in 1680. His wife Elizabeth died in 1688. The final accounting of his estate noted that he owned two slaves; a man, Nat, and a woman, Nancee. **They were valued at £40**.[281] He also had a financial interest in four ships, as well as having connections in Barbados. Barbados was known for sugar cane and slavery. His sons, Jonathan and Edward Jr. died there.

Edward's brother, Richard Raynsford, holds a place of infamy for his ruling that affirmed the continuation of slavery in the English colonies. Richard Raynsford, was the Justice to the King of England, Charles II. In 1677, the case of Butts v Penny gave him the opportunity to inform King Charles II that slavery violated English common law.

Previously, the English slave trade of the 1640s and '50s was described as "*relatively meager and proved insufficient to meet colonial demand – state action would be necessary to guarantee a sufficient bound labor supply and, thus a steady flow of customs and excise duties into the royal exchequer.*"[282]

---

279 Boston Globe, December 17, 1933, p. A1
280 ibid
281 The Great Migration Begins-Immigrants to New England, Ingram Pub Services, 2000, pp. 1544-1548

282 This Species of Property: Slavery and the Properties of Subjecthood in Anglo-American Law and Politics, 1619-1783, John N. Blanton, *Graduate Center, City University of New York, pp.* 206-213

On November 16, 1662, Charles II appointed Sir Richard, *"a baron of the Exchequer"*.[283]

Beginning in the 1660s slavery, especially from Africa, increased. It was very profitable to the investors in the colonies.

In 1664, the Council for Foreign Plantations recognized that slaves, were "*perpetual servants and the most useful appurtenances of a Plantation.*"[284]

In 1677, the Justices of the King's Bench, led by the eminent Sir Richard Raynsford, Chief Justice, found for the plaintiff, Butts, in a special verdict. Raynsford, a confirmed royalist and former MP in the Convention and Cavalier Parliaments, handed down a decision that must have pleased Charles II – no small matter as Raynsford held his seat as Chief Justice *in bene placio*, at the King's pleasure."[285]

The ruling noted that since Africans were *"bought and sold among Merchants, therefore are Merchandise and being Infidels, the slaves were goods the equivalent to any other chattels by English common law."*[286]

I did not locate any burials of African Americans prior to 1854, as such records were poorly kept. Nat & Nancee could be buried there. It is likely they, and other slaves, worked the land.

African Americans who were buried at Rainsford Island between 1854 and 1898:

Age at Death		Men - 79		Women - 17
<1		5		2
Age 10		0		1
11 -- 20		8		1
21 -- 30		15		5
31 -- 40		19		0
41 -- 50		9		6
51 -- 60		11		1
61 -- 70		6		0
71 --80		5		1
82		1		0

283 The Britifh (sic) Chronologift (sic) Vol I. MDCCLXXXIX, Anno, p.264
284 This Species of Property: Slavery and the Properties of Subjecthood in Anglo-American Law and Politics, 1619-1783, John N. Blanton, *Graduate Center, City University of New York, pp.* 206-213
285 ibid
286 ibid

Appendix 4. 2: Inventory of Rainsford Island, 1890

This list is presented for the reader to view the meager amount of materials and supplies allotted to a population of women, children and infants whose numbers often exceeded 400.

The Second Annual Report of the Commissioners of Public Institutions of the City of Boston, for the Year 1890 (pp. 202–207) gives a remarkably detailed inventory of every piece of public property to be found in the Women's Hospital.

SCHEDULE OF PUBLIC PROPERTY AT RAINSFORD ISLAND

Superintendent's House.

Dining-Room. 1 dining-room carpet, 1 sideboard, 1 extension table, 5 linen table cloths, 8 chairs, 3 doz. tumblers, 6 platters, 1 doz. cups and saucers, 1 carving-knife, fork, and steel, window-shades.

Sitting-Room. 1 carpet, 2 lounges, 5 chairs, window-shades.

Parlor. 1 carpet, 1 marble-top table, 1 piano and stool, window-shades, stair and entry carpet.

Doctor's Office. 1 carpet, 1 marble-top table, 1 book-case and writing-desk, 1 leather covered lounge and chair, 3 cane-bottom arm-chairs, window-shades.

Chamber No. 1. 1 carpet, 1 bedstead, 1 spring, mattress and pillows, 1 bureau and washstand, 1 sofa, 3 chairs, 1 marble-top table.

Chamber No. 2. 1 bedstead, spring, mattress, bolster, and two pillows, wardrobe, bureau, washstand, 2 tables, window-shades.

Chamber No. 3. 1 bedstead, carpet, spring, mattress, bolster, 2 pillows, bureau, washstand, 1 table, 1 chair, window-shades.

Clergyman's Room. 1 iron bedstead, spring, mattress, bolster and pillow, bureau, washstand, 2 chairs, 1 rug, window-shades.

Doctor's Chamber. 1 carpet and chamber set, window-shades.

Matron's Room. 1 carpet and chamber set, window-shades.

Kitchen. Range and furniture, 1 table, laundry-stove, clothes-wringer.

Sundries. 6 lamps, 2 clocks, 11, blankets, 8 white spreads, 3 doz. sheets, 4 doz. slips, 3 doz. table napkins

Store

3 desks, 1 platform-scale, 1 counter-scale, 2 hammers, 1 box-opener, 1 soldering-iron, 1 pr. garden shears, 1 meat-knife, 1 steel, 1 cleaver, 1 meat-axe, 1 wood-axe, 1 American flag, 1 kerosene lamp-filler, 1 lard oil-can, 1 watering-pot, 1 clock, 1 receiving-book, 1 day-book, 1 index book, 1 requisition-book, 2 office-chairs, 1 pr. hand-cuffs, 1 meat-table, 2 radiators, 2 fire-extinguishers, 1 shoe peg-cutter, 2 chairs, 3 pails, 1 lantern, 2 lamps, 1 pr. scissors, 1 slate, 1 book-case, 1 tobacco-cutter, 1 waste-basket, 1 bushel basket, 2 inkstands, 2 cuspidors, 2 doz. dinner plates, 8 doz. bowls, 4 doz. mugs, 2 pitchers, 6 wash-basins, 6 dust-pans, 1 doz. brush-brooms, 8 dippers, 1 teapot, 12 pr. women's shoes, 1 doz. pairs carpet slippers, 8 prs. stockings, 10 cotton shirts, 1 meat-chopper, 1 dictionary, 1 bbl. rice, 1 bbl. vinegar, 1 bbl. crackers, 1 bbl. molasses, 1 bbl. sugar, 1 bbl. hard bread, 1 case quilts, 1 ease calico prints, 6 doz. lamp-chimneys, 2 boxes soap, 1 box pepper, 1 box cream tartar, 1 box saleratus [sodium bicarbonate], 1 box starch, 1 box mustard, 1 box rotten stone, 1 box lamp wicking, 1 box clothespins, 1 piece flannel, 5 gro. safety matches, 2 pieces cashmere, 37 lbs. yarn, 2 reams sand-paper, 2 sugar-bowls, 2 pitchers, 100 boxes spool thread, 3 boxes skein thread, 20 gro. buttons, 3 boxes safety pins, 5 bundles common pins, 18 gro. screws, 15 lbs. brads, 20 papers tacks, 2 doz. spoons, 6 doz. knives, 3 doz. forks, 4 boxes tobacco, 4 bundles hairpins, 3 chests tea, 4 window-shades, 12 brushes, 18 brush-brooms, 5 clothes-lines, 5 dippers, 6 hanks window cord, 1 Boston directory, 2 counters, 6 bbls. and covers, 16 pieces 42-in. cotton, 5 pieces 36-in. cotton, 4 stencils. 1 case indelible ink, 1 doz. insect exterminator, 2 doz. door-knobs, 10 files.

Barn

7 rakes, 7 shovels, 3 pickaxes, 7 pitch-forks, 4 harnesses, 2 horses, 4 cows, 3 lanterns, 5 milk-cans, 1 sledge-hammer, 1 hay-cutter, 4 scythes, 6 pails, 5 grain-chests, 1 basket, 2 blocks and tackle, 1 axe, 50 straw beds, 1 tip-cart, 1 water-cart, 1 caravan, 1 jack, 1 ambulance, 2 horse blankets, 2 blocks and tackle.

Piggery

104 pigs, 1 iron kettle, 4 pitchforks, 4 shovels, 7 pails, 2 brooms, 1 stove, 1 saw, 1 crowbar, 1 lamp, 1 clock.

Institution, Main Building

248 beds, 529 blankets, 356 sheets, 158 spreads, 258 pillows, 248 slips. 158 skirts, 158 dresses, 158 chemises, 92 nightgowns, 75 nightcaps, 1 medicine chest, 10 lamps, 137 chairs, 7 dust-pans, 7 brooms, 7 mops, 7 pails, 30 plates, 22 knives, 24 forks, 18 spoons, 1 tray, 1 clock, 1 table.

Institution, Wooden Building

51 beds, 153 blankets, 102 sheets, 51 ticks. 51 slips, 51 spreads, 2 lamps, 2 dust-pans, 2 mops, 2 brooms, 2 pails, 49 shades, 40 night gowns, 48 dresses, 51 chemises, 51 prs. stockings, 51 prs. shoes, 102 skirts, 24 nightcaps.

Halls

5 lamps, 1 broom.

Nursery (Children)

13 cribs, 13 mattresses, 24 sheets, 12 slips, 12 spreads, 12 dresses, 6 prs. stockings, 12 skirts, 6 shirts, 4 prs. shoes.

Nursery (Women)

14 beds, 42 blankets, 28 sheets, 14 pillows, 14 slips, 14 ticks, 13 dresses, 2 chambers, 13 chemises, 6 nightgowns, 13 prs. stockings, 13 prs. shoes, 12 chairs, 1 lamp, 1 dust-pan, 2 brooms, 2 pails, 8 basins, 12 shades.

Matrons' Dining- Room

3 tables, 5 chairs, 1 sideboard, 2 curtains, 1 doz. knives, 3 large spoons, 1 doz. forks, 1 soup-ladle, 1 doz. spoons, 1 carving knife, 6 tablecloths, 6 napkins, 1 doz. plates, 1 doz. cups

and saucers, 2 cream pitchers, 1 milk-pitcher, 1 water-pitcher, 2 meat dishes, 1 dish-pan, 1 ice chest, 8 tumblers, 1 dust-pan, 4 doz. dish-towels.

Officers' Rooms

4 beds, 4 lamps, 8 blankets, 4 spreads, 12 sheets, 16 slips, 4 mattresses, 4 springs, 8 pillows, 11 chairs, 4 dressing-cases, 4 commodes, 3 tables, 4 chambers, 9 shades, 10 towels, 4 carpets.

Chapel

41 settees, 2 lamps, 1 altar, 1 reading-desk, 1 chair, 1 carpet, 2 kneeling-stools, 1 broom, 1 brush, 1 dust-pan.

Laundry

7 flat-irons, 3 clothes-baskets, 5 wash-boards, 1 pail, 1 mop, 1 table, 24 towels.

Dining-Room

15 tables, 200 bowls, 200 plates, 200 knives, 200 forks, 200 spoons, 200 mugs, 1 dust-pan, 2 side-tables, 20 shades, 2 jugs, 2 mops, 2 brooms, 1 brush, 10 lamps, 1 bell, 4 syrup-pitchers, 28 stools, 1 chair, 2 cupboards.

Kitchen

4 steam-kettles, 1 tea-boiler, 2 tables, 1 range, 8 carryalls, 12 tin pails, 10 spoons, 10 knives, 10 forks, 10 plates, 10 bowls, 25 bean pots, 10 stools, 1 skimmer, 4 iron spoons, 1 colander, 1 jug, 1 molasses cup, 1 sieve.

Sewing-Room

200 nightgowns, 16 dresses, 25 skirts, 50 chemises, 400 sheets, 300 slips, 14 baby dresses, 30 shirts, 3 prs. scissors, 2 boxes thread, 2 baskets, 20 chairs, 6 benches, 3 tables.

Barber Shop and (Cottage)

1 barber's chair, 1 settee, 1 table, 2 chairs, 2 razors, 3 mugs, 1 lather brush, 1 stove, 1 basin, 3 towels, 1 coal-hood, 11 beds, 2 tables, 2 lamps, 1 pail, 11 ticks, 22 sheets, 42 blankets, 11 pillows, 11 slips, 11 chambers.

Bakery

1 stove, 14 beds, 14 ticks, 14 slips, 14 pillows, 28 sheets, 50 blankets, 14 chambers. 1 clock, 2 chairs, 1 baker's peel, 1 iron kettle.

Receiving Office

1 desk, 3 chairs, 2 settees, 1 stove, 6 beds, 6 ticks, 6 chambers, 6 pillows, 6 slips, 12 sheets, 36 blankets, 1 flag.

Boat-House

2 boats, 6 oars, 2 sails, 4 blocks and tackle.

Stone Shed

28 iron beds, 6 barrels, 6 snow-shovels.

Blacksmith Shop

1 bellows, 1 anvil, 1 vice, 1 drill-breast, 1 screw-plate and dies, 1 set blacksmith's tools, 900 lbs. iron, 1 forge.

Paint Shop

1 bbl. Venetian red, 1 bbl. plaster Paris, J bbl. Paris white, 25 gals. Porgie oil, 8 gals. varnish, 2 gals. Japan, 10 lbs. zinc white, 25 lbs. white-lead, 3 gals. asphaltum, 3 boxes window-glass, 10 lbs. putty.

Carpenter's Shop

1 long jointer, 2 short jointers, 2 fore planes, 2 smoothing planes, 2 block planes, 1 plough plane, 1 rabbet plane, 1 pr. match planes, 1¼ bead plane, 1 3/4 round plane, 2 cutting-off

saws, 1 splitting saw, 1 panel saw, 1 tennant saw, 2 bit-stocks, 8 bit, 2 screw-drivers, 1 spoke shave, 2 hammers, 1 hatchet, 2 try-squares, 1 steel square, 1 draw-knife, 1 compass saw, 1 stove and pipe, 3 kegs 10d nails, 1 keg 40d. nails, 1 keg 7-in. spikes, 1 gouge, 4 doz. chisels, 1 turning lathe, 2 mallets, 1/2 doz. jack screws, 1 1/2 framing chisel, 400 ft. coffin boards, 1 doz. hand-screws, 100 ft. pine boards, 1 grindstone, 1 whetstone, 1 pr. plyers, 5 coffins.

Cellars

6 tubs butter (inst.), 2 tubs butter (officers), 150 bu. potatoes, 2 bbls. mineral oil, 8 oil barrels, 1 tool chest, 1 refrigerator, 6 whitewash brushes, 1 bbl. lime, 2 trowels, 1 shovel.

Smoking-Houses

2 stoves and pipe.

Store-Room

3 bbls. yellow sugar, 2 bbls. granulated sugar, 3 bbls. crackers, 6 bags beans, 3 bushel-baskets, 2 bbls. hard bread, 3 bags rice, 18 boxes bar soap, 4 bbl. rosin, 1 doz. brooms, 1/2 doz. mop-handles, 50 chambers, 4 oil-skin suits, 1 pr. skids, 1 barber's chair.

Hospital

66 beds. 3 cribs, 198 sheets, 132 slips, 66 spreads, 198 blankets, 265 under garments, 50 chairs and stools, 25 prs. shoes and stockings, 15 lamps, 1 lantern, 25 dresses, 26 tables, 6 tin pans, 1 range, 10 brooms, 15 chambers, 4 bed-pans, 3 doz. roller towels, 4 doz. bowls, 5 doz. spoons, 3 doz. knives and forks, 15 mugs, 12 pails, 1 tea-kettle, 1 clock, 1 stove, smoke-house.

Matrons' Rooms

1 bedstead, 1 spring, 3 blankets, 1 dressing-case, 5 chairs, 3 tables, 1 mattress, 2 pillows, 2 changes linen for same, 1 commode, 1 slop-jar, 1 carpet, 1 lamp, 1 doz. towels, 1 iron bedstead, 1 spring, 1 mattress, 2 pillows, 1 dressing-case, 1 commode, 2 chairs, 1 chamber, 2 window shades, 1 lamp, 1 carpet, 2 tables, 1 wash-bowl, 2 changes of bed linen.

Appendix 7.2: Known burials at Rainsford Island – 1,777

***Civil War Service**

**** War of 1812 Service**

Also posted at Findagrave.com

MONTH	YEAR	NAME	AGE YEARS	AGE MONTHS	CAUSE OF DEATH	BORN
18-Feb	1888	*ALLISON, SAMUEL C	30		PHTHISIS	NEW BRUNSWICK, ST JOHN
19-Jul	1886	*ANDERSON, THOMAS	85		NEPHRITIS	SCOTLAND
23-Sep	1873	*BAILEY, CHARLES M.	28		GANGRENE	NEW HAMPSHIRE, EXETER
20-Sep	1884	*BARRY, JOHN PATRICK	46		LIVER CIRHOSIS	IRELAND
23-Feb	1873	*BEAUJEAN, SIMON	18		TYPHOID FEVER	NOVA SCOTIA
25-Dec	1887	*BEETON, CHARLES A	54		PNEUMONIA	BOSTON
19-Mar	1888	*BENNETT, EDWARD D	61		DEBILITY	BOSTON
19-Oct	1889	*BENT, JOSEPH F	54		HEART MITRAL	CARVER, MA
11-Nov	1865	*BERENGER, ETIENNE	36		PNEUMONIA	FRANCE
16-Mar	1878	*BERRAN, THOMAS	56		SYPHILIS	IRELAND
25-May	1865	*BINNEY, SPENCER	36		SMALL POX	MASS
19-Nov	1884	*BLACK, JOHN	66		DELIRIUM TREMENS	IRELAND
18-Nov	1880	*BLANCHARD, WILLIAM M	59		HEART DISEASE	NEW HAMPSHIRE
1-Aug	1879	*BOYNTON, OZRO	45		CHOLERA	NEW HAMPSHIRE
15-Aug	1888	*BROWN, CHALRES H	53		CEREBRAL HEMORRHAGE	CONNETICUTT, SAYBROOK POINT
25-Jan	1866	*BROWN, JAMES	20		PHTHISIS	VIRGINIA
19-Mar	1885	*BROWN, WILLIAM M	70		ALCHOLISM	BOSTON
23-Mar	1884	*CANNON, JAMES	41		ASTHMA & BRONCHITIS	BOSTON
14-Jan	1877	*CAREY, EDWARD	55		FEVER REMITTENT	BOSTON
7-Jun	1878	*CARNES, PETER	59		HEART DISEASE	MAINE, SACO
11-Feb	1884	*CHANDLER, WILLIAM H	81		BRONCHITIS	PRINCE EDWARD ISLAND
22-Nov	1865	*CHAPMAN, JOHN FRANKLIN	25		DIARRHOEA	BOSTON
11-Jan	1891	*CHEENEY, JOHN M	68		ALCOHOLISM	BARNSTABLE, MA
21-May	1866	*CHRISTY, JAMES	28		DIARRHOEA	PRINCE EDWARD ISLAND
9-Mar	1885	*CLARK, ROBERT	52		PHTHIS & EXHAUSTION	IRELAND
15-Feb	1866	*CLEMENTS, LEWIS E	35		HEART DISEASE	BOSTON
5-Oct	1877	*CLUNA, MICHAEL	66		DYSENTARY	NEW YORK
19-Nov	1886	*COLLIER, FREDERICK M.	73		HEART DISEASE & SENILITY	IRELAND
14-Sep	1863	*CONNELLY, JOHN L	40		LUNG OEDEMA	MAINE, LEEDS
2-Nov	1883	*COUGHLIN, JAMES	43		PHTHISIS	MARYLAND
18-Jan	1886	*COUGHLIN, JOHN	52		AORTIC ANEURISM	BOSTON
28-Dec	1883	*CUNNINGHAM, GEORGE W	66		HEART DISEASE	IRELAND
30-Nov	1877	*CUTHBERT, ANDREW	41		PARALYSIS	VIRGINIA
8-Apr	1889	*DAILY, MICHAEL	71		HEART DISEASE	SCOTLAND
20-Jul	1886	*DAMERY, RICHARD	69		CYSTITIS & DIARRHOEA	IRELAND
22-Jul	1877	*DE COUS, GEORGE	80		OLD AGE	IRELAND
26-Mar	1876	*DOHERTY, MICHAEL	66		ENTERITIS	MANHATTAN
13-Jan	1884	*DURKIN, PATRICK	62		PHTHISIS	IRELAND
5-Oct	1880	*DUSTON, JAMES	79		HEART DISEASE	IRELAND
27-Jan	1885	*DWIGHT, JOSEPH	60		BRIGHT'S DISEASE & MELANCHOLIA	MAINE, BRUNSWICK
10-Feb	1876	*DWYER, JOHN	64		HEART DISEASE	CHARLESTOWN, MA
11-Jul	1891	*ELISHA, JOSEPH H	50		HEART DISEASE AORTIC & MITRAL	BOSTON
14-Aug	1882	*ENNIS, STEPHEN	48		PHTHISIS	
3-Feb	1881	*EVANS, JAMES	43		PHTHISIS	PENNSYLVANIA
22-Apr	1864	*FOSTER, DANIEL O	25		SMALL POX	VIRGINIA
3-Jul	1864	*FOWLE, CLIFFORD B	35		SMALL POX	MASSACHUSETTS
1-Feb	1887	*FRENCH, THOMAS	73		SENILE DEBILITY	WOBURN, MA
26-May	1873	*GALLAGHER, MICHAEL	60		DROPSY	BOSTON

MONTH	YEAR	NAME	AGE YEARS	AGE MONTHS	CAUSE OF DEATH	BORN
12-Mar	1888	*GEARY, DAVID	57		PNEUMONIA & NEPHRITIS	IRELAND
30-Jul	1883	*GOLDEN, EDWARD	38		ULCER GASTRI HEMORRHAGE	BOSTON
29-Mar	1878	*HAMILTON, HUGH	38		CONSUMPTION	IRELAND
16-Oct	1874	*HARLOW, WILLIAM S.	42		PHTHISIS (2 YEARS)	SANDWICH
20-Jul	1876	*HARMON, JAMES W.	34		SYPHILIS & RHEUMATISM	NEW JERSEY
30-Sep	1873	*HARRINGTON, JOHN	32		CONSUMPTION	IRELAND
14-Jan	1874	*HAYES, JOHN P	41		PHTHISIS	BOSTON
4-May	1874	*HEENAN, MICHAEL	40		PHTHISIS (2 YEARS)	NEW BRUNSWICK, ST JOHN
9-Jul	1877	*HERMAN, STEPHEN	63		CONSUMPTION	GERMANY
11-Apr	1887	*HIGGINS, WILLIAM	56		TYPHOID FEVER	IRELAND
7-May	1881	*HOLMES, EDWIN	65		PHTHISIS (12 YEARS)	SHARON
15-Nov	1877	*HOLMES, EZRA S	67		HEART DISEASE	MAINE, MACHIAS
13-May	1878	*HOMER, WILLIAM H	35		PHTHISIS (5 YEARS)	BOSTON
19-Sep	1883	*HURLEY, DENNIS	26		PHTHISIS & EXHAUSTION	BOSTON
20-Feb	1875	*JACKSON, CHARLES	60		PHTHISIS	MARYLAND, BALTIMOE
29-Jul	1880	*JONES, HENRY	66		PULMONARY HEMORRHAGE	WEST VIRGINIA
9-Apr	1876	*KELLEY, JAMES	63		PNEUMONIA	IRELAND
22-Apr	1877	*KNIGHT, HENRY G	73		OLD AGE	WATERTOWN, MA
3-May	1878	*LAVERSHALL (LAROCHELLE), PETER	45		PARALYSIS	CANADA
14-May	1891	*LEWIS, CHARLES	73		FRACTURED FEMUR	VIRGINA, RICHMOND
13-Nov	1878	*LYNCH, PATRICK	70		FRACTURED RIB	IRELAND
4-Oct	1888	*MARSHALL, GEORGE G.	68		CEREBRAL EMBOLISM	BOSTON
22-Jul	1880	*MARSHALL, JOHN	54		CANCER LIVER	IRELAND
10-Mar	1880	*MASSEY, RICHARD	64		RHEUMATISIM	ENGLAND
12-Mar	1873	*MCCARTHY, EUGENE	40		PHTHISIS	IRELAND
1-May	1879	*MCCARTY, CORNELIUS	35			
18-Jan	1893	*MCCUE, BERNARD	65		PNEUMONIA	PNEUMONIA
19-Oct	1877	*MCGIER, PETER	55		PNEUMONIA	IRELAND
2-Aug	1890	*MCGILL, MICHAEL P	59		HEART DISEASE	IRELAND
12-Mar	1879	*MCKEIRNAN (KEIRNAN)	36		PHTHISIS	BOSTON
12-May	1885	*MONAHAN, JOHN	52		DELIRIUM TREMENS & EXHAUSTION	IRELAND
27-Mar	1884	*MOORE, ANTHONY	80		OLD AGE	VIRGINA, RICHMOND
31-Oct	1878	*MORAN, MICHAEL	55		BRIGHT'S DISEASE	IRELAND
18-Sep	1885	*MORSE, WILLIAM H	40		BRIGHT'S DISEASE	SALEM, MA
11-Sep	1885	*MULLEN, ANDREW	39		PHTHISIS	BOSTON
18-May	1882	*MULLIGAN, PATRICK	62		DUODENITES	IRELAND
8-May	1885	*MURPHY, CHARLES H	42		BRIGHTS DISEASE (3 MONTHS)	CHARLESTOWN
10-Oct	1876	*NEWELL, JOHN	59		APOPLEXY	IRELAND
4-Apr	1878	*NOLAN, RICHARD	76		OLD AGE	IRELAND
26-Oct	1884	*NORMAN, THOMAS H	42		PHTHISIS & EXHAUSTION	BOSTON
22-Apr	1874	*O'BRIEN, CHARLES	60		ERYSIPELAS	BOSTON
7-Apr	1887	*O'LEARY, DANIEL	77		BRONCHITIS & EMPHYSEMA	IRELAND
23-May	1881	*O'LEARY, MICHAEL A	50		PHTHISIS	BOSTON
15-Jan	1881	*OLSEN, PETER	42		ASTHMA (2 YEARS)	NORWAY
29-Feb	1884	*QUALLS, ROBERT	37		PNEUMONIA	VIRGINIA
16-Nov	1880	*QUINLAN, PATRICK	47		PHTHISIS	IRELAND
16-Aug	1882	*QUINN, NICHOLAS	53		PHTHISIS	IRELAND
10-Sep	1886	*RANDOLPH, WILLIAM	65		BRONCHITIS & SENILE DEBILITY	VIRGINIA
22-Mar	1887	*REA, EDMUND B	46		PHTHISIS	SCOTLAND
30-Jul	1882	*SHACKFORD, THOMAS	66		BRONCHITIS & EXPOSURE	BOSTON
2-Sep	1875	*SHANAHAN, MICHAEL	61			IRELAND
28-Jun	1877	*SHEEHAN, WILLIAM	42		CONSUMPTION	BOSTON
15-Sep	1882	*SMART, WASHINGTON J	65		SYPHILIS	MAINE, KENNEBUNKPORT
5-Jun	1886	*SMITH, ALFRED W	47		NEPHRITIS	BOSTON
15-Sep	1889	*SMITH, HENRY	48		PHTHISIS	BOSTON
28-Feb	1886	*SMITH, JAMES	45		BRONCHITIS	PRINCE EDWARD ISLAND
28-Nov	1880	*SMITH, PETER	65		BRONCHITIS	IRELAND
11-Sep	1875	*SPURR, CHARLES E	41		PHTHISIS	BOSTON
14-Sep	1884	*TALBOT, JAMES	34		PHTHISIS	PENNSYLVANIA, HARRISBURG
21-Sep	1878	*TEAHAN, JOHN	52		PHTHISIS (2 MONTHS)	IRELAND
23-Sep	1888	*THOMPSON, THOMAS L	54		EPILEPSY	IRELAND
1-Jul	1890	*TROTTMAN, HAMILTON J	45		DEBILITY	BOSTON
19-Jan	1873	*TUCKER, SAMUEL	41		HEART SOFTENING (5 DAYS)	NEW HAMPSHIRE

MONTH	YEAR	NAME	AGE YEARS	AGE MONTHS	CAUSE OF DEATH	BORN
19-Aug	1875	*TURNER, CHARLES A	30		CONSUMPTION	ENGLAND
20-Jun	1881	*WARD, HIRAM F	70		CYSTITIS & INTERMITTENT FEVER	PENNSYLVANIA
26-May	1885	*WEBBER, SAMUEL	53		RHUEMATISIM	MAINE, BYRON
17-Jun	1812	**WHITE, HORACE STOCKTON	21			RUTLAND, MA
19-Jun	1864	*WHITTEMORE, JOHN	26		SMALL POX	VIRGINIA, FREDERICKSBURG
5-Jun	1881	*WILLIAMS, WALTER	60		PHTHISIS	WALES
20-Mar	1884	*WILSON THOMAS A	46		PARALYTIC DEMENTIA & APOPLEXY	BOSTON
12-Feb	1889	*YOUNG, JOSEPH	65		DIARRHOEA	IRELAND
4-Aug	1890	ABBOT, ALICE M		3	CHOLERA INFANTUM	RAINSFORD ISLAND
4-Apr	1857	ABBOT, MOODY	51		HEART ENLARGED	MAINE
7-May	1855	ABBOT, SUSAN	4		WHOOPING COUGH	NEW BRUNSWICK, ST JOHN
29-Oct	1860	ABREL, WILLIAM	24		SMALL POX	NEW HAMPSHIRE, PORTSMOUTH
14-Oct	1861	ADAMS, DAVID	15		TYPHOID FEVER	MAINE, ANSON
13-Jan	1889	ADAMS, LUKE	50		HEART DISEASE	ENGLAND
27-Feb	1880	ADAMS, SAMUEL	70		OLD AGE	IRELAND
12-Feb	1878	ADAMS, WILLIAM	67		PNEUMONIA	NEW HAMPSHIRE
7-Jul	1860	AGIN, BRIDGET (HIGGINS (	32		PHTHISIS	IRELAND
5-Mar	1862	AGIN, MICHAEL	37		PHTHISIS	IRELAND
8-Aug	1898	AHERN, MARY G		4 MONTHS 8 DAYS	FERMENTAL DIARRHOEA	BOSTON
5-Dec	1883	AIKEN, FRANK	40		DELIRIUM TREMENS & EXHAUSTION	DORCHESTER
31-Aug	1882	ALDEN, EDWARD	65		PARALYSIS	BRIDGEWATER, MA
9-Jun	1858	ALGER, ELVIRA	54		LUNG INFLAMMATION	EASTON, MA
28-Aug	1897	ALLAN, SUSAN P		4 MONTHS 12 DAYS	INFANTILE ATROPHY	EVERETT
18-Aug	1898	ALLEN, HAROLD		5 MONTHS 15 DAYS	MALNUTRITION	CAPE BRETTON
12-Feb	1889	ALLENDORF, JEROME A	34		HEART DISEASE	BOSTON
5-Feb	1858	ALLEY, WILLIAM	1	5	MARASMUS	RAINSFORD ISLAND
1-Sep	1886	ANDERSON, EDWARD	69		PARALYSIS & DIARRHOEA	SWEDEN
1-Dec	1860	ANDERSON, JANE	27		INTEMPERANCE	IRELAND
21-Aug	1854	ANDERSON, JOSHUA	23		DYSENTARY	SWEDEN
10-Nov	1859	ANDREWS, JAMES	32		SMALL POX	ENGLAND
25-Apr	1893	ANDREWS, NANCY (MCCAFFREY)	75		MITRAL STENOSIS	IRELAND
31-Jan	1862	ANTHONY, MARY	34		LIVER DISEASE	IRELAND
13-Jul	1877	ARMSTRONG, EDWARD	70		OLD AGE	BOSTON
17-Jun	1856	ARMSTRONG, MATILDA		8	SCROFULA	RAINSFORD ISLAND
12-Jun	1880	ATKINS, JOHN W	66		CEREBRAL HEMORRHAGE	BOSTON
3-Apr	1891	AUKATELLE, BRUDGET (HICKEY)	39		SYPHILIS	IRELAND
18-Jul	1857	AUSTIN, MARY	26		DROPSY	VERMONT, ESSEX
July	1738	BACON, JABEZ			SMALL POX	
15-Sep	1893	BADGE, ELLEN	60			IRELAND
28-Jul	1897	BAGLEY, ANNIE	1	17 DAYS	TUBERCULOSIS	BOSTON
7-Feb	1856	BAILEY, ELI	22		SMALL POX	DELAWARE
24-Jan	1863	BAILEY, JOSEPHINE	20		INTEMPERANCE	BOSTON
26-Jun	1887	BAINE, JOHN	45		PHTHTISIS	SKOWHEGAN, ME
23-Nov	1854	BAKER, JOHN	18		DYSENTARY	BELGIUM
19-Oct	1862	BALCH, ALBERT	34		BRAIN DISEASSE	
10-Aug	1886	BALCH, JAMES W	64		SENILITY & DEBILITY	KEENE, NH
28-Feb	1856	BALL JOSEPH H	27		LUNG INFLAMMATION	ENGLAND
11-Feb	1860	BARKER, MARGETTA	25		....	MAINE
24-Jan	1865	BARKER, THOMAS	69		DYSENTARY	IRELAND
1-May	1889	BARNABY, ELIZABETH (SMITH)	24		TUBERCULOSIS	NEW BRUNSWICK
26-Oct	1890	BARNES, JAMES F		5	BRONCHITIS	RAINSFORD ISLAND
10-Aug	1857-	BARNES, NANCY	26		TYPHOID FEVER	ENGLAND
17-Aug	1863	BARRETT, MARY	70		DIARRHOEA	IRELAND
26-Oct	1857	BARRINGER, ELIZA (PLUMMER)	19		TYPHOID FEVER	ENGLAND
15-Oct	1857	BARRINGER, THOMAS	1	5	TYPHOID FEVER	ENGLAND
9-Jul	1896	BARRON, EUNICE		2	INTESTINAL DISEASE	BOSTON
28-Mar	1857	BARRY, ELLEN	21		CONSUMPTION	IRELAND

MONTH	YEAR	NAME	AGE YEARS	AGE MONTHS	CAUSE OF DEATH	BORN
12-Feb	1858	BARRY, JAMES	39		CONSUMPTION	IRELAND
30-Aug	1891	BARRY, JOHN	72		SENILITY	IRELAND
8-Dec	1878	BARRY, LAURENCE	27		RHEUMATISIM	.....
9-Apr	1880	BARRY, MICHAEL	40		APOPLEXY & PARALYSIS	IRELAND
2-Jul	1862	BARRY, WILLIAM	35		BRAIN DISEASSE	IRELAND
1-May	1862	BATTISTE, JOHN	40		PHTHISIS	CANADA
16-Oct	1858	BAXTER, MARY	59		HEART DISEASE	IRELAND
4-Oct	1859	BEAN, MICHAEL	25		INTEMPERANCE	BOSTON
27-Apr	1863	BEATTY, ELIZABETH (GILLIS)	38		HEART DISEASE	NOVA SCOTIA
13-Jul	1889	BEAVER, FRANCIS	66		HEART DISEASE	EAST INDIES
12-Feb	1889	BEDDIGS, CATHARINE (MORAN)	55		NEPHRITIS	IRELAND
1-Jun	1860	BEERS, ROBERT	24		SMALL POX	IRELAND
23-Jul	1862	BELL, HANNAH (CRONAN)	22		BURNS (2 MONTHS)	CAMBRIDGE, MA
4-Jun	1889	BELL, MARY (KELLEY)	49		PHTHISIS	IRELAND
13-Jun	1862	BENNETT, EDWARD	63		PHTHISIS	MAINE
23-May	1859	BENSON, JAMES	24		INTEMPERANCE	NEW HAMPSHIRE
22-Nov	1878	BENT, WILLIAM	70		EPILEPSY	BOSTON
25-Jul	1854	BERGESON, ANDRES	26		LUNG DISEASE	SWEDEN
21-Jun	1864	BERGESON, BENJAMIN	24		DIARRHOEA	SWEDEN
18-Jun	1898	BERNHARDT, MATILDA		2	FERMENTAL DIARRHOEA	BOSTON
30-Aug	1862	BERRY, BURDICK	30		KNEE INFLAMMATION	MAINE, PORTLAND
7-Apr	1886	BERRY, DANIEL	35		PHTHISIS	NOT LISTED
10-Mar	1890	BERRY, ELLA (BELL)	36		PHTHISIS	BOSTON
3-Nov	1859	BERRY, H. C.	25		SMALL POX	MAINE, RICHMOND
23-Jan	1860	BERRY, LAWRENCE	32		SMALL POX	SALEM, MA
27-May	1864	BERSE, JOSEPH	26		SYPHILIS	MARYLAND
17-Feb	1888	BJORKLUND, FRANCIS ADRIAN		4	INTESTINAL DISEASE	RAINSFORD ISLAND
15-Jan	1891	BLACK, ELIZABETH	47		RHEUMATISIM	KENTUCKY
23-Jul	1860	BLACK, JAMES	34		SMALL POX	MAINE
2-Aug	1889	BLACK, MARY		2	INTESTINAL DISEASE	LONG ISLAND HOSPITAL
17-Sep	1860	BLAKE, EDWARD	39		ANAEMIA	IRELAND
29-Jan	1863	BLESSINGTON, JOHN E.		1	SYPHILIS	
15-Sep	1875	BLIGH, GEDDES	68		OLD AGE	NOVA SCOTIA, CORNWALLIS
29-Aug	1894	BLOOM, ROSA		7 MONTHS 10 DAYS	CHOLERA INFANTUM	BOSTON
19-May	1862	BOHNER, JOSEPH	57		PARALYSIS RHEUMATIC	FRANCE
15-Mar	1863	BOLAN, JOHN	50		PHTHISIS	ENGLAND
1-Aug	1860	BOLAND, WILLIAM	22		TYPHOID PNEUMONIA	BOSTON
19-Oct	1890	BOOTH, CHARLES	49		HEART DISEASE	
16-Aug	1898	BORNSTEIN, HARRY		1 MONTH 7 DAYS	FERMENTAL DIARRHOEA	BOSTON
11-Aug	1896	BOUCHE, PAULINE		5 MONTHS 18 DAYS	INFANTILE ATROPHY	BOSTON
14-May	1857	BOWERS, JAMES	22		SPINE DISEASE	NOVA SCOTIA
13-Apr	1856	BOYD, ISAAC H	29		LUNG INFLAMMATION	NEW YORK, ALBANY
19-Aug	1863	BOYLE, CORNELIUS (ALIAS GILL)	35		PNEUMONIA	IRELAND
28-Apr	1866	BOYLE, JANE	28		PHTHISIS	IRELAND
17-Nov	1861	BOYLE, JOHN	55		BRAIN DISEASE	IRELAND
5-Sep	1861	BRADBURN, MARTIN		7	TABES MESENTERICA	BOSTON
29-Jul	1862	BRADFORD, MARTHA	27		PHTHISIS	IRELAND
29-Aug	1897	BRADY, JOHN		6 MONTHS 18 DAYS	FERMENTAL DIARRHOEA	BOSTON
23-Sep	1835	BRAZIER, JAMES		11 MONTHS	SMALL POX	CHARLESTOWN
27-Oct	1887	BRENNAN, BRIDGET	60		DEBILITY	IRELAND
28-Nov	1858	BRENNAN, ELLEN	40		HEART DISEASE	IRELAND
11-Jul	1861	BRENNAN, PETER	32		DELIRIUM TREMENS	IRELAND
24-Feb	1888	BRENNAN, WILLIAM	24		HEART VALVE DISEASE	BOSTON
11-Aug	1886	BRESLOW, CHARLES	34		PHTHISIS	IRELAND
29-Dec	1891	BRIDE, ALICE (PORPERLY)	73		ATHEROMA	IRELAND
4-Jul	1826	BRIGGS, GEORGE	27		TYPHUS FEVER	COHASSET
18-May	1890	BRIGHAM, CLARA (SUMMER)	76		SENILE DEBILITY	BOSTON
22-May	1891	BRISCOE, WILLIAM	55		CHRONIC INTESTINAL CATARH	IRELAND

MONTH	YEAR	NAME	AGE YEARS	AGE MONTHS	CAUSE OF DEATH	BORN
26-Jan	1863	BRISTON, HENRY	47		SMALL POX	NOVA SCOTIA
4-Jul	1888	BRISTOW, JOHN	42		NEPHRITIS	ENGLAND
7-Jan	1880	BROOKS, MARTIN W	75		RHEUMATISIM	MEDFORD, MA
10-Oct	1861	BROOKS, PETER	36		BRAIN DISEASE	IRELAND
27-Aug	1898	BROWN, ALICE		3 MONTHS 15 DAYS	FERMENTAL DIARRHOEA	BOSTON
29-Aug	1857	BROWN, CATHARINE (ROBERTSON)	35		CONSUMPTION	ENGLAND
29-May	1856	BROWN, CYNTHIA	43		SMALL POX	NEW HAMSHIRE, THORNTON
26-Dec	1891	BROWN, EMMA (HARRIS)	30		CHRONIC INTESTINAL CATARH	BOSTON
26-Mar	1857	BROWN, EUNICE (DAVIS)	50		TYPHOID FEVER	MAINE, SACO
22-Aug	1864	BROWN, FANNY	18		SMALL POX	FRANCE
16-Sep	1858	BROWN, HANNAH		1	SYPHILIS - CONGENITAL	BOSTON
25-Sep	1855	BROWN, JOHN	34		LUNG INFLAMMATION	BOSTON
24-Jul	1877	BROWN, JOHN	53		ALCHOLISM	SWEDEN
13-Dec	1872	BROWN, JOHN F	63		CONVULSIONS	BOSTON
29-Jan	1859	BROWN, JOHN H	26		TYPHOID FEVER	ENGLAND
18-Aug	1861	BROWN, JOHN H	31		SPINE DISEASE	VIRGINIA
30-Oct	1861	BROWN, JOSHUA	27		PHTHISIS	DELAWARE
13-Oct	1860	BROWN, MARY	20		INTEMPERANCE	IRELAND
16-Sep	1896	BROWN, NELLIE F		5	ATROPHY	CAMBRIDGE, MA
23-Aug	1897	BROWN, ROSE		6 MONTHS 10 DAYS	INFANTILE ATROPHY	BOSTON
15-Jun	1886	BROWN, WALTER B	52		ATAXIA LOCOMOTOR & ASTHENIA	FAIRHAVEN, MA
2-Aug	1895	BROWN, WILLIAM	1	10	MENINGITIS	BOSTON
11-Feb	1851	BRUCE, MARY (SPEAR)	50		CONSUMPTION	BOSTON
29-Aug	1897	BRULAND, EARL H		2 MONTHS 19 DAYS	INFANTILE ATROPHY	BOSTON
29-Apr	1888	BUCHANAN, MARY A (MCGUIRE)	56		HEART DISEASE	IRELAND
12-Aug	1856	BUCHET, PETER	69		SMALL POX	NOVA SCOTIA, CAPE BRETON
21-Nov	1887	BUCK, JOSEPHINE (EDWARDS)	44		HEART DISEASE	PENNSYLVANIA, PITTSBURGH
5-May	1864	BUCKINGHAM, CHARLES	35		SMALL POX	ENGLAND
18-Jan	1862	BUCKLEY, DENNIS	39		KIDNEY DISEASE	IRELAND
1-Mar	1862	BUCKLEY, JAMES	40		HEART DISEASE	IRELAND
20-May	1854	BUCKLEY, MARY	78		DIARRHOEA	IRELAND
20-Aug	1862	BUGBEE, MARY	35		EXHAUSTION	IRELAND
11-Apr	1884	BULLARD, ISAAC	70		BRONCHITIS & OLD AGE	SHARON
16-Oct	1822	BUNKER, WILLIAM A				
16-Aug	1859	BURKE, FRANK A/K/A BUSH	27		SMALL POX	MAINE
27-Sep	1858	BURKE, JULIA	23		CONSUMPTION	IRELAND
7-May	1866	BURKE, MARY	40		CANCER	IRELAND
31-Mar	1857	BURNS, PATRICK		3	MARASMUS	RAINSFORD ISLAND
16-Jul	1895	BURT, EMILY	1	8	MARASMUS	BOSTON
16-Aug	1859	BUSH, FRANK A/K/A BURKE	27		SMALL POX	MAINE
24-Jun	1877	BUTLER, EDWARD	87		OLD AGE	BOSTON
23-Jan	1856	BUTTERFIELD, GEORGE L	32		SMALL POX	MAINE, PORTLAND
13-Oct	1856	BUTTERS, GEORGE	50		DIARRHOEA	NEW HAMPSHIRE, PORTSMOUTH
15-Feb	1885	BYAM, EPHRAIM L	77		RHEUMATISIM & DEBILITY	CHELMSFORD, MA
29-Jun	1880	BYRNES, THOMAS	65		CEREBRAL HEMORRHAGE	IRELAND
14-Jan	1891	CALDER, MARY	68		SENILE DEBILITY	IRELAND
4-Mar	1855	CALLAGHAN, DENNIS	22		PERIONITIS	IRELAND
26-Oct	1888	CALLAHAN, ANNIE		11	TUBERCULAR MENINGITIS	BOSTON
19-Aug	1861	CALLAHAN, BRIDGET (MCLAUGHLIN)	38		UTERUS INFLAMMATION	IRELAND
16-Mar	1858	CALLAHAN, DAVID		7	LUNG INFLAMMATION	RAINSFORD ISLAND
18-Aug	1857	CALLAHAN, ELLEN (O'BRIEN)	30		UTERINE HEMORRHAGE	IRELAND
16-Jul	1856	CALLAHAN, JAMES	50		CONSUMPTION	IRELAND
18-Aug	1890	CALLAHAN, JULIA (DOHERTY)	72		HEMIPLEGA &HEART FAILURE	IRELAND
15-Apr	1865	CALLAHAN, MARTIN	40		DELIRIUM TREMENS	IRELAND
28-Sep	1857	CAMPBELL, JAMES	23		BRONCHITIS	IRELAND

MONTH	YEAR	NAME	AGE YEARS	AGE MONTHS	CAUSE OF DEATH	BORN
19-Oct	1883	CAMPBELL, JOHN	18		PHTHISIS & EXHAUSTION	ROXBURY, MA
14-Apr	1855	CAMPBELL, MATTHEW	20		CONSUMPTION	IRELAND
12-Dec	1856	CAMPBELL, RODERICK	30		TYPHOID FEVER	PRINCE EDWARD ISLAND
21-Oct	1859	CAMPBELL, THOMAS	22		SMALL POX	
17-Jul	1826	CANADY, WALTER	34		CONSUMPTION	SCOTLAND
2-Aug	1896	CANDOW, HUGH W		3 MONTHS 27 DAYS	CEREBRAL CONGESTION	BOSTON
11-Sep	1881	CANNON, JOHN	60		PHTHISIS	IRELAND
23-Feb	1860	CARLIN, THOMAS	21		SMALL POX	IRELAND
10-Oct	1856	CARNES, JOHN	45		APOPLEXY	NORWAY
30-Jul	1856	CARNEY, JANE (FULTON)	45		HEART DISEASE	IRELAND
31-Jul	1840	CARNEY, JOHN	20		SMALL POX	
31-Aug	1894	CARPENTER, AGNES		7 MONTHS 25 DAYS	CHOLERA INFANTUM	WOBURN
8-Oct	1888	CARR, MARY (SARGENT)	52		ULCER VARICOSE	NEW HAMPSHIRE
8-Aug	1855	CARROLL, MARY A		2	ATELECTASIS	RAINSFORD ISLAND
16-Nov	1859	CARROLL, ANN	34		NOT NOTED	IRELAND
10-Aug	1856	CARROLL, CATHARINE (CLARK)	35		DIARRHOEA	IRELAND
25-Aug	1898	CARTER, BLANCHE		19 DAYS	PNEUMONIA	EVERETT
22-Jan	1856	CARTER, FRANCIS		3	SMALL POX	BRIGHTON, MA
28-Sep	1854	CARTER, SARAH	25		DIARRHOEA	NOVA SCOTIA
6-Sep	1854	CASE, GEORGE	22		SMALL POX	NEW HAMPSHIRE, KEENE
15-Sep	1857	CASEY, DENNIS	23		CONSUMPTION	IRELAND
15-Aug	1862	CASHER, JOHN	36		KIDNEY & LIVERDISEASE	IRELAND
29-Jan	1857	CASS, CATHARINE	30		CONSUMPTION	IRELAND
6-Dec	1859	CASTANO, JOSEPH	29		SMALL POX	AZORES
27-Oct	1863	CHAMBERLIN, JOHN	40		PARALYSIS	IRELAND
9-Jul	1803	CHANDLER, JOHN			DROWNED	LEWISTOWN, MAINE
3-Jan	1893	CHANDLER, JOHN H	39			
27-Apr	1891	CHASE, CATHARINE (MCLAUGHLIN)	38		TUBERCULOSIS	MASS
5-Apr	1863	CHASE, CHARLES D	34		SMALL POX	MAINE
16-Apr	1876	CHEEVER, FREDERICK AUGUSTUS	59		PNEUMONIA (5 DAYS)	LOWELL, MA
19-Oct	1890	CHICK, JOSEPH P	66		SENILE MARASMUS	NEW HAMPSHIRE, PORTSMOUTH
11-Feb	1890	CHISHOLM, ELVINA	60		HEART DISEASE	MAINE
11-Oct	1854	CHURCH, JOHN	46		TYPHOID FEVER	PORTUGAL
6-Feb	1893	CLANCEY, MARY (MURRAY)	78		PLUERISY	IRELAND
16-Mar	1863	CLANCY, ANN (CONWAY)	35		NECROSIS	IRELAND
27-Sep	1881	CLANCY, JOHN	67		ASTHMA	IRELAND
25-Mar	1858	CLARK, BRIDGET	22		DROPSY	IRELAND
23-Dec	1890	CLARK, CAROLINE (DANBRIDGE)	80		SENILE GANGRENE	VIRGINIA
9-Jun	1860	CLARK, GEORGE	20		TYPHOID FEVER	VERMONT
13-Dec	1891	CLARK, JAMES A	55		DIARRHOEA	MAINE
23-Jun	1879	CLARK, JOHN D MD	66		HEART DISEASE	MASS
10-Apr	1864	CLARK, MARIA (RICH)	24		PHTHISIS	CANADA
4-Aug	1895	CLAUSS, CHARLES		4	MALNUTRITION	BOSTON
11-Aug	1858	CLAYTON, ELIZA (KAIN)	50		CONSUMPTION	ENGLAND
20-May	1890	CLEARE, ELLEN (HALEY	79		BRONCHITIS	IRELAND
27-Oct	1856	CLIFFORD, CHARLES	29		CONSUMPTION	NEW HAMPSHIRE, PORTSMOUTH
4-Oct	1854	CLIFFORD, JULIA	24		DYSENTARY	IRELAND
29-Mar	1857	CLIFFORD, THOMAS	31		ERYSIPELAS	IRELAND
11-Aug	1856	CLINCH, GEORGE	36		HIP DISEASE	IRELAND
5-Dec	1889	CLINE, HENRY	61		PHTHISIS	GERMANY
28-Jul	1897	CLOSE, AMBER		3 MONTHS 10 DAYS	FERMENTAL DIARRHOEA	HORTON, MAINE
2-Aug	1897	CLOSE, CEDRIC		4	FERMENTAL DIARRHOEA	HORTON, MAINE
27-Jul	1857	CLOUGH, JOHN	21		CONSUMPTION	MICHIGAN
30-Aug	1857	CODY, NICHOLAS	34		CONSUMPTION	NOVA SCOTIA
26-Jul	1865	COFFEE, JEREMIAH	52		GANGRENE	MASS
7-Apr	1866	COFFEE, JOHN	39		SYPHILIS	ITALY
21-Feb	1890	COFFRAN, JOHN W	70		DEMENTIA & PARALYSIS	NEW HAMPSHIRE, CONCORD

MONTH	YEAR	NAME	AGE YEARS	AGE MONTHS	CAUSE OF DEATH	BORN
13-Aug	1890	COGGINA, FANNY	60		ANAEMIA	NEW BRUNSWICK, ST JOHN
3-Aug	1896	COHEN, DORA	1	2	ENTERITISS	BOSTON
17-Sep	1890	COHEN, JOHN		2	DIARRHOEA & SYPHILIS	RAINSFORD ISLAND
21-Aug	1865	COIN, MARGARET	54		LUNG HEMORRHAGE	IRELAND
31-May	1883	COLBURN, ORLANDO	68		BRIGHT'S DISEASE	NEW YORK, ROME
May	1827	COLBY, NATHANIEL			SMALL POX	
28-May	1830	COLE, RICHARD	20		SMALL POX	
14-Oct	1855	COLEMAN, MARGARET (DODD)	64		TYPHOID FEVER	IRELAND
10-Feb	1893	COLLINS, ANN (COLLINS)	38		MITRAL VALVE INSUFFIECIENCY	IRELAND
5-Jun	1861	COLLINS, DAVID	45		BRAIN DISEASE	IRELAND
11-Apr	1880	COLLINS, JAMES	69		PHTHISIS	IRELAND
16-Mar	1861	COLLINS, JOHN	65		CANCER	IRELAND
13-Dec	1855	COLLINS, MARY	1	9	LUNG INFLAMMATION	NEW YORK
8-Oct	1860	COLLINS, ROBERT	22		DELIRIUM TREMENS	BOSTON
30-Sep	1875	COLLINS, TIMOTHY	62		CONSUMPTION	IRELAND
5-Apr	1866	COMSTOCK, GILDER LEROY	5		PHTHISIS	MASS
8-Feb	1889	CONDON, JOHN	28		PHTHISIS	BOSTON
10-Jul	1898	CONDON, JOSEPH		1 MONTH 7 DAYS	FERMENTAL DIARRHOEA	BOSTON
16-Jul	1855	CONGDON, BENJAMIN	63		BLADDER INFLAMMATION	RHODE ISLAND, NEWPORT
25-Aug	1885	CONLEY, MICHAEL J	34		PHTHISIS (17 MONTHS)	IRELAND
31-Mar	1891	CONLEY, PATRICK	24		TUBERCULOSIS	BOSTON
12-Jun	1854	CONNELLY, BRIDGET	1	4	MARASMUS	BOSTON
17-Apr	1892	CONNELLY, SARAH (FLAHERTY)	44		RHEUMATISIM	IRELAND
2-Nov	1856	CONNELLY, TIMOTHY	60		LUNG INFLAMMATION	IRELAND
12-Nov	1877	CONNERS, JOHN	85		OLD AGE	IRELAND
31-Aug	1890	CONNOLLY, CATHARINE (LEARY)	75		CANCER UTERUS	IRELAND
12-Sep	1863	CONNOLLY, JOHN	45		LUNG GANGRENE	IRELAND
16-Mar	1890	CONNOLLY, MARY		3 DAYS	ASPHYXIA	RAINSFORD ISLAND
14-Oct	1864	CONNOLLY, OWEN	50		PHTHISIS	IRELAND
26-Jun	1865	CONNOR, CATHARINE	5		CANCRUM ORIS	BOSTON
2-Jun	1888	CONNOR, MARY L (MCDONALD)	75		BRONCHITIS	NEW HAMPSHIRE
1-Aug	1898	CONNORS, ELLEN		1 MONTH 14 DAYS	FERMENTAL DIARRHOEA	BOSTON
4-Oct	1856	CONNORS, MICHAEL	43		CONSUMPTION	IRELAND
6-Sep	1862	CONNORS, MICHAEL	29		PHTHISIS	IRELAND
2-Jul	1883	CONNORS, MICHAEL	71		SENILTY	PENNSYLVANIA, PHILADELPHIA
26-Sep	1893	CONNORS, SUSAN (DOHERTY)	59		CEREBRAL HEMORRHAGE	IRELAND
16-Aug	1898	CONNORS, THERESA		8	INFANTILE ATROPHY	BOSTON
26-Mar	1892	CONROY, ELIZA (CAMPBELL)	67		DIARRHOEA	CANADA
29-Jan	1881	CONWAY, STEPHEN	58		BRONCHITIS	IRELAND
14-Dec	1857	COOK, MICHAEL	50		LUNG GANGRENE	IRELAND
13-Nov	1894	CORCORAN, CATHARINE (MCHUE)	69		DEBILITY	IRELAND
6-Jan	1888	CORCORAN, MARY HANNIGAN)	47		PERIONITIS	IRELAND
15-Nov	1857	CORCORAN, PATRICK	32		DIARRHOEA	IRELAND
6-Jan	1858	CORDY, KARL	27		CONSUMPTION	SWEDEN
2-Aug	1897	COSTIE, WILLIAM		7	INFANTILE ATROPHY	BOSTON
5-Mar	1862	COSTIGAN, WILLIAM C	24		CANCER STOMACH	CANADA
7-Mar	1891	COSTIN, CATHARINE	60		DIARRHOEA	IRELAND
16-Mar	1860	COTTER, EDWARD	28		CONSUMPTION	NEW BRUNSWICK, ST JOHN
11-Sep	1895	COTTER, HAROLD		3	MARASMUS	MEDFORD, MA
31-Aug	1826	COTTER, MICHAEL	17		BILIOUS FEVER	
26-Oct	1891	COTTRELL, PATRICK	32		TUBERCULOSIS	ENGLAND
12-Feb	1858	COUGHLAN, CORNELIUS	1	2	CONSUMPTION	BOSTON
4-Dec	1857	COUGHLAN, ELLEN (MORRISON)	35		CONSUMPTION	NOVA SCOTIA
4-Aug	1855	COUGHLAN, MARY	24		SHIP FEVER	IRELAND
1-Jul	1890	COUGHLIN, ANN (HERLIHY)	69		BRONCHITIS	IRELAND

MONTH	YEAR	NAME	AGE YEARS	AGE MONTHS	CAUSE OF DEATH	BORN
16-Oct	1862	COUGHLIN, ELIZABETH	34		PHTHISIS & ASTHMA	IRELAND
19-Aug	1889	COUGHLIN, HANNAH (CONNOR)	40		CANCER HEPATIC	IRELAND
27-Feb	1863	COURTNEY, ELLEN	29		SYPHILIS	IRELAND
17-Jul	1857	COWAN, MARY	19		CONSUMPTION	IRELAND
28-Dec	1883	COWDEN, JOSEPH	42		PNEUMONIA (7 DAYS)	BOSTON
9-Oct	1835	COX, JOHN	19		SMALL POX	
18-Jan	1889	CRAWFORD, MARY (ROACH)	43		PHTHISIS	NEW HAMPSHIRE, HAMPTON
8-Apr	1859	CRAWFORD, WILLIAM	60		RHEUMATISIM	MAINE
14-Aug	1897	CREARY, THOMAS		5 MONTHS 17 DAYS	ASPHYXIA	CAMBRIDGE
3-Jan	1857	CREIGHTON, CATHARINE (O'NEAL)	30		CONSUMPTION	IRELAND
26-Oct	1890	CRONIN, ELLEN (MAHONEY)	61		SENILE DEBILITY	IRELAND
3-Sep	1890	CRONIN, MARY (GLAVIN)	61		HEART FAILURE	IRELAND
19-Mar	1890	CRONIN, MARY (KELLEY)	61		PNEUMONIA	IRELAND
14-Apr	1884	CROSS, JEREMIAH	56		DEBILITY	RICHMOND, VA
28-Nov	1856	CROTTY, DAVID	35		LIVER CANCER	IRELAND
9-Aug	1884	CROWLEY, DANIEL	74		PARALYSIS & DIARRHOEA	IRELAND
27-Aug	1857	CROWLEY, HANNAH (HANNEGAN)	41		CONSUMPTION	IRELAND
19-Sep	1860	CROWLEY, MARGARET	27		TYPHOID FEVER	IRELAND
27-Jul	1897	CROWLEY, MARGARET		4	FERMENTAL DIARRHOEA	BOSTON
10-Feb	1889	CROWLEY, MARGARET (O'BRIEN)	70		DYSENTARY	IRELAND
18-Jul	1889	CROWLEY, MARY (MCCARTHY)	65		HEMIPLEGA & EXHAUSTION	IRELAND
15-Jul	1888	CROWLEY, SUSAN		14 DAYS	ECLAMPSIA	RAINSFORD ISLAND
12-Jun	1866	CULLEN, GEORGE	33		PHTHISIS	IRELAND
2-Apr	1888	CULLEN, GEORGE	78		SENILE DEBILITY	IRELAND
4-Jul	1861	CULLINAN, JOANNA (CRADEN)	33		PHTHISIS	IRELAND
10-Aug	1858	CUMMINGS, BRIDGET	19		CONSUMPTION	IRELAND
6-Sep	1881	CUMMINGS, LEPRELET	75		RHEUMATISIM	DIGHTON, MA
25-Mar	1889	CUMMINGS, MARY	28		PHTHISIS	BOSTON
25-Apr	1888	CUMMINGS, OLIVE (DONNELLY)	59		HEART DISEASE	MAINE, SACO
20-Feb	1824	CUMMINGS, RACHEL			SMALL POX	NOTTINGHAM, NH
20-Sep	1856	CUNNINGHAM, ANN		1	MARASMUS	RAINSFORD ISLAND
21-Mar	1856	CUNNINGHAM, BRIDGET	28		BRONCHITIS	IRELAND
23-Nov	1884	CUNNINGHAM, DAVID	34		PHTHISIS & EXHAUSTION	BOSTON
17-May	1864	CUNNINGHAM, JAMES	30		SMALL POX	IRELAND
12-Nov	1884	CUNNINGHAM, PATRICK	39		BRONCHITIS & EXHAUSTION	NEW BRUNSWICK, ST JOHNS
21-Jun	1885	CURLEY, JAMES	57		PHTHISIS & EXHAUSTION	IRELAND
3-May	1856	CURLEY, MARY		10	HEART DISEASE	BRIDGEWATER, MA
7-Mar	1890	CURRAN, BRIDGET	36		PHTHISIS	IRELAND
30-Dec	1887	CURRAN, JOHN F	51		PHTHISIS	IRELAND
4-Jul	1896	CURRY, MARGERY	1	2	TUBERCULOSIS	BOSTON
20-Sep	1898	CURTAIN, HENRY		2 MONTHS 15 DAYS	FERMENTAL DIARRHOEA	BOSTON
6-Sep	1827	CURTIS, GEORGE	40		SMALL POX	GEORGETOWN, COLUMBIA
7-Aug	1895	CUSHMAN, GEORGE E.		4	IMPROPER FEEDING	BOSTON
9-May	1890	CUTTING, EDWARD W	70		ATHEROMA	BOSTON
1-Jan	1892	DAILY, MICHAEL				
5-Oct	1860	DALEY, CATHARINE	12		SCROFULA	ENGLAND
7-Aug	1888	DALTON, CARRIE	54		SENILE DEMENTIA	MANHATTAN
17-Jul	1876	DALTON, JOHN	52		PHTHISIS	IRELAND
10-Jul	1856	DALTON, JULIA	28		SMALL POX	NEW BRUNSWICK, ST JOHNS
15-Nov	1857	DALY, HANNAH	27		CONSUMPTION	IRELAND
4-Sep	1854	DALY, WILLIAM		1	DIARRHOEA	IRELAND
28-Oct	1888	DAMON, MAURICE	56		ERYSIPELAS & GANGRENE	HINGHAM, MA
6-Mar	1865	DANIELS, JOHN	49		PARALYSIS	ENGLAND
19-Jun	1883	DANIELS, MICHAEL	63		DIARRHOEA	MAINE, WISCASSET
17-Oct	1858	DANIELS, VINCENT	52		CYSTITIS	ENGLAND
21-Mar	1888	DAVERY, MARY (KENNEY)	30		PHTHISIS	IRELAND

MONTH	YEAR	NAME	AGE YEARS	AGE MONTHS	CAUSE OF DEATH	BORN
4-Oct	1855	DAVES, CHARLES	30		CONSUMPTION	NOVA SCOTIA
28-Jun	1859	DAVIS, BENJAMIN	24		SMALL POX	CONNECTICUTT
13-Nov	1805	DAVIS, JACOB	22			
4-Jan	1857	DAVIS, JAMES	70		DEBILITY	IRELAND
18-Jan	1875	DAVIS, JOHN	75		HEART DISEASE	WALES
25-Feb	1894	DAVIS, MARY (BROWN)	72		PNEUMONIA	BOSTON
20-May	1893	DAVIS, MARY E	38		CANCER RECTUM	IRELAND
14-Jun	1861	DAVIS, MARY M		1	PREMATURE BIRTH	RAINSFORD ISLAND
25-Jul	1830	DAWES, WILLIAM		5	SMALL POX	
27-Mar	1855	DAY, JOHN	21		CONSUMPTION	ENGLAND
11-Jun	1855	DEAN, ISABELLA	43		SPINE CARIES	IRELAND
23-Jan	1889	DEERY, EDWARD	40		TUBERCULOSIS	IRELAND
12-Jan	1863	DELANEY, JOHN	40		DIARRHOEA	IRELAND
9-Mar	1890	DELAY, ELLEN (WALSH)	39		PHTHISIS	BOSTON
20-Sep	1891	DEMPSEY, JOHN	55		ATAXIA LOCOMOTOR	IRELAND
30-Jan	1881	DENGLER, CHRISTIAN	65		DEBILITY	GERMANY
9-Mar	1859	DEPAYNE, ANTONI	22		CONSUMPTION	
7-May	1864	DERRICK, JOSEPH	18		SMALL POX	ANTIQUA
18-May	1893	DESMOND, ANN (CROWLEY)	72		SENILITY	IRELAND
12-Oct	1855	DESMOND, MARGARET (MADDEN)	32		TYPHOID FEVER	IRELAND
30-Apr	1858	DESMOND, TIMOTHY	40		UNKNOWN	
10-Nov	1863	DEVER, JAMES	40		DELIRIUM TREMENS	IRELAND
17-Jun	1864	DEVINE, JAMES	27		SMALL POX	SALEM
24-Jun	1882	DEVINE, JOHN	62		HEART DISEASE & DROPSY	IRELAND
9-Oct	1856	DEVINE, MARY (O'CONNELL)	27		CONSUMPTION	IRELAND
9-Mar	1883	DEVINE, WILLIAM	58		PHTHISIS	IRELAND
7-Jun	1883	DEVLIN, PATRICK	70		BRONCHITIS	IRELAND
21-Apr	1857	DEWITT, CHARLES A	33		SPINE CARIES	MADEIRA
11-Jul	1896	DI BENEDETTA, KATHERINE	1	3	CEREBRAL CONGESTION	BOSTON
4-Nov	1888	DICKEY, CATHERINE (HOPE)	31		PHTHISIS & EPILEPSY	
22-Mar	1861	DINAN, DANIEL	24		CYANOSIS	IRELAND
2-Jan	1864	DIXON, ANN	21		DIARRHOEA	BOSTON
17-Jul	1866	DIXON, OVID	16		FRACTURE OF THIGH	NEW ORLEANS
9-Aug	1865	DOHERTY, ANN	29		PHTHISIS	IRELAND
3-Jul	1894	DOHERTY, ANN	76		SENILITY	IRELAND
16-Apr	1857	DOHERTY, BARNEY	22		CONSUMPTION	CANADA
26-Mar	1858	DOHERTY, BRIDGET	3		CONSUMPTION	BOSTON
24-Nov	1859	DOHERTY, BRIDGET	21		CONSUMPTION	IRELAND
24-Jun	1888	DOHERTY, DANIEL		1	INTESTINAL CATARRH & MARASMUS	LONG ISLAND HOSPITAL
6-Dec	1891	DOHERTY, JAMES	33		PNEUMONIA	IRELAND
13-Jul	1896	DOHERTY, JOSEPH		2	INFANTILE	
17-Jul	1857	DOHERTY, MARY J	2	5	BRAIN INFLAMMATION	BOSTON
12-May	1891	DOHERTY, SARAH (MCCARRON)	43		WOUND ON HAND GANGRENE	IRELAND
25-Jul	1891	DOLAN, DELIA (PALMER)	60		NEPHRITIS	MAINE
8-Jun	1889	DOLAN, JAMES	46		BRONCHITIS & HEART DISEASE	IRELAND
1-Jul	1890	DOLAN, MARY	64		HEART DISEASE	IRELAND
6-Feb	1863	DOLAND, CHARLES	21		UNKNOWN	WESTERN ISLANDS
8-May	1888	DONAHOE, ANN	96		SENILITY	IRELAND
22-Mar	1888	DONAHOE, ELIZABETH (HOLLAND)	80		DIARRHOEA	IRELAND
28-Dec	1892	DONAHOE, HANNAH	55		DEBILTIY	IRELAND
29-Oct	1887	DONEGAN, JAMES	75		BRONCHITIS	IRELAND
28-Jun	1860	DONEGAN, TIMOTHY	32		PHTHISIS	IRELAND
10-Mar	1882	DONLEY, JAMES	63		BRONCHITIS	IRELAND
25-Jan	1859	DONOVAN, DANIEL	74		PARALYSIS	IRELAND
25-Mar	1878	DONOVAN, DENNIS	35		CONSUMPTION	BOSTON
18-Oct	1890	DONOVAN, JEREMIAH	52		PHTHISIS	
7-Jul	1863	DONOVAN, JOHN	55		INTEMPERANCE	IRELAND
6-Dec	1884	DONOVAN, JOHN	41		PHTHISIS	IRELAND
7-Aug	1882	DOONAN, JOHN	58		DIARRHOEA	IRELAND
21-Dec	1888	DORAN, ANASTASIA	58		BRIGHT'S DISEASE	IRELAND

MONTH	YEAR	NAME	AGE YEARS	AGE MONTHS	CAUSE OF DEATH	BORN
17-Apr	1880	DORSEY, THOMAS	81		OLD AGE	IRELAND
8-May	1888	DOUBLER, ELLEN (FOLEY)	53		CANCER UTERUS	IRELAND
3-Dec	1882	DOUGHERTY, JAMES	62		PARALYSIS & APOPLEXY	IRELAND
11-Apr	1858	DOWD, MARY	12		SPINE CRIES	IRELAND
29-Jun	1891	DOWNEY, CATHARINE (SHEA)	72		SENILITY	IRELAND
27-Apr	1864	DOWNEY, FANNY	35		SMALL POX	NEW BRUNSWICK
6-Aug	1888	DOWNEY, JOHN	30		PHTHISIS	BOSTON
30-Dec	1888	DOWNING, HANNAH (MULLENS)	40		PHTHISIS	IRELAND
20-Sep	1856	DOWNING, JOHN	66		DIARRHOEA	IRELAND
13-May	1856	DOWNS, RICHARD	38		TYPHOID FEVER	ENGLAND
25-Oct	1892	DOYLE, ANN (CALLAN)	55		INTESTINAL OBSTRUCTION	IRELAND
15-Jun	1857	DOYLE, CATHARINE	30		DYSENTARY	BOSTON
23-Jun	1865	DOYLE, JOHN	39		EPILEPSY	IRELAND
1-Aug	1886	DOYLE, JOSEPH H	39		PHTHISIS	BOSTON
28-Jul	1877	DOYLE, MATTHEW	18		EPILEPSY	BOSTON
5-Aug	1865	DOYLE, RICHARD	64		HEART DISEASE	IRELAND
3-Apr	1891	DRAPER, DAVID	22		DROWNED	VIRGINIA
15-Nov	1859	DRINAN, MARGARET	35		CANCER	IRELAND
13-Jan	1890	DRISCOLL, CATHARINE (DONOVAN)	45		PHTHISIS	IRELAND
30-Apr	1863	DRISCOLL, JOHN G	43		PHTHISIS	IRELAND
31-May	1889	DRISCOLL, MARGARET (O'NEILL)	50		HEART DISEASE	IRELAND
4-Sep	1854	DROUD, HENRY	33		LIVER DISEASE	FRANCE
23-Jan	1860	DRUMMY, MARY	22		SMALL POX	IRELAND
9-Apr	1860	DUDDY, SIDNEY	24		CONSUMPTION	IRELAND
6-Aug	1885	DUFFY, JAMES	19		PHTHISIS	BOSTON
23-Oct	1859	DUGAN, CATHARINE	54		ANEMIA	NOVA SCOTIA
15-Sep	1859	DUGAN, MARY	46		INTUSSUSEPTION	IRELAND
27-Dec	1857	DUGAN, WILLIAM	41		TYPHOID FEVER	MAINE, EASPORT
9-May	1889	DUKE, MARY (MURRAY)			DEBILITY	PRINCE EDWARD ISLAND
24-Aug	1865	DUMAS, RUFUS	38		HEART DISEASE	PORTUGAL
5-Aug	1889	DUNCAN, SIMEON	77		HEART VALVE DISEASE & HERNIA	BOSTON
31-Jul	1864	DUNLAVEY, CATHARINE	72		CANCER BREAST	
11-Mar	1889	DUNLAVEY, JAMES	83		HEART DISEASE	IRELAND
31-Jul	1864	DUNLAVEY, JOHN	72		CANCER BREAST	SCOTLAND
29-Apr	1886	DUNN, JAMES	36		PHTHISIS & PNEUMONIA	BOSTON
19-Jan	1889	DUNN, JOHN J	27		NEPHRITIS	BOSTON
1-Dec	1864	DUNN, MARY A	34		TYPHOID FEVER	IRELAND
2-Aug	1860	DUNN, PETER	45		SYPHILIS (31 DAYS)	IRELAND
20-Jul	1865	DUNN, WILLIAM	28		PHTHISIS	NOVA SCOTIA
4-Dec	1864	DUNN, WILLIAM H		11	MARASMUS	BOSTON
8-Aug	1898	DYER, EDNA		10	PNEUMONIA	BOSTON
5-Sep	1882	EAGAN, EDWARD	44		PHTHISIS	NOT KNOWN
5-Aug	1863	EAGAN, JOHN	28		HEART DISEASE	IRELAND
30-May	1863	EASON, WILLIAM	49		PHTHISIS	ENGLAND
3-Jan	1889	EATON, JAMES	64		PARALYSIS & DIARRHOEA	BOSTON
15-Apr	1892	EATON, THADDEUS	66		SENILE DEMENTIA	
13-Jun	1873	EDWARDS, FREEMAN	19		SCROFULA (CONGENITAL) & TUBERCULOSIS	DORCHESTER, MA
October	1819	EDWARDS, WILLIAM				MANCHESTER
12-Apr	1888	EGLESTON, SARAH	65		DYSENTARY	IRELAND
28-Aug	1819	ELDER, JAMES				
10-Apr	1889	ELIOTT, CHARLES O	69		HEART DISEASE	BOSTON
24-Feb	1889	ELKINS, EDWARD	61		DEMENTIA	MAINE, PORTLAND
2-Jun	1822	ELWELL, ALBAN	51			NORTHPORT, MAINE
22-Dec	1855	EMMONS, HARRIET	28			NEW HAMPSHIRE
16-May	1864	ENGLISH, JAMES	25		SMALL POX	IRELAND
7-Aug	1863	ESPINOLA, MARTIN	20		PHTHISIS	CAPE VERDE
1-Jan	1893	ESSEX, ELLEN (MCCARTHY)	79			IRELAND
2-Sep	1821	EUGLEY, GEORGE			SHIP FEVER	
20-Mar	1865	EVANS, RICHARD	38		SMALL POX	TENNESSE
26-Dec	1854	EVANS, SAMUEL	22		SHIP FEVER	ENGLAND
3-Feb	1858	EVERETT, MANUEL		1 DAY	SYPHILIS	RAINSFORD ISLAND

MONTH	YEAR	NAME	AGE YEARS	AGE MONTHS	CAUSE OF DEATH	BORN
16-Jan	1860	EVERETT, THOMAS R	80		OLD AGE	ENGLAND
12-Apr	1860	FADER, MARY TOOT		1	SMALL POX	RAINSFORD ISLAND
27-Feb	1889	FAGIN, SARAH (JONES)	47		BRIGHTS DISEASE	ENGLAND
15-Sep	1857	FAHEY, MARY	29		SPINE DISEASE	IRELAND
10-Aug	1888	FALLON, MARIA	24		PNEUMONIA	IRELAND
16-Sep	1863	FARRELL, CATHARINE (HOGAN)	40		LIVER & LUNG DISEASE	IRELAND
8-Sep	1856	FARRELL, JOHN	15		CONSUMPTION	IRELAND
15-Aug	1865	FARRELL, MARY E	23		PHTHISIS	MAINE
25-Jan	1890	FARRELL, NANCY	68		HEART DISEASE	NOVA SCOTIA
5-Apr	1860	FARREN, CATHARINE	27		LUNG INFLAMMATION	BOSTON
13-Aug	1898	FATHEY, WILLIAM		2	MALNUTRITION	BOSTON
13-Feb	1888	FAULKNER, CATHARINE	50		DEBILTY	IRELAND
8-Apr	1888	FAULKNER, ELIZA	50		PHTHISIS	IRELAND
16-Mar	1859	FAULKNER, SAMUEL T	45		SHIP FEVER	IRELAND
14-Oct	1891	FAY, MARGARET (MALONEY)	65		NEPHRITIS	IRELAND
28-Jan	1859	FEELEY, PATRICK	60		CONSUMPTION	IRELAND
6-Sep	1897	FEENEY, PETER	1	1 MONTH 6 DAYS	FERMENTAL DIARRHOEA	BOSTON
5-Sep	1894	FEINBERG, ISAAC		1 MONTH 19 DAYS	CHOLERA INFANTUM	BOSTON
2-Jun	1854	FERGUSON, DARBY	60		SHIP FEVER	IRELAND
20-Apr	1891	FERGUSON, ELIZABETH (WELLINGTON)	38		CEREBRAL HEMORRHAGE	MAINE
24-Aug	1896	FERGUSON, GEORGE		3	ECLAMPSIA	RAINSFORD ISLAND
25-Feb	1861	FERGUSON, HANNAH (KOHANE)	33		PARALYSIS	IRELAND
30-Sep	1887	FERRIER, EDWARD	23		PHTHISIS	BOSTON
4-Jul	1880	FIELD, WILLIAM	80		CANCER	DORCHESTER, MA
23-May	1886	FINGER, FRANCIS G	59		HEMIPLEGIA	AUSTRIA
21-Jan	1858	FINLEY, FRANCIS	60		ASCITIES	IRELAND
24-Nov	1873	FINN, CHARLES	33		PHTHISIS	NEW YORK
16-Mar	1857	FINN, MARGARET (SULLIVAN)	30		PHTHISIS	IRELAND
6-Jul	1857	FINNERTY, MARY (FALLAON)	40		SPINE DISEASE	IRELAND
20-Jun	1884	FITZGERALD, EDWARD	68		DIARRHOEA (2 YEARS) & DEBILITY	IRELAND
10-May	1889	FITZGERALD, JOHN F				
21-Jun	1881	FITZGERALD, LAURENCE	68		BOWEL OBSTRUCTION	IRELAND
19-Jun	1859	FITZGERALD, MARY	23		LUNG INFLAMMATION	IRELAND
3-Oct	1889	FITZGERALD, MICHAEL T	26		NEPHRITIS	BOSTON
17-Jun	1856	FITZGIBBONS, CHARLES		1 DAY	SPINA BIFIDA	RAINSFORD ISLAND
9-Oct	1860	FITZGIBBONS, ELLEN	50		PHTHISIS	IRELAND
10-Dec	1857	FITZPATRICK, ELIZA	49		DROPSY IN THE HEAD	IRELAND
18-Jun	1862	FITZSIMMONS, LUCINDA (MCGUINNIS)	48		PARALYSIS	IRELAND
17-Sep	1881	FLAHERTY, MICHAEL	59		BRONCHITIS	IRELAND
14-Apr	1864	FLAMER, DAVID	33		SMALL POX	PENNSYLVANIA
8-Oct	1854	FLETCHER, GEORGE	25		TYPHOID FEVER	GERMANY
26-Jan	1856	FLOOD, JAMES		10 DAYS	SPINE DISEASE	RAINSFORD ISLAND
3-Jan	1859	FLORINE, MANUEL		1 DAY	INFANTILE	RAINSFORD ISLAND
25-Jun	1861	FLYNN, CATHARINE (HARTLAND)	40		SPINE CARIES	IRELAND
10-Apr	1878	FLYNN, JAMES	52		CONSUMPTION	IRELAND
22-Jun	1894	FOLEY, ELLEN (SULLIVAN)	80		SENILITY	IRELAND
1-Feb	1860	FORAN, MARY	42		CONSUMPTION	IRELAND
21-Apr	1858	FORD, MARIA	23		LUNG INFLAMMATION	MAINE, DAMARISCOTTA
4-Jul	1859	FORD, OWEN	1		MARASMUS	BOSTON
5-Feb	1893	FOSS, SILAS W	65		DIARRHOEA	MAINE
20-Dec	1889	FOSTER, ANN (CROWLEY)	39		TUBERCULOSIS	IRELAND
3-Apr	1874	FOSTER, CHRISTOPHER	70		DEBILITY	BOSTON
1-Oct	1859	FOSTER, HARRIET	24		LUNG INFLAMMATION	ENGLAND
26-Jun	1859	FOSTER, MARY	50		CONSUMPTION	IRELAND
17-Aug	1891	FOWLER, ELEANOR F (DYER)	77		ELEPANTIASIS LEG	IRELAND
12-Jul	1889	FOWLER, JOHN M	70		BRONCHITIS	MARYLAND, BALTIMOE

MONTH	YEAR	NAME	AGE YEARS	AGE MONTHS	CAUSE OF DEATH	BORN
13-Jul	1891	FOX, ANN	76		HEART DISEASE	IRELAND
1-Oct	1857	FRANCIS, EDWARD	32		CONSUMPTION	NOVA SCOTIA
7-Oct	1858	FRANCOIS, MARIA (HOOPER)	19		CONSUMPTION	BOSTON
29-Mar	1888	FRANKLIN, JANE (KNOX)	40		HEART DISEASE	IRELAND
19-Jan	1866	FRAVERS, JAMES	28		NECROSIS	MAINE
21-Feb	1865	FRAZIER, JOSEPH	21		SMALL POX	WESTERN ISLANDS
21-Sep	1865	FREEMAN, MARY		1 DAY	SYPHILIS	RAINSFORD ISLAND
2-Dec	1859	FRISBEE, CATHARINE	20		HEART DISEASE	
26-Jan	1858	FUREY, PATRICK	30		CONSUMPTION	IRELAND
3-Jul	1892	GAFFNEY, MARY (GAFFNEY)	76		SENILTY	IRELAND
21-Feb	1855	GALE, HARRISON	30		SMALL POX	NEW HAMPSHIRE
21-Nov	1839	GALE, WILLIAM	50		SMALL POX	WALTHAM
13-Jan	1878	GALLAGHER, FRANCIS	59		CONSUMPTION	IRELAND
14-Dec	1887	GALLAGHER, JOHN G	29		PHTHISIS	BOSTON
28-Sep	1856	GALLAGHER, MARTHA (WILSON)	30		TYPHOID FEVER	IRELAND
29-Mar	1856	GALLAGHER, ROSANNA	31		SYPHILIS	IRELAND
7-Apr	1862	GALLUP, GEORGE G	56		PNEUMONIA	VERMONT, WOODSTOCK
26-Jul	1897	GALVIN, ELLEN		2	FERMENTAL DIARRHOEA	BOSTON
1-Sep	1857	GALVIN, PETER	32		CONSUMPTION	IRELAND
15-Aug	1894	GAMBON, SARAH (STEWARD)	41		PHTHISIS	PRINCE EDWARD ISLAND
20-Jul	1890	GARAGHTY, MARY (CAHILL)	53		DIARRHOEA	IRELAND
16-Sep	1890	GARDNER, ALICE (CARROLL)	38		HEART DISEASE	RHODE ISLAND, NEWPORT
6-Apr	1866	GARDNER, BENJAMIN B	30		SYPHILIS	MASSACHUSETTS
1-Jan	1893	GARLAND, ELLEN (MCKENZIE)	62			
28-Jun	1857	GARTLAND, CHARLES H. W.	1	2	LUNG INFLAMMATION	RAINSFORD ISLAND
19-Apr	1888	GAUL, SHARLANDA (PETERS)	82		SENILTY	CONNECTICUTT
30-Nov	1891	GAVIN, JOHN W.	36		PHTHISIS	BOSTON
8-Oct	1882	GEARY, LAWRENCE	24		ALCHOLOISM	BOSTON
9-Aug	1896	GENTLE, LUCIA		3	PNEUMONIA	BOSTON
13-Sep	1889	GEORGE, BRAZILLA (GORMAN)	60		HEART DISEASE	AT SEA
21-Oct	1880	GERMAIN, JOHN	60		HEART DISEASE	BOSTON
24-Mar	1893	GIBBEN, JAMES E				
4-May	1864	GIBBENS, WILLIAM	27		SMALL POX	PRINCE EDWARD ISLAND
3-Aug	1861	GIBBONS, BRIDGET	20		PERICARDITIS ADHESIVE	IRELAND
13-Aug	1892	GIBBONS, CATHARINE (MATTHEWS)	35		SYPHILIS	IRELAND
29-Nov	1856	GIBBS, BRIDGET		5	MARASMUS	BRIGHTON, MA
9-Sep	1893	GIBBS, ELIZABETH	83		CELLULITIS & SENILITY	ENGLAND
27-Oct	1856	GIBBS, ELLEN	24		PERITONITIS	IRELAND
15-Nov	1834	GIBBS, RUFUS	32		SMALL POX	
25-Aug	1876	GIBSON, HENRY L	75		OLD AGE	BOSTON
25-Aug	1858	GIBSON, JOHN	47		ASCITIES	IRELAND
19-Feb	1876	GIBSON, LEMUEL T	70	4 MONTHS	PHTHISIS	DORCHESTER, MA
29-Nov	1863	GIBSON, ROBERT	45		PARALYSIS	SCOTLAND
7-Oct	1855	GILL, MARY A	5		PLURISY	BOSTON
17-Aug	1856	GILLEN, JULIA (HALLEY)	24		PNEUMONIA	IRELAND
22-May	1889	GILLIS, AUGUSTA (DONVAN)	42		SYPHILIS	NEW BRUNSWICK, ST JOHN
2-Feb	1896	GILLIS, MARY S	5		ENTERITIS ACCUTE CATARRHAL WITH VIOLENT SYMPTOMS	BOSTON
1-Apr	1893	GILMAN ADDIE	22		SYPHILIS	BOSTON
2-Mar	1856	GLEASON, CATHARINE	20		INTEMPERANCE	PENNSYLVANIA, PHILADELPHIA
17-Jun	1891	GLEASON, MARY	85		SENILITY	IRELAND
5-Jun	1861	GLENNON, MARTIN	60		CYSTITIS	IRELAND
15-Sep	1855	GLINES, GEORGE F	17		SMALL POX	NEW HAMPSHIRE, MOUTONBOUROGH
14-Aug	1898	GLITSEN, ETTA		5	FERMENTAL DIARRHOEA	BOSTON

MONTH	YEAR	NAME	AGE YEARS	AGE MONTHS	CAUSE OF DEATH	BORN
22-Nov	1861	GLYNN, MARY (HOWARD)	31		PHTHISIS	IRELAND
3-Oct	1861	GLYNN, THOMAS		2	DEBILITY	BOSTON
6-Mar	1876	GODFREY, HENRY	48		HEART DISEASE	FALL RIVER, MA
6-Oct	1828	GODFREY, MARIA	23		CONSUMPTION	
5-Aug	1898	GOLDMAN, ROSA	2		FERMENTAL DIARRHOEA	BOSTON
13-Jun	1876	GOODRICH, LEWELL	70		NEPHRITIS	MASSACHUSETTS
20-Jan	1837	GORE, LOUISA ANN	3		SMALL POX	
6-Jul	1860	GORMAN, CATHARINE	40		DROPSY	IRELAND
3-Sep	1885	GOSS, JAMES	38		DELIRIUM TREMENS	RHODE ISLAND, PROVIDENCE
7-Mar	1855	GOULD, GRANVILLE B	41		PALSY	NEW HAMPSHIRE, HILLSBORO
27-Oct	1888	GOULD, MARY (KEVLIN)	50		PARALYSIS	IRELAND
14-Jul	1864	GOULDING, PATRICK	23		SMALL POX	IRELAND
3-Jun	1862	GOVE, ALICE		11	SYPHILIS	BOSTON
25-May	1893	GRACE, JOHN	46		CANCER GASTRIC	IRELAND
19-Aug	1892	GRACE, SARAH (LAPSE)	70		SENILTY	FRANCE
17-Jul	1857	GRADY, CATHARINE (BRADY)	56		CANCER	IRELAND
2-Jan	1857	GRAHAM, MICHAEL	35		LIVER DISEASE	IRELAND
14-Apr	1855	GRANT, DANIEL	20		ERYSIPELAS	PENNSYLVANIA, PHILADELPHIA
17-Apr	1881	GRANT, JAMES	36		PHTHISIS	NEWFOUNDLAND
17-Apr	1856	GRAVES, MARY	18		SMALL POX	MAINE, CHINA
8-Feb	1855	GRAY, BETSEY	70		DROPSY	VIRGINIA, ALEXANDRIA
19-May	1837	GRAY, JOHN	38		SMALL POX	
19-Mar	1856	GRAY, NANCY (JAMES)	55		SMALL POX	IRELAND
23-Mar	1888	GRAY, WILLIAM H.		8 DAYS	SYPHILIS	LONG ISLAND HOSPITAL
18-Aug	1894	GREALY, JOSEPH F		4	CHOLERA INFANTUM	READING
26-Jul	1897	GREEN, ANNIE		2	FERMENTAL DIARRHOEA	BOSTON
10-May	1874	GREEN, DANIEL	70		TYPHOID FEVER	IRELAND
31-Aug	1862	GREEN, ELIZABETH	21		SPINE CARIES	LOWELL, MA
9-Aug	1858	GREEN, MARY	34		CANCER	NOVA SCOTIA
15-Aug	1861	GREEN, MARY A		1	STARVATION	BOSTON
13-Oct	1892	GREEN, ROBERT	83		SENILITY	IRELAND
3-Sep	1888	GREER, JOHN	63		SENILITY	IRELAND
1-Sep	1898	GREW, SYLVIA		1 MONTH 15 DAYS	ECZEMA	BOSTON
21-Jan	1863	GRIFFIN, FRANCIS	30		ERYSIPELAS	NEW HAMPSHIRE
31-Aug	1854	GROMBERG, CHARLES A	18		DYSENTARY	SWEDEN
9-Nov	1889	GROSSPIETSCH, AUGUST A	51		CANCER FACE	GERMANY
20-Apr	1831	GROVES, THOMAS	61		SMALL POX	
20-Apr	1860	GUNN, RICHARD	48		EMPHYSEMA	BOSTON
10-Oct	1865	GUYNAN, WILLIAM	45		PARALYSIS	IRELAND
29-Sep	1862	HAGGERTY, JANE (BATERLY)	35		CANCER LIVER	IRELAND
26-Jul	1897	HAGGERTY, MARY		4	FERMENTAL DIARRHOEA	BOSTON
4-Sep	1889	HAINES, MARY E (BARNSFIELD)	74		DYSENTARY	IRELAND
8-Aug	1888	HALES, AGNES	40		GANGRENE	ENGLAND
1-Jan	1855	HALEY, JULIA	23		CONSUMPTION	IRELAND
18-Dec	1893	HALEY, MARY	38		CANCER RECTUM	IRELAND
9-Jul	1885	HALEY, MICHAEL	35		PHTHISIS	BOSTON
18-Oct	1856	HALEY, THOMAS	34		TYPHOID FEVER	IRELAND
27-Sep	1855	HALEY, WILLIAM W	1	1	WHOOPING COUGH	BOSTON
7-Jan	1890	HALL, CATHARINE (JOHNSON)	45		PHTHISIS	DISTRICT OF COLUMBIA
17-Jan	1864	HALL, FRANCES	33		CRIMINAL ABORTION	MAINE
20-Mar	1885	HALL, HENRY	33		PHTHISIS	MARYLAND
7-Aug	1874	HALL, HOPRETILL	65		HEART DISEASE	ROXBURY, MA
17-Apr	1858	HALLIMAN, ELIZA	5		CONSUMPTION	NATICK, MA
7-Mar	1883	HALLOWELL, MARTIN	60		PHTHISIS	IRELAND
8-Oct	1888	HAMILTON, FREDERICK		6	TUBERCULOSIS	LONG ISLAND
24-Nov	1891	HAMILTON, MARY (CREGAN)	33		PHTHISIS	NEW BRUNSWICK, ST JOHN
7-Feb	1894	HAMILTON, SOPHIA (MORRISON)	67		BRONCHITIS	NEW BRUNSWICK

MONTH	YEAR	NAME	AGE YEARS	AGE MONTHS	CAUSE OF DEATH	BORN
1-Jan	1862	HAMMEL, FREDERICK	22		CANCER THIGH	GERMANY
19-Apr	1893	HAMMOND, JENNY LOUISE		2	HEART DISEASE	RAINSFORD ISLAND
4-Jan	1889	HANAFORD, B. FRANK	66		PHTHISIS	IRELAND
30-Mar	1856	HANCOCK, SIMON W	18		CONSUMPTION	MAINE, BUXTON
20-Sep	1821	HANDY, RICHARD S	22			COHASSET
11-Jun	1855	HANLEY, ROSANNA		8	INFLAMMATION OF NAVEL	RAINSFORD ISLAND
27-Aug	1894	HANNE, CHARLES		6	CHOLERA INFANTUM	BOSTON
23-Jul	1854	HANSEN, GEORGE	22		LIVER DISEASE	SWEDEN
31-Jul	1832	HARDY, PATRICK	30		INTERMITTENT FEVER	
5-Jul	1898	HARLEY, WILLIAM		7	INFANTILE ATROPHY	BOSTON
12-Feb	1893	HARNEY, MARY	75		RHEUMATISIM	IRELAND
27-Jul	1895	HARNISH, MARGUERITE		11	TUBERCULOSIS	BOSTON
20-Apr	1866	HARRIGAN, FRANCIS		3 DAYS	INTERAL HEAMORRHAGE	RAINSFORD ISLAND
20-Dec	1873	HARRIGAN, WILLIAM	37		PNEUMONIA	IRELAND
1-Aug	1855	HARRINGTON, EDWARD		2	MARASMUS	RAINSFORD ISLAND
17-Aug	1873	HARRINGTON, HENRY	60		DIARRHOEA	MAINE
28-Jan	1873	HARRINGTON, JEREMIAH	70		ASCITIES	IRELAND
4-Sep	1875	HARRINGTON, TIMOTHY	69		PHTHISIS	IRELAND
24-May	1887	HARRINGTON, TIMOTHY	39		ASTHMA & EMPHYSEMA	IRELAND
2-Dec	1859	HARRIS, GEORGE	22		SMALL POX	
15-Mar	1886	HARRIS, LOUIS	34		DEMENTIA	BOSTON
25-Mar	1878	HARTWELL, THOMAS	89		OLD AGE	ALLSTON, MA
6-Jul	1889	HARTY, HENRY O	44		HEART DISEASE	BOSTON
30-Nov	1887	HARVEY, ELLEN (KEARINS)	40		PHTHISIS	IRELAND
12-Jun	1885	HARVEY, JOHN	24		PHTHISIS & PARALYSIS	SCITUATE, MA
24-Mar	1861	HARVEY, S ANNA (DAVIS)	29		DROPSY	SUTTON, MA
13-Aug	1890	HARVEY, SARAH (MINAHAN)	39		PHTHISIS	IRELAND
11-Mar	1881	HARWOOD, GEORGE W	66		DEBILITY	RHODE ISLAND, COVENTRY
17-Oct	1830	HASKELL, CAROLINE		7	SMALL POX	
20-Oct	1864	HASSETT, THOMAS	50		INTEMPERANCE	IRELAND
25-Sep	1826	HATCH, NATHANIEL	20		BILIOUS FEVER	KENNEBUNK
15-Jun	1883	HAWKINS, EDWARD	25		MEASLES & HIP DISEASE & EXHAUSTION	MARYLAND, BALTIMOE
20-Sep	1888	HAWLEY, MARY (DORMAN)	38		HEMIPLEGIA (OLD) & ASTHENIA	BOSTON
9-Feb	1866	HAYDEN, MICHAEL	48		HEART DISEASE	IRELAND
27-Jun	1889	HAYDEN, WILLIAM	57		DIARRHOEA	IRELAND
10-Aug	1897	HAYES, JAMES		6 MONTHS 10 DAYS	FERMENTAL DIARRHOEA	BOSTON
6-Mar	1856	HAYES, MARGARET	28			IRELAND
3-Dec	1854	HAYES, PATRICK	37		SHIP FEVER	IRELAND
17-Sep	1860	HEALY, BRIDGET	31		DROPSY	IRELAND
10-May	1865	HEARD, SYLVANUS	20		SMALL POX	NEW HAMPSHIRE
10-Jul	1885	HEINSELMANN, CHRISTIAN	62		PARALYSIS & DIARRHOEA	GERMANY
22-Apr	1891	HEMPLE, HANNAH (CARROLL)	49		PHTHISIS	IRELAND
1-Sep	1838	HENDERBO, THOMAS	28		BILIOUS FEVER	NEWPORT, RI
23-May	1889	HENDERSON, LOUISA	1	1	PNEUMONIA	TEWKSBURY, MA
15-Feb	1888	HENDERSON, THOMAS	70		NEPHRITIS	PENNSYLVANIA, PHILADELPHIA
12-Sep	1819	HENLY, WILLIAM				
21-Dec	1887	HENNESSEY, ANASTASIA (CARROLL)	75		EPITHELIOMA ANASTENIA	IRELAND
15-Jan	1890	HENNESSEY, ELIZA	65		HEART DISEASE & BRONCHITIS	IRELAND
15-Sep	1887	HENNESSEY, ELLEN	46		PHTHISIS	IRELAND
13-Sep	1863	HENNESSEY, JAMES	1	6	DIARRHOEA	RAINSFORD ISLAND
4-Dec	1873	HENNESSEY, JAMES L	60		DEMENTIA	BOSTON
10-Jan	1878	HENNESSEY, JOHN	47		PNEUMONIA	IRELAND
15-Jan	1889	HENNIE, FRANK	60		CEREBRAL HEMORRHAGE (21 DAYS)	GERMANY
9-Oct	1882	HENRATTY, ANDREW	82		SENILITY	IRELAND
1-Sep	1898	HENSON, AMY		9	FERMENTAL DIARRHOEA	BOSTON
13-Jan	1865	HEWEY, LOUISA	25		SMALL POX	MAINE
5-Dec	1891	HEWITT, JESSIE (FLYNN)	60		CANCER CEREBRAL	SCOTLAND

MONTH	YEAR	NAME	AGE YEARS	AGE MONTHS	CAUSE OF DEATH	BORN
18-Apr	1862	HICKEY, MATTHEW	27		BURNS	IRELAND
23-Jun	1865	HICKEY, THOMAS	31		DYSENTARY	ENGLAND
29-Jan	1889	HICKS, STEPHEN	37		PHTHISIS	DISTRICT OF COLUMBIA
8-Aug	1889	HIGGINS, JOHN	69		SENILITY	IRELAND
5-Aug	1897	HIGGINS, MARY		9 MONTS 5 DAYS	PNEUMONIA	BOSTON
22-Feb	1858	HIGGINS, WILLIAM	49		PHTHISIS & EXHAUSTION	BOSTON
31-Oct	1857	HILAND, WILLIAM	21		DIARRHOEA	IRELAND
28-May	1865	HILL, GEORGE	24		SMALL POX	MAINE
20-Nov	1882	HILL, GEORGE	74		BRIGHTS DISEASE	IRELAND
9-May	1856	HILL, MARY	23		SYPHILIS	IRELAND
19-Jan	1891	HILL, WILLIAM	72		SENILE MARASMUS	RHODE ISLAND, PROVIDENCE
19-Aug	1821	HINCKLEY, JOHN CAPTAIN	23			BLUE HILL
22-Jun	1857	HINDS, WILLIAM	56		CONSUMPTION	IRELAND
17-Mar	1888	HINES, ANDREW	38		PNEUMONIA	BOSTON
23-May	1889	HINES, CATHARINE (O'BOYLE)	69		CANCER STOMACH	IRELAND
23-Jun	1865	HIRL, MARY	22		TYPHOID FEVER	IRELAND
10-Apr	1855	HIRLEHY, MARY	29		HEART DISEASE	IRELAND
26-Aug	1856	HODGKINS, ESTHER	41		CONSUMPTION	GLOUCESTER, MA
27-May	1837	HOFF, ABIGAIL N	19		SMALL POX	
10-Apr	1863	HOGAN, DENNIS	70		PHTHISIS	IRELAND
31-Aug	1860	HOGAN, MARGARET	27		SMALL POX	IRELAND
28-Aug	1858	HOGAN, MARY	30		CONSUMPTION	IRELAND
5-Nov	1882	HOGG, JAMES	29		PHTHISIS	ROXBURY, MA
15-Aug	1865	HOIN, LEWIS	25		DIARRHOEA	
24-Jun	1889	HOLLAND, TIMOTHY	26		PHTHISIS	CAMBRIDGE, MA
February	1738	HOLLAND, WILLIAM				
15-Jun	1865	HOLM, MARCELLUS	58		DYSENTARY	SWEDEN
25-Sep	1887	HOLMES, ADELINE	78		HEART DISEASE	NEWHAMPSHIRE, GRAFTON
16-Dec	1865	HOLMES, FRANK	33		SMALL POX	BOSTON
27-Aug	1861	HOLMES, SIDNEY	50		PHTHISIS	DEER ISLAND
7-Sep	1888	HOLMES, THOMAS J	1		MARASMUS	LONG ISLAND HOSPITAL
10-Dec	1887	HOLMES, WILLIAM D	67		EPITHELIOM TONGUE & ASTHENIA	BOSTON
5-Sep	1819	HOOT, MARY	11			
15-Dec	1888	HOPKINS, BRIDGET		1	INANITION	BOSTON
18-Feb	1888	HORRIGAN, CATHERINE	1		PNEUMONIA	BOSTON
11-Nov	1857	HORRIGAN, DANIEL	50		APOPLEXY	IRELAND
28-Sep	1889	HORRIGAN, MICHAEL	36		TUBERCULOSIS	IRELAND
30-Jul	1881	HORRIGAN, TIMOTHY	60		DEBILITY	IRELAND
27-Jan	1860	HORSON, WILLIAM	29		SMALL POX	
10-Jul	1856	HOUGHTON, CHARLES S	19		SMALL POX	HARVARD, MA
29-Mar	1856	HOWARD, ANN (JAMES)	55		SMALL POX	
24-Sep	1892	HOWARD, CATHARINE	26		PHTHISIS	BOSTON
1-May	1860	HOWE, CYRUS	3		CEREBRITIS	MAINE
2-Dec	1888	HOWLEY, JOHN	62		NEPHRITIS	IRELAND
30-Jul	1883	HOYT, ALBERT P	79		DIARRHOEA & DEBILTY	REHOBOTH, MA
29-Mar	1880	HUBBARD, MARY		2	SYPHILIS CONGENITAL	DEER ISLAND
20-Aug	1858	HUGHES, ELIZABETH	1		SMALL POX	IRELAND
30-Sep	1855	HUGHES, HENRY H		5 DAYS	CONVULSIONS	RAINSFORD ISLAND
23-Apr	1855	HUGHES, JOHN	16		CONSUMPTION	ENGLAND
26-Feb	1883	HUGHES, JOHN	68		BRONCHITIS	EASTPORT, MAINE
17-Nov	1888	HUMPHREY, NIXON	38		HEART DISEASE	CONNECTICUTT, NEW HAVEN
26-Aug	1859	HURLEY, ALICE	70		PARALYSIS	IRELAND
21-Jun	1856	HURLEY, DANIEL	32		CONSUMPTION	IRELAND
8-Jun	1889	HYNES, MARY (DONNELLY)	50		HEART DISEASE	IRELAND
2-Oct	1877	HYPOLITO, PEROT	66		PARALYSIS	FRANCE
26-Feb	1889	IDE, CHARLES	37		HEART DISEASE	BOSTON
13-Sep	1886	INGALLS, JAMES	85		PARALYSIS	GROTON, MA
2-Apr	1864	JACKSON, EDWARD	26		SMALL POX	NEW YORK
12-Apr	1858	JACKSON, ELIZABETH (MILLER)	22		ULCERS	PENNSYLVANIA
17-Apr	1865	JACKSON, GEORGE	32		SMALL POX	GEORGIA
27-Dec	1875	JACKSON, GEORGE R	53		CONSUMPTION	BOSTON

MONTH	YEAR	NAME	AGE YEARS	AGE MONTHS	CAUSE OF DEATH	BORN
31-Jul	1892	JACKSON, MARY E (WILLIAMS)	44		GANGRENE	VIRGINIA
24-Feb	1858	JACOBS, ELIZABETH (CRONE)	26		LUNG INFLAMMATION	NOVA SCOTIA
10-Mar	1858	JACOBS, JOSEPH		6	DIARRHOEA	RAINSFORD ISLAND
27-Jan	1857	JACOBS, SIMON	39		LUNG INFLAMMATION	MAINE
5-Mar	1861	JAMES, ANDREW	43		SMALL POX	CAPE VERDE
19-Oct	1861	JAMES, SUSAN (AVERILL)	25		SYPHILIS	NEW YORK
4-Apr	1856	JAQUITH, STEPHEN	45		SMALL POX	NEW HAMPSHIRE, SANBORN CORERS
20-May	1860	JARVIS, EDWARD	18		SMALL POX	NOVA SCOTIA
11-Oct	1856	JEFFERS, MICHAEL	26		SPINE CARIES	IRELAND
21-Mar	1866	JEFFERS, MOSES	26		PHTHISIS	PENNSYLVANIA
23-Dec	1894	JENKINS, ELLEN	60		BRONCHITIS	IRELAND
27-Sep	1864	JEREMY, SAINT	22		GANGRENE AFTER AMPUTATION	HAITI
9-Oct	1859	JESSUP, EMILY	31		HEART DISEASE	ENGLAND
17-Feb	1890	JEWETT, PHOEBE	44		PHTHISIS	BOSTON
21-Jul	1891	JOHNSON, ALBERT		21 DAYS	SYPHILIS	CLINTON, MA
1-Feb	1866	JOHNSON, FREDERICK	20		PHTHISIS	NOVA SCOTIA
7-Nov	1859	JOHNSON, GEORGE	30		SMALL POX	VIRGINIA, RICHMOND
24-Sep	1861	JOHNSON, GIVAN	56		HEART DISEASE	VIRGINIA
2-Jan	1866	JOHNSON, HARRIET	72		SMALL POX	NEWBURYPORT, MA
12-Apr	1860	JOHNSON, ISAAC	40		SMALL POX	
8-May	1864	JOHNSON, JAMES	35		BRAIN INFLAMMATION	
2-Mar	1886	JOHNSON, JOHN G	50		ALCHOLOISM	BOSTON
13-Jun	1888	JOHNSON, MARY	60		HEART DISEASE	NOVA SCOTIA
16-Aug	1865	JOHNSON, MARY A	10		SPINE CARIES	CANADA
23-Nov	1889	JOHNSON, MARY A (HARNER)	54		PLUERITIS	ENGLAND
6-Dec	1856	JOHNSON, MARY J.E. (FATHEY)	22		SYPHILIS	IRELAND
7-Sep	1888	JOHNSON, VICTORIA (GOUNART)	40		PHTHISIS	GERMANY
5-May	1889	JONES, BRIDGET (EKE)	81		SENILITY	ENGLAND
14-Jan	1884	JONES, CHARLES	23		PHTHISIS (1 WEEK)	GEORGIA, SAVANAH
27-Mar	1883	JONES, SAMUEL	75		BRONCHITIS	VIRGINIA
29-Jun	1819	JONES, SAMUEL	32			SCITUATE
19-Feb	1888	JONES, SARAH (FENTON)	26		PHTHISIS	MARYLAND
17-Aug	1865	JONES, THOMAS	54		TYPHOID FEVER	NEW HAMPSHIRE
25-Feb	1858	JORDAN, SARA E (NOTT)	30		HEMORRHAGE	ENGLAND
27-Mar	1860	JOY, SAMUEL	47		HYPOCHONDRIASIS (FEAR OF BEING ILL)	MAINE
14-Feb	1855	JOYCE, MARGARET	44		SHIP FEVER	IRELAND
2-Feb	1888	JUDGE, BERNARD	61		PHTHISIS	SPAIN
24-Mar	1893	JUDGE, JOHN	56		PLEURISY	BOSTON
6-May	1881	KANE, JAMES	36		RHEUMATISIM & ENDOCARDITIS	IRELAND
16-Aug	1891	KANE, MARY (SHARKEY)	69		DIARRHOEA	IRELAND
12-Dec	1859	KEATING, JAMES	34		SMALL POX	NEW YORK
21-Mar	1858	KEATING, JOANNA (BARRY)	70		CONSUMPTION	IRELAND
24-Aug	1898	KEEFE, ELLA		10	ILEO COLITIS	BOSTON
2-Jul	1865	KEEFE, MARGARET (HOAR)	45		PHTHISIS	IRELAND
22-Jul	1856	KEEFE, SARAH	26		GANGRENE	IRELAND
25-Jan	1891	KEHOE, WILLIAM	50		PARALYSIS	IRELAND
23-Mar	1865	KELLEY, CATHARINE (MCCLOUD)	22		SMALL POX	NOVA SCOTIA
28-Aug	1858	KELLEY, ELLEN (MCCARTY)	20		EXHAUSTION	IRELAND
30-Dec	1892	KELLEY, FREDERICK	42		DELIRIUM TREMENS	BOSTON
24-Jan	1890	KELLEY, MARGARET (TUCKER)	39		CEREBRAL HEMORRHAGE	IRELAND
2-Oct	1889	KELLEY, MARY (CALLAHAN)	40		ALCOHOLISM & TUBERCULOSIS	WOBURN, MA
8-Jun	1888	KELLY, CATHARINE	45		PHTHISIS	IRELAND
14-Feb	1860	KELLY, DANIEL	22		SMALL POX	MAINE
23-Aug	1895	KELLY, FRANCIS HAROLD		3	MALNUTRITION	SUMMER HOSPITAL
26-May	1881	KELLY, JAMES	61		PNEUMONIA DOUBLE	IRELAND

MONTH	YEAR	NAME	AGE YEARS	AGE MONTHS	CAUSE OF DEATH	BORN
26-Oct	1859	KELLY, JOHN	39		LUNG INFLAMMATION	IRELAND
30-Jul	1897	KELLY, LOUISE		5	FERMENTAL DIARRHOEA	BOSTON
18-Jun	1857	KELLY, MARIA (WILSON)	68		CONSUMPTION	ENGLAND
28-Dec	1855	KELLY, MARY	22		SHIP FEVER	IRELAND
26-Jun	1865	KELLY, MARY A		4 DAYS	SYPHILIS	RAINSFORD ISLAND
14-Jul	1888	KENNARD, ELLEN (FLEMING)	70		DEMENTIA & HEART FAILURE	BOSTON
10-Oct	1860	KENNEDY, JAMES	28		DELIRIUM TREMENS	IRELAND
21-Feb	1859	KENNEDY, LUCIUS	47		HEART DISEASE	BOSTON
12-Sep	1861	KENNEDY, PATRICK	66		DEBILITY	IRELAND
27-Nov	1857	KENNEDY, PHILIP	22		PLEURISY	IRELAND
25-Jun	1891	KENNEY, CATHARINE		1 DAY	SYPHILIS	RAINSFORD ISLAND
13-Sep	1891	KENNEY, ELIZABETH (MCDONALD) LIZZIE	46		HEART DISEASE	NEW BRUNSWICK, ST JOHN
26-Jul	1891	KENNEY, FREDERICK		1 DAY	SYPHILIS	RAINSFORD ISLAND
3-Jul	1889	KENNEY, GEORGE HENRY	BORN 3/15	4	GASTRO INTESTINAL CATARRH	LONG ISLAND HOSPITAL
23-Dec	1884	KENNEY, THOMAS	43		DEBILTY & EXHAUSTION	IRELAND
9-Aug	1888	KERRIGAN, CATHARINE (GILLIGAN)	70		PHTHISIS	IRELAND
16-Jul	1854	KILGARE, MARTIN	42		BRAIN DISEASE	IRELAND
3-Jul	1859	KIMBALL, GEORGIANNA	22		SYPHILIS	BOSTON
11-Apr	1860	KING, ALEXANDER	24		SMALL POX	AZORES
5-Apr	1860	KING, MARY	38		UNKNOWN	IRELAND
23-May	1855	KING, WILLIAM	8		SMALL POX	IRELAND
21-Apr	1880	KINGSBURY, ASA C	80		HEART DISEASE	NORFOLK, MA
16-Jul	1858	KIRBY, TIMOTHY	58		CONSUMPTION	IRELAND
17-Apr	1862	KNIGHT, NANCY	32		PHTHISIS	MAINE
7-May	1866	KNIGHTS, JOHN	44		BLADDER INFLAMMATION	IRELAND
29-Jul	1855	KNOFLOCK, WILLIAM	22		CONSUMPTION	GERMANY
2-Apr	1887	KNOX, JOHN	77		HEART DISEASE	IRELAND
30-Jul	1895	KRANKE, ANNIE		6	MALNUTRICIAN	ENGLAND
14-Jun	1885	KUGLINSKI, JOHN	71		SENILE DEBILITY	POLAND
18-Jul	1812	LAFTON, DAVID			SMALL POX	WASHINGTON, NC
22-Mar	1864	LAHY, THOMAS	28		CANCER SHOULDER	IRELAND
22-May	1890	LAMB, AGNES (FLEMING)	67		NEPHRITIS & PULMONARY ODEMA	SCOTLAND
9-Jul	1856	LAMB, MICHAEL	20		TYPHOID	IRELAND
3-Jul	1862	LANE, CATHARINE	37		DELIRIUM TREMENS	IRELAND
16-Nov	1883	LANE, WILLARD	69		DYSPEPSIA & DEBILITY	MAINE
5-Jun	1860	LANG, SARAH	37		HEART DISEASE	IRELAND
11-Sep	1896	LANGENTHAL, CHARLES M		8 MONTHS 7 DAYS	DIARRHOEA CAUSING HEART FAILURE	SCHENECTADY, NY
19-Jun	1855	LANSING, GERARD	22		SMALL POX	NEW YORK
3-Mar	1864	LARKEY, DANIEL	45		SMALL POX	CANADA, NEW BRUNSWICK
31-May	1888	LARKIN, WILLIAM	60		PHTHISIS	IRELAND
14-Mar	1862	LARKINS, NICHOLAS	21		SYPHILIS	IRELAND
6-Feb	1864	LASSEN, ELLEN	30		BOWEL HEMORRHAGE	IRELAND
22-Sep	1863	LAVERTY, WILLIAM	44		PHTHISIS	IRELAND
11-Feb	1890	LAWLER, MARY (DUNN)	55		PARALYSIS	IRELAND
24-Mar	1893	LAWLESS, MARIA	61		DEBILITY	IRELAND
5-Feb	1860	LAWRENCE, ELIZABETH	23		LUNG INFLAMMATION	LOWELL, MA
7-Jan	1866	LEADER, HARRIET	50		DELIRIUM TREMENS	ENGLAND
3-Nov	1888	LEAHY, JEREMIAH	31		PARALYSIS, HEART FAILURE AND DIARRHOEA	IRELAND
4-Jun	1863	LEARY, CORNELIUS	37		PHTHISIS & FISTULA	IRELAND
31-Dec	1881	LEARY, DANIEL	36		PNEUMONIA	IRELAND
24-Apr	1858	LEARY, JOHN	59		ERYSIPELAS	IRELAND
28-May	1856	LEARY, MARY (MCGRATH)	50		DIARRHOEA	IRELAND
11-Aug	1876	LEAVEY, JOSEPH	70		PARALYSIS	NEW HAMPSHIRE
24-Jan	1860	LEE, NICHOLAS		14 DAYS	SMALL POX	RAINSFORD ISLAND
24-Jul	1897	LEE, THOMAS		10	FERMENTAL DIARRHOEA	BOSTON
17-Oct	1863	LEFTWICH, JAMES L	50		EPILEPSY	ENGLAND
24-Jun	1859	LEMERE, LOUIS	36		SPINE DISLOCATION	CHILE
26-Sep	1887	LEONARD, THADDEUS M	72		BRONCHITIS & SENILE DEBILITY	ROXBURY, MA
25-Mar	1889	LESPEE, H W	47		PHTHISIS	GERMANY
10-Jun	1802	LESSLIE, JAMES ESQ.	53			

MONTH	YEAR	NAME	AGE YEARS	AGE MONTHS	CAUSE OF DEATH	BORN
14-Jun	1862	LETCHER, ANDREW	59		DELIRIUM TREMENS	KENTUCKY
11-Mar	1866	LEVERD, MARY D	20		PHTHISIS	WESTERN ISLANDS
27-Jul	1865	LEWIS, DANIEL	17		TYPHOID	VIRGINIA
18-Jul	1858	LEWIS, JOHN	32		CONSUMPTION	IRELAND
21-Aug	1880	LEWIS, JOSEPH	45		BRIGHTS DISEASE	AZORES
7-Apr	1864	LEWIS, WINIFRED (MCLAUGHLIN)	32		CANCER UTERUS	IRELAND
21-Nov	1859	LIBBY, DE LAN	59		CONSUMPTION	MAINE
7-Dec	1873	LINCOLN, SAMUEL A. V.	52		DEBILITY	....
19-Apr	1858	LINNAHAN, CORNELIUS	69		CONSUMPTION	IRELAND
10-Dec	1884	LINNEHAN, JOHN	37		PHTHISIS	
8-May	1840	LINNELL, SAMUEL	21		SMALL POX	
29-Sep	1890	LINSCOTT, CAROLINE M (THORNTON)	42		DIARRHOEA	BOSTON
30-Dec	1865	LIVINGSTON, ELIZABETH	30		BRAIN SOFTENING	CANADA, NEW BRUNSWICK
22-Jun	1860	LIVINGSTON, MARY	26		INTESTINAL STRICTURE	GERMANY
17-Aug	1895	LIVINGSTONE, FRANK	1	6	PNEUMONIA (12 DAYS)	BOSTON
31-May	1892	LOGAN, BRIDGET	66		CEREBRAL EMBOLISM	IRELAND
10-May	1890	LOGOMASINO, ANGELINA	50		CEREBRAL SCLEROSIS	ITALY
12-Sep	1895	LONDSKOG, RALPH EMERSON		4	MARASMUS	BOSTON
22-Dec	1857	LONG, MARY		4	BRONCHITIS	RAINSFORD ISLAND
Sept	1815	LONG, NATHAN				AMEBURY
3-Sep	1898	LORENZO, PETER		2 MONTHS 5 DAYS	NEPHRITIS	BOSTON
23-Oct	1890	LOTRIDGE, ADA (ST JOHNS)	36		PARALYSIS (9 MONTHS)	MAINE
6-Jun	1885	LOVE, WILLIAM	92		SENILITY	IRELAND
20-Nov	1882	LOVIS, WILLIAM	72		SENILITY	BOSTON
26-Jun	1859	LOWE, JAMES M	23		SMALL POX	GLOUCESTER, MA
2-Nov	1863	LOWNEY, JOHN	25		AMPUTATION OF FOOT	NEW YORK
17-Jun	1824	LUDWIG, JOSPEH			SMALL POX	
24-May	1861	LUNDY, SARAH (GILLESPIE)	25		PARALYSIS	IRELAND
12-Sep	1898	LYNCH, ALICE		3	FERMENTAL DIARRHOEA	BOSTON
28-Aug	1897	LYNCH, EDWARD		5 MONTHS 4 DAYS	PNEUMONIA	BOSTON
20-Feb	1888	LYNCH, MARY	68		CEREBRAL HEMORRHAGE	IRELAND
15-Aug	1889	LYNN, JAMES	32		PHTHISIS	BOSTON
29-May	1866	LYONS, MARY	41		CANCER	IRELAND
26-Mar	1857	MACK, JOHN	24		CONSUMPTION	IRELAND
30-Jul	1882	MACK, ROBERT	57		BRONCHITIS & DEBILITY	CAMBRIDGEPORT, MAINE
24-Sep	1891	MADDEN, ANNIE (MCDONALD)	70		TUBERCULOR MENIGITIS	SCOTLAND
12-Mar	1889	MADDEN, BRIDGET	60		CANCER BREAST	IRELAND
18-Dec	1865	MADDEN, MARY	20		PHTHISIS	BOSTON
7-Sep	1861	MAHAN, CATHARINE (ROGERS)	74		DYSENTARY	IRELAND
5-May	1861	MAHAN, JAMES	49		ULCERS	IRELAND
3-Aug	1856	MAHAN, JOSEPHINE		2	CHOLERA INFANTUM	RAINSFORD ISLAND
12-Dec	1888	MAHER, ELLEN	80		DEBILITY & BRONCHITIS	IRELAND
11-Sep	1861	MAHONEY, BRIDGET (KILCAIN)	32		PHTHISIS	IRELAND
30-Aug	1892	MAHONEY, ELLEN	76		SENILTY	IRELAND
20-Jan	1889	MAHONEY, ELLEN (MCCARTHY)	80		DIARRHOEA	IRELAND
22-Oct	1889	MAHONEY, JULIA (HICKEY)	50		CANCER BREAST	IRELAND
27-Feb	1861	MAHONEY, MARIA	20		SYPHLILIS & BRAIN CONGESTION	CONCORD, MA
7-Mar	1860	MAHONEY, MARY	20		SMALL POX	IRELAND
4-Aug	1892	MAHONEY, MARY				
22-Aug	1891	MAHONEY, MARY (MAHONEY)	70		DIARRHOEA	IRELAND
16-Mar	1885	MAHONEY, MICHAEL	64		DEMENTIA & DEBILITY	IRELAND
29-May	1892	MAHONEY, PATRICK	40		PNEUMONIA	BOSTON
13-Aug	1891	MALLEN, CATHARINE	35		PURPURA HEMORRHAGE	BOSTON

MONTH	YEAR	NAME	AGE YEARS	AGE MONTHS	CAUSE OF DEATH	BORN
6-Oct	1861	MALLET, ELIZABETH (CASEY)	41		BRAIN DISEASE	IRELAND
26-Aug	1897	MALONEY, HUGH		5 MONTHS 19 DAYS	FERMENTAL DIARRHOEA	BOSTON
30-Aug	1856	MALONEY, MARY A	6		DYSENTARY	RAINSFORD ISLAND
28-Jul	1861	MANCHESTER, SARAH	19		SYPHILIS	MANHATTAN
7-Mar	1889	MANKLE, JOHN	78		HEART DISEASE	GERMANY
28-Jan	1860	MANN, GEORGE	47		NOT NOTED	NEW YORK
25-Sep	1894	MANNING, ELLEN	67			ENGLAND
17-Jul	1855	MANNING, HANNAH	23		SHIP FEVER	IRELAND
26-Aug	1897	MANSFIELD, GRACE		2 MONTHS 8 DAYS	INFANTILE ATROPHY	BOSTON
24-Sep	1864	MANSFIELD, THOMAS	48		KIDNEY INFLAMMATION	IRELAND
20-Feb	1862	MARCY, JANE (WILLIAMS)	30		INTEMPERANCE	SCOTLAND
21-Aug	1873	MARK, JOHN E	52		PHTHISIS	FALL RIVER, MA
7-Sep	1865	MARS, CATHARINE		2 MONTHS	MARASMUS	BRIDGEWATER
16-Apr	1889	MARSHALL, ANN	80		DIARRHOEA	IRELAND
6-Jul	1862	MARSHALL, MARY (MCNAMEE)	23		PHTHISIS	BOSTON
24-Jan	1866	MARTIN, BENJAMIN	37		PHTHISIS	IRELAND
28-Mar	1864	MARTIN, HENRY	44		SMALL POX & DELIRIUM TREMMENS	SCOTLAND
1-Sep	1894	MARTINA, PASQUALE		9	CHOLERA INFANTUM	BOSTON
17-May	1891	MASON, JOSEPH	78		BRONCHITIS	BOSTON
16-Apr	1864	MASTERS, PHILIP	35		SMALL POX	CANADA, PRINCE EDWARD ISLAND
13-Oct	1862	MAXWELL, HANNAH		2	SYPHILIS	RAINSFORD ISLAND
13-Feb	1890	MCANERLIN, MARY J. (MONTGOMERY)	67		NEPHRITIS	IRELAND
14-Sep	1898	MCATEER, HELEN		10 MONTHS 2 DAYS	ILEO COLITIS	BOSTON
11-Apr	1857	MCAULEY, THOMAS		1	MARASMUS	RAINSFORD ISLAND
4-Mar	1866	MCAVOY, JOHN	22		SMALL POX	MAINE
21-Feb	1862	MCBOYLE, MARGARET		3	HEART MALFORMATION	RAINSFORD ISLAND
16-May	1889	MCCABE, MARGARET	80		SENILE	IRELAND
24-Jan	1887	MCCAFFERTY, WILLIAM	40		PHTHISIS	IRELAND
25-Mar	1855	MCCALEB, DANIEL	24		SMALL POX	NOVA SCOTIA
5-Aug	1854	MCCALLIGAN, JOHN	28		CHOLERA	IRELAND
11-Oct	1876	MCCALLUM, JOHN	80		DYSENTARY	NOVA SCOTIA
15-Oct	1888	MCCANN, ANN (CONNORS)	75		GASTRITIS	IRELAND
17-Sep	1858	MCCANN, JOHN	23			
28-Jun	1896	MCCARRON, GERTRUDE	2	2 MONTHS 2 DAYS	ATROPHY	BOSTON
29-Jun	1884	MCCARTHY, CORNELIUS	60		CIRRHOSIS OF THE LIVER (4 MONTHS)	IRELAND
21-Jul	1896	MCCARTHY, CORNELIUS		7 MONTHS 4 DAYS	FERMENTAL DIARRHOEA	CAMBRIDGE
17-Apr	1891	MCCARTHY, FRANCIS		3	INFANTILE ATROPHY	RAINSFORD ISLAND
16-Jun	1889	MCCARTHY, JULIA (O'NEIL)	60		CEREBRAL HEMORRHAGE	IRELAND
23-Feb	1891	MCCARTHY, MARGARET (GRAY)	70		BRONCHITIS	IRELAND
28-Mar	1891	MCCARTHY, MARY				
4-Apr	1888	MCCARTHY, MARY (SHEEHAN)	50		PHTHISIS	IRELAND
22-Nov	1887	MCCARTHY, MICHAEL	40		PHTHISIS	IRELAND
29-May	1882	MCCARTHY, PATRICK	65		DEBILTY	IRELAND
2-Apr	1893	MCCARTHY, SUSAN (GILMARTIN)	65			IRELAND
17-Feb	1890	MCCARTHY, THOMAS	57		ELEPHANTIASIS	IRELAND
18-Jan	1887	MCCARTHY, WILLIAM	63		HEMIPLEGGIA	IRELAND
5-Jun	1857	MCCARTY, ANN (MINTON)	62		CANCER	IRELAND
7-Dec	1859	MCCARTY, CATHARINE	30		CONSUMPTION	IRELAND
3-Aug	1862	MCCARTY, DENNIS	47		PHTHISIS	IRELAND
2-Nov	1861	MCCARTY, JOHN	70		ATRAEMIA	IRELAND
3-Jan	1865	MCCARTY, JOHN		4	SMALL POX	BOSTON
15-Dec	1865	MCCARTY, JOHN	23		BRIGHTS DISEASE	BOSTON

MONTH	YEAR	NAME	AGE YEARS	AGE MONTHS	CAUSE OF DEATH	BORN
5-Feb	1860	MCCARTY, MARY	50		DEBILITY	IRELAND
15-Apr	1865	MCCARTY, MARY	20		SMALL POX	IRELAND
24-Jan	1865	MCCARTY, MARY (MURPHY	38		SMALL POX	IRELAND
25-Apr	1858	MCCARTY, MARY A (CLARK)	30		CONSUMPTION	PRINCE EDWARLD ISLAND
20-Sep	1855	MCCLOSKEY, NANCY	33		CARIES OF THE SPINE	SCOTLAND
19-Mar	1889	MCCLUSKEY, HUGH	31		PHTHISIS	BOSTON
2-Apr	1882	MCCORMICK, JAMES	33		CIRHOSIS OF LIVER	BOSTON
22-Sep	1888	MCCORMICK, MICHAEL	55		DIARRHOEA	IRELAND
28-Jun	1863	MCCORMICK, WILLIAM	44		PHTHISIS	IRELAND
19-Oct	1861	MCCORRY, JAMES S	44		PHTHISIS	SCOTLAND
4-May	1859	MCCOURT, SUSAN	21		CONSUMPTION	IRELAND
3-Mar	1863	MCCUDDY, JOHN	22		SYPHILIS	IRELAND
17-Jan	1889	MCCUE, CATHARINE	49		CEREBRAL HEMORRHAGE	IRELAND
17-Jan	1891	MCCUE, JAMES	32		ANEURISM AORTIC	BOSTON
9-Aug	1864	MCDERMOTT, ANN (FLORICK)	64		PARALYSIS	IRELAND
28-Jan	1886	MCDERMOTT, JOHN	68		NEPHRITIS	IRELAND
10-Aug	1897	MCDERMOTT, PATRICK G.		4 MONTHS 14 DAYS	FERMENTAL DIARRHOEA	BOSTON
14-Aug	1896	MCDERMOTT, STEPHEN		5	INFANTILE	BOSTON
13-Mar	1889	MCDEVITT, GEORGE	50		PHTHISIS	BOSTON
10-Aug	1889	MCDEVITT, SARAH	75		DIARRHOEA	IRELAND
16-Apr	1858	MCDEVITT, WILLIAM	26		CONSUMPTION	BOSTON
18-Dec	1857	MCDONALD, ALEXANDER	47		CONSUMPTION	NOVA SCOTIA
27-Oct	1858	MCDONALD, ANN	30		LUNG INFLAMMATION	IRELAND
25-May	1863	MCDONALD, BRIDGET	40		HEART DISEAE	IRELAND
26-May	1887	MCDONALD, HUGH	11		PNEUMONIA & EPILEPSY	BOSTON
29-Mar	1865	MCDONALD, JAMES	28		SMALL POX	PRINCE EDWARD ISLAND
17-Dec	1854	MCDONALD, JOHN	22		LUNG INFLAMMATION	NOVA SCOTIA, CAPE BRETON
31-Jul	1864	MCDONALD, JOHN	23		SMALL POX	SCOTLAND
6-Jul	1896	MCDONALD, MARY A		1	INANITION	BOSTON
5-Dec	1855	MCDONALD, NEAL	33		SMALL POX	SCOTLAND
13-Jun	1856	MCDONALD, STILLBORN DEMALE		0	STILLBORN	RAINSFORD ISLAND
15-Oct	1890	MCDONOUGH, DELIA (MCDONOUGH)	44		PHTHISIS	IRELAND
11-Apr	1893	MCDONOUGH, MARY	21		PUERPERAL & ECLAMPSIA	AT SEA
13-Feb	1859	MCDONOUGH, MICHAEL	56		CONSUMPTION	IRELAND
18-Oct	1889	MCENELLY, JAMES	73		SENILITY	BOSTON
20-Jul	1896	MCEWEN, LILLIAN L		7	INFANTILE ATROPHY	BOSTON
9-Aug	1889	MCFARLAND, ISABELLA (ADAMS)	68		HEART DISEASE	SCOTLAND
4-Nov	1856	MCGAHAGAN, BERNARD	44		GANGRENE	IRELAND
7-Oct	1892	MCGHAN, MARGARET (CAMPBELL)	76		LUNG OEDEMA	IRELAND
26-Aug	1856	MCGINNIS, THOMAS	56		CONSUMPTION	IRELAND
21-Oct	1891	MCGONNIGLE, MARY	62		NEPHRITIS	IRELAND
1-Jul	1859	MCGOWAN, JAMES	45		CONSUMPTION	IRELAND
30-Jul	1890	MCGOWAN, MARGARET	32		PHTHISIS	NEW BRUNSWICK, ST JOHN
17-Feb	1888	MCGOWAN, MARY (DOHERTY)	90		SENILITY	IRELAND
16-Oct	1856	MCGRATH, BRIDGET (BOYLE)	30		GASTRITIS	IRELAND
14-Mar	1855	MCGRATH, DENNIS	66		DYSENTARY	IRELAND
29-Aug	1883	MCGRATH, JOHN	58		PHTHISIS	IRELAND
17-Aug	1885	MCGRATH, JOHN	60		HEART DISEASE	IRELAND
24-Dec	1859	MCGREGOR, MALCOLM	21		SMALL POX	CAPE BRETON
2-May	1856	MCGUIRE, ANN (DOHERTY)	60		PLEURISY	IRELAND
1-Nov	1860	MCGUIRE, CATHARINE	78		OLD AGE	NEWFOUNDLAND
6-Oct	1858	MCGUIRE, MARY	50		CONSUMPTION	IRELAND
24-Sep	1864	MCGUIRE, PHILIP	29		DYSENTARY	IRELAND
8-Aug	1895	MCGUIRE, WILLIAM		5	MARASMUS	BOSTON
16-Mar	1885	MCINERNEY, JOHN	55		HIP DISEASE & EXHAUSTION	IRELAND
18-Aug	1892	MCINTOSH, DANIEL	28		PHTHISIS	BOSTON

MONTH	YEAR	NAME	AGE YEARS	AGE MONTHS	CAUSE OF DEATH	BORN
10-Sep	1887	MCINTYRE, EDWARD	35		HEART MITRAL VALVE	NOT LISTED
2-Jan	1862	MCINTYRE, JAMES	24		LUNG GANGRENE	IRELAND
18-Aug	1897	MCINTYRE, LORETTA		2 MONTHS 14 DAYS	FERMENTAL DIARRHOEA	BOSTON
8-Jan	1893	MCKAY, ELIZA	68		PNEUMONIA	IRELAND
31-Jul	1856	MCKAY, HANNAH (MURPHY)	31		INTEMPERANCE	IRELAND
2-Oct	1885	MCKENNA, DANIEL	73		SENILE & BOWEL OBSTRUCTION	IRELAND
28-Aug	1863	MCKENNA, JAMES	38		PHTHISIS	IRELAND
8-Sep	1892	MCKENNA, JAMES	70		SENILE DEMENTIA	IRELAND
7-Mar	1866	MCKENZIE, FREDERICK E		3	MARASMUS	RAINSFORD ISLAND
19-May	1855	MCKENZIE, JAMES	20		SMALL POX	NOVA SCOTIA
26-Jan	1856	MCKINNAN, PETER	25		SMALL POX	NEW YORK
18-Aug	1893	MCKINNON, AGNES N (MCMULLEN)	99		SENILTY	SCOTLAND
29-Nov	1854	MCLAUGHLIN, ALEXANDER	24		SMALL POX	IRELAND
5-May	1885	MCLAUGHLIN, EDWARD	39		PHTHISIS	NEW BRUNSWICK
15-Feb	1874	MCLAUGHLIN, HUGH	69		ASTHMA	IRELAND
16-Jul	1854	MCLAUGHLIN, JOHN	21		CONSUMPTION	IRELAND
3-May	1883	MCLAUGHLIN, JOHN J	30		CIRHOSIS OF LIVER	BOSTON
12-Sep	1856	MCLAUGHLIN, MARY (ROURKE)	21		CONSUMPTION	DRACUT, MA
12-Jul	1874	MCLAUGHLIN, NEIL	69		DIABETIS	IRELAND
12-Jun	1884	MCLAUGHLIN, WILLIAM	69		PNEUMONIA	NOVA SCOTIA
17-Dec	1859	MCLENNON, MARY A	37		SCROFULA	SALEM, MA
8-Nov	1875	MCMAHAN, JOHN A/K/A MCMANN	68		OLD AGE	IRELAND
27-Aug	1865	MCMAHON, BRIDGET	41		INTEMPERANCE	IRELAND
11-Oct	1891	MCNAMARA, BRIDGET (KIERNAN)	63		DIARRHOEA	BOSTON
9-Mar	1890	MCNAMARA, JOANNA	56		HEART DISEASE	IRELAND
20-Sep	1884	MCNAMARA, JOHN	71		SENILITY	IRELAND
9-Jun	1856	MCNEIL, JOHN	51		CONSUMPTION	IRELAND
17-Jun	1856	MCNEIL, NEIL	25		CONSUMPTION	NOVA SCOTIA
27-Feb	1888	MCNULTY, MARY (CURRAN)	50		PNEUMONIA	IRELAND
10-Jun	1854	MCPHERSON, MARY		5	SCROFULA	HOUSE OF INDUSTRY BOSTON
4-Aug	1889	MCSORLEY, DAVID	40		PNEUMONIA	BOSTON
13-Mar	1888	MCTEAGUE, ROSANNA	47		PHTHISIS	IRELAND
19-Aug	1862	MCVANEY, ELIZABETH	55		INTEMPERANCE	IRELAND
18-May	1860	MEAD, CHARLES	40		DELIRIUM TREMENS	IRELAND
9-Oct	1862	MEEHAN, THOMAS	65		DEBILITY	IRELAND
9-Aug	1888	MEHEGAN, MARY				
22-Oct	1860	MELFER, PROSPER	30		PHTHISIS	ITALY
13-Aug	1898	MENDELSHON, LOUIS	1	6	FERMENTAL DIARRHOEA	BOSTON
21-Aug	1889	MERRYFIELD, ELIZABETH (HENDERSON)	60		INTESTINAL CATARRH	NOVA SCOTIA
11-Sep	1896	MESERVE, MARION		4 MONTHS 29 DAYS	INFANTILE ATROPHY	BOSTON
24-May	1893	METZLER, GEORGE	80		PROSTATIS	FRANCE
14-Jun	1886	MIDDLETON, DAVID	66		BRONCHITIS	SCOTLAND
2-Jul	1860	MILES, WILLIAM	23		PHTHISIS	IRELAND
9-Jul	1897	MILLER, ALICH	2		PNEUMONIA	LYNN
27-Jul	1886	MILLER, ALLEN H	65		DIARRHOEA & DEBILTY	SEEKONK, MA
19-Feb	1862	MILLER, ELIZABETH (BLAISDELL)	44		PHTHISIS & GANGRENE	MAINE, THOMASTON
10-May	1861	MILLER, JOSEPH	33		PSOAD ABCESS	BOSTON
8-Aug	1898	MILLER, WILLIAM		7	FERMENTAL DIARRHOEA	BOSTON
16-Jan	1865	MILLIKEN, JOHN		14 DAYS	MARASMUS	RAINSFORD ISLAND
4-Jun	1893	MINEHAN, CORNELIUS	62		HEART DISEASE	IRELAND
3-Nov	1891	MINER, ELIZA (GREGG)	28		HEART DISEASE	HAVERHILL, MA
22-Jul	1888	MINTON, ELLEN (MURPHY)	36		ULCER VARICOSE	IRELAND
19-Mar	1891	MINTON, MALE CHILD		1 DAY	INANITION	RAINSFORD ISLAND
5-Aug	1889	MINTON, MARY	65		PARALYSIS	
7-Sep	1865	MITCHELL, MARY	50		PARALYSIS	VIRGINIA
1-Aug	1854	MITCHELL, PATRICK	29		CHOLERA	IRELAND

MONTH	YEAR	NAME	AGE YEARS	AGE MONTHS	CAUSE OF DEATH	BORN
17-Aug	1897	MOCKETT, VOUCHEY P		2MONTHS 25 DAYS	VOMITING	BOSTON
29-Nov	1860	MONAHAN, JOHN	40		ANASARCA	IRELAND
29-Jul	1865	MOORE, BRIDGET	40		BRONCHITIS	IRELAND
10-Aug	1891	MOORE, EILZABETH (HOLESTON)	58		DIARRHOEA	ENGLAND
17-Feb	1892	MOORE, ELIZABETH (FALLON)	59			NOVA SCOTIA
23-Jun	1860	MOORE, FANNIE	22		SMALL POX	MAINE
20-Aug	1896	MOORE, JOHN		11	PHTHISIS	BOSTON
5-Aug	1855	MOORE, ROBERT	35		SMALL POX	SOUTH CAROLINA
6-Apr	1892	MORAN, JANE (MORAN)	32		SHOCK FOLLOWING INJURY	ENGLAND
12-May	1886	MORAN, MICHAEL	50		BLADDER STRICTURE	IRELAND
27-Jul	1881	MORAN, WILLIAM	22		PHTHISIS	BOSTON
6-Oct	1860	MOREY, ETHELINE		1	UNKNOWN	RAINSFORD ISLAND
16-Jul	1854	MORGAN, CATHARINE	20		CONSUMPTION	IRELAND
18-Dec	1859	MORGAN, JAMES	31		SMALL POX	IRELAND
12-Oct	1888	MORLEY, ALICE (DUFFEY)	43		PHTHISIS	BRIGHTON, MA
26-Aug	1858	MORRILL, AMELIA (GIBSON)	82		DIARRHOEA	ENGLAND
7-Jun	1865	MORRILL, CHARLES	55		SMALL POX	NOVA SCOTIA
20-Jul	1889	MORRILL, JOHN	76		HEART & LUNG DISEASE	IRELAND
18-Apr	1877	MORSE, SAMUEL	75		RHEUMATISIM	NEW HAMPSHIRE, ALSTEAD
13-Jul	1862	MORTELLE, ELLEN (NEENAN)	43		DIARRHOEA	IRELAND
23-Mar	1808	MOTTS, PAUL			SMALL POX	
5-Mar	1889	MOYNIHAN, CATHARINE (SULLIVAN)	27		ALCOHOLIC PARAPLEGIA	IRELAND
13-Apr	1889	MULHERN, MARGARET (COONEY)	65		NEPHRITIS	IRELAND
6-Jun	1862	MULLANY, MARGARET	40		RHEUMATISIM & BED SORES	IRELAND
13-Jun	1888	MULLEN, JAMES	56		BRONCHITIS	NEW YORK
16-Apr	1892	MULLEN, JOSEPHINE (MULLEN)	38		DIARRHOEA	NEW BRUNSWICK, ST JOHN
27-Jul	1858	MULLEN, MARGARET	60		CONSUMPTION	IRELAND
21-Oct	1887	MULLEN, PATRICK	32		PHTHISIS	BOSTON
10-Jul	1861	MULLIGAN, MARY (MAHONEY)	40		PHTHISIS	IRELAND
24-Aug	1875	MULLIGAN, THOMAS	43		POPLITEAL ABCESS	IRELAND
21-Aug	1897	MULLOY, ANNIE		4 MONTHS 7 DAYS	FERMENTAL DIARRHOEA	BOSTON
9-Aug	1888	MULVANEY, CATHARINE (KELLEY)	60		DIARRHOEA	IRELAND
21-Apr	1856	MUNROE, JULIA	36		KIDNEY DISEASE	IRELAND
30-Oct	1888	MURPHY, CATHARINE				
22-Jan	1858	MURPHY, DAVID	60		CONSUMPTION	IRELAND
28-Oct	1856	MURPHY, DENNIS	37		CONSUMPTION	IRELAND
20-Dec	1887	MURPHY, ELLEN (HAYES)	48		HEART DISEASE VALVE	ENGLAND
16-Aug	1898	MURPHY, EVELYN		17 DAYS	FERMENTAL DIARRHOEA	BOSTON
3-Aug	1896	MURPHY, FRANCIS		21 DAYS	INANITION	BOSTON
1-Jun	1893	MURPHY, HANNAH	66		CANCER	IRELAND
7-Aug	1890	MURPHY, HANNAH (MULLINS)	76		SENILE MARASMUS	IRELAND
19-May	1885	MURPHY, JAMES H	27		PHTHISIS	BOSTON
19-Jun	1856	MURPHY, JOHN	56		CONSUMPTION	IRELAND
31-Mar	1859	MURPHY, THADDEUS	32		PHTHISIS	BOSTON
31-Mar	1859	MURRAY, CATHARINE	20		LUNG INFLAMMATION	IRELAND
29-Jan	1874	MURRAY, CHARLES	38		ENTERITIS	IRELAND
6-Jul	1859	MURRAY, DANIEL	42		CONSUMPTION	IRELAND
25-Sep	1863	MURRAY, DANIEL	16		FEMUR INFLAMMATION	RHODE ISLAND, NEWPORT
19-Jun	1855	MURRAY, HUGH	30		SMALL POX	LOWELL, MA
19-Jul	1887	MURRAY, JAMES	77		BRONCHITIS & AORTIC REGURGITATION	IRELAND
18-Feb	1893	MURRAY, JOHANNA (SULLIVAN)	85		SENILITY	IRELAND
11-Mar	1888	MURRAY, MARTHA (BROWN)	24		PHTHISIS	PENNSYLVANIS, HARRISBURG
9-Aug	1896	MURRAY, MARY	1	11	SCARLET FEVER	BOSTON

MONTH	YEAR	NAME	AGE YEARS	AGE MONTHS	CAUSE OF DEATH	BORN
26-Feb	1892	MURRAY, SOPHIA H. (INGALLS)	80		SENILTY	LITTLESTON, MA
19-Feb	1855	MUTE, MARY	16		SMALL POX	VERMONT, WOODSTOCK
1-Sep	1898	NALLY, JAMES A.		2 MONTHS 13 DAYS	HEART DISEASE CONGENITAL	WALTHAM
29-Apr	1857	NASON, EDWARD	24		CONSUMPTION	MARYLAND, BALTIMORE
27-Jan	1856	NEAGLE, JAMES	26		SMALL POX	IRELAND
15-Jun	1854	NEAGLE, WILLIAM	20		SHIP FEVER	IRELAND
15-Dec	1854	NEAMAN, JAMES	20		SHIP FEVER	IRELAND
9-Jun	1855	NEEDHAM, BRIDGET	17		SMALL POX	NOVA SCOTIA
14-Jun	1892	NEIL, CATHARINE (LANNIGAN)	75		SENILITY	IRELAND
23-Jul	1889	NEITHOLDT, AUGUSTA (FREIDMAN)	80		OLD AGE & DIARRHOEA	GERMANY
14-Apr	1865	NELSON, AGNES (HENDERSON)	34		SYPHILIS	OHIO
5-Mar	1892	NELSON, JOSEPH D	27		DIABETIS AND PHTHISIS	BOSTON
11-Jun	1837	NELSON, WILLIAM	20		SMALL POX	
4-Feb	1889	NEVILLE, ANDREW	68		SENILITY	BOSTON
18-May	1854	NEVILLE, THOMAS	54		OLD AGE	IRELAND
9-Jun	1857	NEWCOMB, WILLIAM FREEMAN	43		APOPLEXY	NOVA SCOTIA
21-Mar	1892	NEWMAN, ANNA M (EPPS)	84		SENILITY	GERMANY
18-Jul	1889	NEWTON, JOANNA (HURLEY)	50		PHTHISIS	BOSTON
14-Aug	1895	NEWTON, MARY A		10	TUBERCULOSIS	BOSTON
10-Oct	1857	NILES, MARY (CARTER)	59		CONSUMPTION	BOSTON
31-Jan	1889	NOLAN, JAMES	82		HEART DISEASE	BOSTON
20-Jul	1895	NOLAN, JOHN		5	DIARRHOEA	BOSTON
4-May	1865	NOLAN, THOMAS	60		UNKNOWN	IRELAND
12-Jul	1855	NOONAN, CORNELIUS	25		SMALL POX	NOVA SCOTIA
13-Jun	1892	NOONAN, MARGARET (MAHAR)	80		CEREBRAL EMBOLISM	IRELAND
30-Jan	1889	NOONE, MICHAEL	40		PHTHISIS	IRELAND
1-Aug	1890	NORTON, MARY	15		HEART FAILURE	BOSTON
17-Jan	1890	NORTON, MICHAEL	48		CEREBRAL HEMORRHAGE	NEW YORK
25-Aug	1889	NORTON, MICHAEL J	55		PHTHISIS	LOWELL, MA
25-Jul	1891	NOYES, SAMUEL	76		SENILITY	VERMONT
1-Nov	1888	O'BRIEN, CATHARINE (FINNEGAN)	64		HEART DISEASE AORTIC	IRELAND
8-Sep	1855	O'BRIEN, CATHARINE (KEANE)	30		CONSUMPTION	IRELAND
23-Nov	1865	O'BRIEN, DANIEL	50		EXHAUSTION	IRELAND
2-Jun	1863	O'BRIEN, DELIA	28		PHTHISIS	IRELAND
18-Sep	1898	O'BRIEN, ELIZABETH		7 MONTHS 5 DAYS	ILEO COLITIS	CAMBRIDGE
13-Sep	1856	O'BRIEN, FRANCIS C	22		TYPHOID FEVER	NOVA SCOTIA
20-Sep	1854	O'BRIEN, HENRY	24		LARYNGITIS	IRELAND
28-Mar	1880	O'BRIEN, JOHN	28		HEART DISEASE	ENGLAND
2-Jun	1893	O'BRIEN, JOHN	72		HEART DISEASE MITRAL STENOSIS	IRELAND
15-Feb	1858	O'BRIEN, SARAH (KELLY)	40		CONSUMPTION	BOSTON
22-Sep	1855	O'BRIEN, TERRANCE		1	MARASMUS	RAINSFORD ISLAND
17-Jun	1881	O'BRIEN, WILLIAM	78		OLD AGE	IRELAND
5-Aug	1889	O'BRIEN, WILLIAM E	19		PHTHISIS	BRIDGEWATER, MA
17-May	1885	O'BRYNE, PATRICK	55		CIRHOSIS OF LIVER	IRELAND
27-Aug	1895	O'CONNELL, ELLEN E		3	DIARRHOEA & EXHAUSTION	
11-Feb	1886	O'CONNELL, JEREMIAH	25		PHTHISIS	BOSTON
21-Aug	1896	O'CONNOR, HENRY J		5	INFANTLE	BOSTON
1-Nov	1891	O'CONNOR, JULIA (O'SULLIVAN)	45		ALCOHOLISM	NEW HAMPSHIRE
20-Sep	1885	O'CONNOR, WILLIAM	16		PNEUMONIA	BOSTON
21-Feb	1858	O'DAY, PATRICK	22		TYPHOID FEVER	IRELAND
4-Sep	1884	O'DONNELL, JAMES	77		DYSENTARY	IRELAND
5-Sep	1895	O'DONNELL, JOHN		1	GASTRO ENTERITIS	BOSTON
26-Jul	1896	O'DONNELL, MARY		4 MONTH 3 DAYS	INFANTILE ATROPHY	BOSTON
27-Dec	1889	O'DOWD, MARY J		2	DIARRHOEA	ST MARY INFANT ASYLUM, BOSTON

MONTH	YEAR	NAME	AGE YEARS	AGE MONTHS	CAUSE OF DEATH	BORN
26-Jan	1855	O'HARA, HUGH	20		SHIP FEVER	ENGLAND
26-Mar	1889	O'HEARN, MARY	21		PHTHISIS	NEW YORK
4-Dec	1855	OISTER, SOLOMON	30		SMALL POX	NEW HAMPSHIRE, WALDOBORO
14-Oct	1889	O'KEEFE, WILLIAM	76		SENILITY	IRELAND
12-Jun	1860	OLD, CHARLES N	25		SMALL POX	NOVA SCOTIA
18-Sep	1889	O'LEARY, EUGENE	18		PHTHISIS	BOSTON
24-Jun	1837	OLIVER, CATHARINE	48		SMALL POX	
4-Jul	1885	OLIVER, CHARLES	66		SENILE DEBILITY	MAINE, GEORGETOWN
29-Apr	1857	O'NEAL, CATHARINE	20		SYPHILIS	IRELAND
22-Jul	1854	O'NEIL, JOHN	25		SHIP FEVER	IRELAND
31-Jul	1860	O'NEIL, JOHN	35		DIARRHOEA	IRELAND
9-Mar	1860	O'NEIL, MARGARET	21		SMALL POX	NOVA SCOTIA
10-Oct	1855	O'NEIL, MARGARET (COX)	27		DYSENTARY	IRELAND
16-Aug	1855	O'ROURKE, CATHARINE	54		DIARRHOEA	IRELAND
4-Aug	1884	O'ROURKE, EDWARD	49		RHEUMATISM	BOSTON
25-Apr	1855	ORR, JAMES	35		SMALL POX	ENGLAND
19-Jul	1857	OSBORN, CHAUNCEY		1	SYPHILIS	RAINSFORD ISLAND
6-Oct	1865	OSMOND, OSMAN	57		CANCER	NORWAY
12-Aug	1892	OWEN, ANN (MCLEAN)	44		PHTHISIS	NOVE SCOTIA, CAPE BRETON
24-Jan	1856	OWENS, THOMAS	29		SMALL POX	MAINE, PORTLAND
30-May	1864	PAINE, GRACE (HILL)	46		SMALL POX	NOVA SCOTIA
6-Jun	1858	PALLASSE, JOSEPH	18		CONSUMPTION	SPAIN
19-Aug	1821	PALMER, JOHN D				
20-Aug	1855	PAPA, JOHN	25		CONSUMPTION	SWEDEN
30-Aug	1896	PARKER, EMMA G		5	INFANTILE	BOSTON LYING-IN
10-May	1864	PARKER, JANE	20		SMALL POX	NEW HAMPSHIRE
17-Oct	1830	PARKER, THOMAS	18		SMALL POX	
18-Jan	1884	PARKER, WILLIAM	73		BRONCHITIS	BOSTON
7-Oct	1888	PATTEN, GEORGE W	69		PARALYSIS	NEWBURYPORT, MA
27-Mar	1825	PATTERSON, CORNELIUS D	2		SMALL POX	
6-Jun	1861	PATTERSON, JAMES	35		PHTHISIS	SCOTLAND
26-Nov	1891	PAYNE, SARAH	86		SENILITY	NEW HAMPSHIRE
31-Aug	1897	PEARLSTEIN, CECELIA		2 MONTHS 18 DAYS	FERMENTAL DIARRHOEA	BOSTON
20-May	1855	PEARSON, HARRIET	22		SMALL POX	MAINE
29-Jul	1888	PENDERGAST, ABBIE	81		SENILE DEMENTIA	NEW HAMPSHIRE
4-Sep	1898	PETERS, GLADYS		9	FERMENTAL DIARRHOEA	BOSTON
9-Oct	1854	PETERSON, ANDRES	45		DIARRHOEA	SWEDEN
22-Dec	1889	PHILLIPS, ANN	90		SENILITY	CHARLESTOWN, MA
25-Aug	1884	PHILLIPS, ISAAC	74		RHEUMATISIM & DEBILITY	CHARLESTOWN, MA
9-Jun	1857	PIDDEPAN, ANDREW	21		LUNG INFLAMMATION	NOVA SCOTCIA
6-Mar	1886	PIERCE, BENJAMIN	75		CEREBRAL HEMORRHAGE	BOSTON
26-Nov	1891	PIKE, JULIA A (O'BRIEN)	27		SYPHILIS	SALEM, MA
14-Aug	1826	PIKE, WILLIAM R	26		DROPSY IN CHEST	
25-May	1855	PITMAN, JOSEPH	22		SMALL POX	NOVA SCOTIA
22-Aug	1887	PLUMMER, ALDEN	75		DIARRHOEA	NOTLISTED
18-Mar	1864	PLUMMER, GEORGE	20		SMALL POX	DISTRICT OF COLUMBIA
4-Dec	1861	PLUMMER, HENRY	45		DYSENTARY	NOVA SCOTIA, HALIFAX
28-Sep	1861	PLUMMER, ROBERT P	29		DYSENTARY	DELAWARE
19-Sep	1821	POPP, JOHN				
22-Jun	1836	PORTER, HUNTINGTON	22		SMALL POX	NEW HAMSHIRE, RYE
2-Jul	1857	PORTER, MARGARET	23		CONSUMPTION	NOVA SCOTIA
17-Feb	1856	POTTER, CALEB A	20		SMALL POX	RHODE ISLAND, WARWICK
22-Aug	1896	POTTER, HAROLD		3	INFANTILE ATROPHY	SPRINGFIELD
19-Dec	1857	POWELL, ANN	17		CONSUMPTION	BOSTON
28-Dec	1858	POWERS, ANN	80		CONSUMPTION	IRELAND
5-Jun	1892	POWERS, CHARLES	22		PHTHISIS	BOSTON
31-Jul	1887	POWERS, JAMES	52		PHTHISIS	IRELAND
5-Aug	1856	POWERS, JOHN H		5	CHOLERA INFANTUM	BOSTON
20-Oct	1891	POWERS, MARY	62		PHTHISIS	IRELAND
29-Dec	1854	POWERS, MARY A	41		CONSUMPTION	IRELAND
6-May	1856	PRAY, CHARLES	24		SMALL POX	MAINE, VASSALBORO
7-Oct	1860	PRINCE, CHARLES F	33		TYPHOID FEVER	MAINE

MONTH	YEAR	NAME	AGE YEARS	AGE MONTHS	CAUSE OF DEATH	BORN
9-Jul	1896	PRINDABLE, ETHEL E		7	FERMENTAL DIARRHOEA	BOSTON
26-Jun	1888	PUNCH, MARGARET (DUGGAN)	73		DIARRHOEA	IRELAND
22-Jun	1898	PURCELL, JOHN		8	PNEUMONIA	BOSTON
18-Jun	1891	PURTELL, ANNIE	40		PHTHISIS	IRELAND
31-May	1866	QUINLAN, ALFRED		1	MARASMUS	RAINSFORD ISLAND
18-Jun	1888	QUINN, BRIDGET (DONNELLY)	75		CEREBRAL HEMORRHAGE	IRELAND
28-Aug	1863	QUINN, CATHARINE (MURPHY)	52		PHTHISIS	IRELAND
24-Apr	1857	QUINN, ELIZA	21		SHIP FEVER	IRELAND
21-Jan	1877	QUINN, JOHN	52		PNEUMONIA	IRELAND
8-16	1855	QUINN, MARY	40		CANCER	IRELAND
9-Jun	1891	RABBAT, JOHN	81		HEART DISEASE MITRAL STENOSIS	IRELAND
21-Jul	1896	RAE, MARY ELIZABETH		3	INFANTILE	EVERETT, MA
1-Aug	1889	RAFFERTY, ALICE		5	CHOLERA INFANTUM & ECLAMPSIA	LONG ISLAND HOSPITAL
2-Oct	1891	RANKEN, FREDERICK		4	GASTRO INTESTINAL CATARRH	RAINSFORD ISLAND
27-Mar	1865	RANKIN, WILLIAM	36		SMALL POX	MAINE
20-Oct	1890	RAY, MARGARET	64		HEART DISEASE	NEW BRUNSWICK
8-May	1874	READY, JEREMIAH	30		HEART DISEASE	BOSTON
2-Feb	1855	REARDAN, MICHAEL E	48		SHIP FEVER	IRELAND
30-Jun	1892	REARDON, NORA	34		PHTHISIS	IRELAND
11-Aug	1898	REARDON, WILLIAM		7 MONTHS 15 DAYS	FERMENTAL DIARRHOEA	BOSTON
4-Apr	1855	REDDING, CHARLES	58		DYSENTARY	NEW JERSEY
7-Apr	1864	REED, CHARLES	49		PHTHISIS	MASSACHUSETTS
28-Dec	1881	REESE, JOHN	72		OLD AGE	CAPE VERDE
25-Nov	1857	REGAL, GEORGE	40		APOPLEXY	GERMANY
11-Aug	1865	REGAN, CATHARINE	25		PERITONITIS	IRELAND
22-May	1862	REICHSTADLER, ANTON	60		PNEUMONIA	GERMANY
13-Mar	1860	REID, PETER	30		SMALL POX	PRINCE EDWARD ISLAND
19-Aug	1896	RENO, JOHN		4 MONTHS 10 DAYS	INFANTILE ATROPHY	EAST CAMBRIDGE
2-Apr	1882	REXTROW, JAMES EDWARD "EDWARD"	64		PNEUMONIA	CHARLESTOWN, MA
24-Oct	1862	REYNOLDS, CATHARINE	20		MENINGITIS	IRELAND
5-Feb	1857	REYNOLDS, ELIZA A	4		SPINE CARIES	BOSTON
4-Mar	1865	REYNOLDS, SARAH H	22		PHTHISIS	MAINE
August	1817	RICHARDS, JOHN				
3-Aug	1891	RICHARDSON, ELLEN A		1	GASTRO INTESTINAL CATARRH	
20-Dec	1876	RICHARDSON, LORENZO	63		CYSTITIS	WOBURN, MA
18-Jul	1861	RILEY, EDWARD	35		PHTHISIS	ENGLAND
2-Apr	1862	RILEY, ELLEN (HENNEKY)	31		CANCER UTERUS	IRELAND
26-Jul	1896	RILEY, GRACE	1	6	ECLAMPSIA	BOSTON
28-Aug	1861	RILEY, MARY (WARD)	37		HOMICIDE	IRELAND
21-Sep	1854	RIORDAN, DENNIS	38		DROPSY	IRELAND
20-Sep	1856	RIORDAN, JOHN		8	DYSENTARY	BOSTON
17-Apr	1881	RIORDAN, JOHN	36		PHTHISIS	IRELAND
21-Apr	1857	RIVAS, ANTIONIO	30		APOPLEXY	SPAIN
26-Jul	1892	ROACH, ELLEN	75		ARTHRITIS DEFORMANS	IRELAND
25-Sep	1860	ROACH, JAMES	34		PHTHISIS	IRELAND
15-Nov	1874	ROACH, JAMES	46		PHTHISIS	IRELAND
3-Mar	1862	ROACH, MARGARET (ROACH)	30		HEART DISEASE & PLEURISY	IRELAND
10-Jan	1888	ROACH, MARTIN	77		HEART DISEASE VALVE	IRELAND
1-Jan	1891	ROACH, MARY	89		PARALYSIS	IRELAND
11-Jul	1875	ROBBINS, LEVERETTE	58		OLD AGE & DEBILITY	IPSWICH, MA
13-Jul	1837	ROBBINS, MARY			SMALL POX	
11-Dec	1856	ROBERTS, ELLEN, (MALONEY)	30		HEART DISEASE	IRELAND
26-Aug	1898	ROBERTSON, ELIZABETH	1		ANAEMIA	NEWTON
16-Sep	1898	ROBERTSON, JOHN		7 MONTS 7 DAYS	FERMENTAL DIARRHOEA	BOSTON
30-Oct	1830	ROBERTSON, MARY	21		SMALL POX	
24-Oct	1855	ROBERTSON, MARY	17		SHIP FEVER	IRELAND
15-Mar	1861	ROBINS, MARY ANN	27		PHTHISIS	BOSTON
24-Feb	1862	ROBINSON HANNAH (PRICE)	20		SYPHILIS & PHTHISIS	BOSTON

MONTH	YEAR	NAME	AGE YEARS	AGE MONTHS	CAUSE OF DEATH	BORN
9-Nov	1858	ROBINSON, GEORGE W	45		LIVER DISEASE	MAINE
12-Aug	1888	ROBINSON, JAMES	60		CEREBRAL HEMORRHAGE	IRELAND
6-Mar	1876	ROBINSON, JOHN	78	4 MONTHS	OLD AGE & EXHAUSTION	NEW HAMPSHIRE
10-Aug	1884	ROBINSON, JOHN C	74		DIARRHOEA & DEBILITY	IRELAND
30-Jul	1857	ROBINSON, MARGARET(LAHY)	28		LIVER DISEASE	IRELAND
2-Mar	1891	ROBINSON, MARY (BREEN)	69		CEREBRAL HEMORRHAGE	BOSTON
21-Sep	1855	ROBINSON, SUSAN	22		CANCER	BOSTON
7-Jul	1864	ROCK, BRIDGET	27		SHIP FEVER	IRELAND
11-Aug	1890	RODDAY, MARTHA (MILLER)	38		CANCER WOMB	RHODE ISLAND
25-Nov	1864	RODNEY, SAMUEL	32		SMALL POX	NEW BRUNSWICK
21-Jan	1889	ROGERS, PATRICK	23		TUBERCULOSIS	IRELAND
4-Apr	1887	ROGERS, SAMUEL F	66		CEREBRAL HEMORRHAGE	NEW HAMPSHIRE, TAMWORTH
17-May	1858	ROGERS, THOMAS	40		INTEMPERENCE	IRELAND
19-May	1893	ROGERS, TIMOTHY	76		CEREBRAL HEMORRHAGE	IRELAND
20-Apr	1889	ROGERS, WILLIAM A	71		CEREBRAL HEMORRHAGE & HEART DISEASE	BOSTON
7-Aug	1891	ROLAND, MARY (COLLINS)	60		NEPHRITIS & HEART DISEASE	IRELAND
4-Nov	1891	RONAN, MICHAEL	70		BRONCHITIS	IRELAND
7-Oct	1887	ROONEY, JOSEPH L	20		PHTHISIS	BOSTON
8-Aug	1880	ROONEY, TERENCE	68		CANCER STOMACH	IRELAND
14-Jan	1860	ROSANDOLPH, CHRISTINA	51		DROPSY	GERMANY
23-Sep	1859	ROSE, ANN M	27		EPILEPSY	WESTERN ISLANDS
18-Sep	1858	ROSIAS, HANNAH	22		CONSUMPTION	ITALY
18-Sep	1896	ROTHERMEL, EMMA		7	PNEUMONIA	BOSTON
11-Aug	1821	ROUNDY, RAY				
8-Oct	1887	ROWELL, ISAIAH	65		HEART DEISEASE & DEBILITY	NEW HAMSHIRE, SALEM
11-Aug	1891	ROWEN, HONORA (HARRISON)	39		CANCER INTESTINES	WALES
3-Jul	1854	RUDDOCK, CAROLINE	30		SHIP FEVER	ENGLAND
7-Nov	1873	RUNEY, MICHAEL	64		PNEUMONIA	IRELAND
10-Aug	1865	RUSSELL, ANNA	23		SMALL POX	MAINE
7-Apr	1858	RUSSELL, BARTHOLOMEW	36		LUNG INFLAMMATION	ENGLAND
14-Apr	1856	RUSSELL, CYRUS	36		SMALL POX	VERMONT
6-Sep	1889	RUSSELL, EDWARD F.		8 DAYS	SYPHILIS	LONG ISLAND HOSPITAL
3-Jun	1856	RUSSELL, JAMES	1		MARASMUS	RAINSFORD ISLAND
29-Jul	1886	RUSSELL, JOHN	33		PHTHISIS	MAINE, PORTLAND
9-Sep	1898	RUSSELL, RICHARD A.		3	FERMENTAL DIARRHOEA	CHELSEA
21-May	1857	RYAN, EDWARD	36		PLEURISY	IRELAND
20-May	1865	RYAN, ELLEN	20		SMALL POX	NOVA SCOTIA
13-Aug	1898	RYAN, FRANK		3 MONTHS 9 DAYS	FERMENTAL DIARRHOEA	BOSTON
31-Jan	1893	RYAN, JAMES F.	35		PHTHISIS	BOSTON
11-Oct	1888	RYAN, JANE P (DAY)	77		HEART DISEASE	MAINE
22-Feb	1882	RYAN, JOHN	37		ENTERITIS	IRELAND
28-Jul	1882	RYAN, JOHN	72		ALCOHOLISM & PARALYSIS	IRELAND
6-Sep	1897	RYAN, MARY E	1	9 MONTHS 20 DAYS	PHTHISIS	BOSTON
9-Jun	1857	RYAN, PATRICK	28		CONSUMPTION	IRELAND
20-Aug	1889	SACCO, PASQUALE	37		PERITYPHLITIS	ITALY
21-Mar	1864	SAIF, MATTHEW	45		HEART DISEASE	GERMANY
12-Nov	1836	SAMPSON, MARY	40		SMALL POX	
5-Jan	1857	SANBORN, DANIEL E		9	DIARRHOEA	
11-Sep	1856	SANBORN, SARAH	21		DYSENTARY	MAINE
9-Jun	1854	SANDLIN, HANNAH	8		HEART DISEASE	BOSTON
17-Aug	1836	SANTO, CARLO	12		LUNG INFLAMATION	
11-Jun	1886	SAVAGE, WILLIAM C	71		PARALYSIS	NEW HAMPSHIRE, FRANCESTOWN
25-Dec	1857	SCALES, SARAH (JACKSON)	24		CONSUMPTION	OHIO, CINNCINNATI
18-Aug	1858	SCANLAN, DENNIS	50		INTEMPERENCE	IRELAND
7-Jan	1890	SCANLON, PATRICK	55		DEBILITY	IRELAND

MONTH	YEAR	NAME	AGE YEARS	AGE MONTHS	CAUSE OF DEATH	BORN
26-Nov	1856	SCANNELL, JOHN		6	DROPSY IN HEAD	RAINSFORD ISLAND
10-Oct	1890	SCHILLING, BRIDGET (MONDAY)	83		NEPHRITIS	IREALND
1-Feb	1855	SCHULLER, MARIA		1	MARASMUS	RAINSFORD ISLAND
18-Aug	1889	SCHUSTER, ANNIE				
30-Sep	1859	SCHUYLER, JOHN	26		BOWELL INFLAMMATION	BOSTON
5-Aug	1854	SCHWALL, FELIX	30		LIVER DISEASE	GERMANY
27-Oct	1856	SCOFIELD, JAMES	30		CONSUMPTION	BOSTON
2-Aug	1864	SCOTT, ABRAHAM	50		SMALL POX	MARYLAND, BALTIMORE
26-Nov	1890	SCOTT, JAMES	50		URAEMIC PROBABLY	
16-Oct	1822	SCOTT, MAURICE				
9-Mar	1825	SCRIBNER, MARY	25			
27-Apr	1881	SCRIGGINS, JOSEPH G	68		DEBILITY	NEW HAMPSHIRE (PORTSMOUTH)
12-Sep	1819	SEAMAN, JOHN				
14-Oct	1864	SEAMAN, JOHN N.	25		SMALL POX	
6-Jul	1837	SEAVEY, WARREN	37		SMALL POX	
16-Feb	1863	SEAVY, MARY		1 DAY	PERITONITIS	RAINSFORD ISLAND
2-Nov	1854	SEBASTIAN,	25		TYPHOID FEVER	GERMANY
14-Mar	1855	SEEARY, PATRICK A/K/A SEALY	26		HEMORRHAGE	IRELAND
15-Aug	1894	SEELEY, MARY E		8 MONTHS 4 DAYS (2 WEEKS)	CHOLERA INFANTUM	BOSTON
10-Mar	1817	SEGER, SARAH	21			NEWTON
18-Nov	1888	SEYMOUR, VICTORIA	35		EPITHELIOMA	CANADA
20-Sep	1861	SHADY, WILLIAM	1	6	SCROFULA	
18-Aug	1889	SHANAHAN, TIMOTHY	86		HEART DISEASE	IRELAND
29-Jan	1859	SHARP, CATHARINE	30		BLADDER INFLAMMATION	IRELAND
6-Oct	1884	SHAUGHNESSEY, JOHN	48		PARALYSIS	IRELAND
19-Jan	1890	SHAW, MARIA (GILMORE)	46		PNEUMONIA	ENGLAND
8-Apr	1856	SHEA, MARGARET	25		DYSENTARY	IRELAND
23-Jul	1855	SHEEHAN, PATRICK	22		HEMORRHAGE	IRELAND
7-Aug	1889	SHEEHAN, WILLIAM	38		ALCOHOLISM	BOSTON
24-Dec	1887	SHEPARD, ALBERT	80		HEART DISEASE	DORCHESTER
15-Sep	1863	SHERIDAN, EDWARD	36		HEART DISEASE	IRELAND
18-Jul	1860	SHERMAN, MARGARET	32		PHTHISIS	CANTON, MA
9-Jun	1861	SHERRY, JOSEPH	34		PHTHISIS	IRELAND
7-Jul	1891	SHULTZ, MARY (STAFFORD)	62		SENILITY	IRELAND
8-Aug	1825	SIBLEY, NAPOLEON B	20		SMALL POX	
16-Apr	1865	SILVA, FRANK	16		BURNS	WESTERN ISLANDS
31-Oct	1888	SILVER, CATHARINE	58		PHTHISIS & PNEUMONIA	IRELAND
26-May	1855	SILVER, JOSEPH	24		SMALL POX	VERMONT
9-Nov	1857	SIMMONS, ROBERT D	39		TYPHOID FEVER	NOVA SCOTIA
9-Dec	1872	SIMMS, HENRY	82		ERYSIPELIAS	GEORGIA
22-May	1865	SIMPSON, ANN	25		BRAIN SOFTENING	IRELAND
23-Jun	1860	SIMPSON, ELLEN	30		PHTHISIS	NOVA SCOTIA, HALIFAX
16-Jan	1864	SIMPSON, THOMAS	3		SYPHILIS	RAINSFORD ISLAND
20-Sep	1854	SMEERDON, GEORGE	22		CANCER	NEW BRUNSWICK, ST JOHNS
12-Oct	1873	SMITH, ARTIMAS	73		SENILE GANGRENE	NATICK, MA
7-Sep	1875	SMITH, DAVID	67		PHTHISIS & HEART DISEASE	SCOTLAND
20-Jun	1883	SMITH, EDWARD	29		DELIRIUM TREMENS	BOSTON
31-Aug	1898	SMITH, ELLIOT B		7 MONTHS 9 DAYS	MALNUTRITION	NEW YORK
22-Jul	1898	SMITH, GERTRUDE		6 MONTHS 1 DAY	PNEUMONIA	EVERETT
25-Aug	1878	SMITH, HECTOR	60		RHUEMATISIM	NEW YORK, BROOKLYN
6-Feb	1860	SMITH, JAMES	38		SMALL POX	PRINCE EDWARD ISLAND
1-Jul	1861	SMITH, JANE	21		UNKNOWN	IRELAND
15-Sep	1854	SMITH, JOANNA	19		TYPHOID FEVER	IRELAND
18-Dec	1855	SMITH, JOANNA (HICKMAN)	40		PLEURISY	IRELAND
11-Nov	1865	SMITH, JOHN	50		PHTHISIS	ENGLAND
29-Apr	1858	SMITH, JULIA	40		CONSUMPTION	MAINE, DRESDEN
7-May	1859	SMITH, LETITIA	26			NEW BRUNSWICK
7-Sep	1854	SMITH, MARGARET	31		DYSENTARY	IRELAND
14-Sep	1855	SMITH, MARGARET	19		CONSUMPTION	IRELAND

MONTH	YEAR	NAME	AGE YEARS	AGE MONTHS	CAUSE OF DEATH	BORN
5-Sep	1898	SMITH, MARY		3	INPROPER FEEDING	BOSTON
7-Jun	1889	SMITH, MARY (AHERN)	66		PERTUSIS	IRELAND
11-May	1893	SMITH, MARY A (HAWKES)	79		PNEUMONIA	BIRDGEWATER, MA
29-May	1837	SMITH, MORES	28		SMALL POX	
14-Nov	1862	SMITH, NANCY	45		CANCER RECTUM	IRELAND
18-Sep	1860	SMITH, NELLIE B	1	6	SYPHILIS	RAINSFORD ISLAND
1-Sep	1896	SMITH, ROBERT E		3 MONTHS 22 DAYS	INFANTILE ATROPHY	EVERETT
18-Sep	1860	SMITH, THOMAS	24		DELIRIUM TREMENS	IRELAND
5-Aug	1865	SMITH, WILLIAM		2 DAYS	SYPHILIS	RAINSFORD ISLAND
15-Jan	1888	SMITH, WILLIAM O	74		DEBILITY	MAINE, READFIELD
23-Jan	1856	SMITHIEL, MICHAEL	40		LUNG INFLAMMATION	IRELAND
3-Nov	1857	SNOW, HANNAH, (HAMAN)	30		PLEURISY	MAINE, CALAIS
7-Feb	1882	SNOWDEN, WILLIAM W	53		RHEUMATISM	BOSTON
27-Jul	1887	SOMERVILLE, ROBERT	47		TUBERCULOSIS	BOSTON
27-Sep	1890	SOUTHARD, WILLIAM R	64		PHTHISIS	PENNSYLVANIA, PHILADELPHIA
18-Dec	1864	SOUTHERLAND, JAMES	7		STARVATION & SMALL POX	BOSTON
12-Dec	1864	SOUTHERLAND, JAMES C	39		SMALL POX	NOVA SCOTIA
4-Nov	1863	SOUTHWELL, ANN (FALLON)	37		BURNS (1 MONTH)	IRELAND
31-Jul	1888	SPARROW, CATHARINE (MALONE)	70		SENILTY	IRELAND
	1799	SPEAR, GEORGE				
22-Apr	1812	SPEAR, THOMAS	58			FOR MANY YEARS KEEPER OF RAINSFORD ISLAND
May	1738	SPEARE, JOSEPH III			SMALL POX	
21-Feb	1881	SPENCE, EDWARD	54		ASTHMA	SCOTLAND
10-Sep	1896	SPILLANE, GERTRUDE		8	INFANTILE	BOSTON
12-Sep	1898	SPILLANE. LIZZIE		3 MONTHS 15 DAYS	FERMENTAL DIARRHOEA	BOSTON
18-Jul	1892	SPILOKEN, CATHARINE (FRYE)		67	HEART DISEASE MITRAL VALVE	GERMANY
4-Dec	1861	SPOFFORD, DANIEL	62		DYSENTARY	MAINE
27-Jul	1896	SPRAGUE, HAROLD		2	INFANTILE	BOSTON
7-Jun	1876	SPRAGUE, WILLIAM	59		APOPLEXY	HINGHAM
27-Jun	1889	SPRINGER, EDWIN S.	33		PHTHISIS	BOSTON
20-Feb	1875	SPURR, OTIS W	69		PNEUMONIA	BOSTON
15-Apr	1865	ST. CROIX, MARY	20		SMALL POX	NEWFOUNDLAND
16-Aug	1898	STANTON, ADELAIDE		11	FERMENTAL DIARRHOEA	BOSTON
10-Jun	1822	STAPLES, LEVI	22			PROSPECT
8-Oct	1861	STAPLETON, HANNAH (EVANS)	30		DYSENTARY	ENGLAND
7-Sep	1825	STARK, DAVID	21		TYPHUS FEVER	DUNBAR, NH
2-Sep	1883	STEARNS, EDWARD	45		PHTHISIS	
22-Feb	1855	STEBBINS, WILLIAM C	32		CARIES	NORTHAMPTON, MA
13-Feb	1891	STETSON, AGNES JULIA		1	MARASMUS	RAINSFORD ISLAND
25-May	1889	STETSON, FRANK	12/18/1888	5	MARASMUS	BOSTON
5-May	1890	STETSON, MARY E		1	BRONCHITIS	RAINSFORD ISLAND
14-Jan	1887	STEVENS, HENRY F	51		PHTHISIS	BERMUDA
13-Sep	1884	STEVENS, JOHN M	59		ATAXIA LOCOMOTOR & DIARRHOEA	BOSTON
9-Nov	1854	STEWARD, JAMES	16		CONSUMPTION	ENGLAND
13-Jan	1856	STEWART, MARY (CAMPBELL)	25		CONSUMPTION	SCOTLAND
22-Oct	1891	STEWART, SARAH J. (KELLEY)	64		ATAXIA LOCOMOTIVE	IRELAND
30-Apr	1856	STHOEN, JOHN G	48		CANCER	GERMANY
24-Jun	1891	STINSON, THOMAS	31		ALCOHOLISM	BOSTON
OCT	1798	STONE, ELEANOR				
1-Jun	1883	STONE, JOHN	68		INSANITY & EXHAUSTION	
21-Oct	1887	STRATTON, MARY	80		HEART DISEASE	BOSTON
18-Nov	1862	STRONG, CARL W	42		BRAIN DISEASE	SWEDEN
11-Dec	1887	SULLIVAN, ALEXANDER		1	SYPHILIS & INTESTINAL CARARRH	BOSTON
14-Dec	1856	SULLIVAN, ANN	32		CONSUMPTION	IRELAND
10-Aug	1890	SULLIVAN, ANN	67		HEART DISEASE VALVE	IRELAND

MONTH	YEAR	NAME	AGE YEARS	AGE MONTHS	CAUSE OF DEATH	BORN
3-Mar	1892	SULLIVAN, CATHARINE	68		SENILITY	IRELAND
22-Oct	1865	SULLIVAN, DENNIS	40		WOUND	IRELAND
26-Aug	1889	SULLIVAN, ELLEN		3	INTESTINAL CARRTAH	BOSTON
16-Feb	1857	SULLIVAN, JEREMIAH	2		SCROFULA	RAINSFORD ISLAND
13-Apr	1864	SULLIVAN, JOHN P	21		SMALL POX	IRELAND
8-Jul	1897	SULLIVAN, JOSEPH		3	FERMENTAL DIARRHOEA	SOMERVILLE
20-Jan	1861	SULLIVAN, JULIA	28		LIVER DISEASE	IRELAND
23-May	1856	SULLIVAN, MARY		10	SMALL POX	BOSTON
15-Feb	1889	SULLIVAN, MARY (SULLIVAN)	60		HEART DISEASE	IRELAND
3-Mar	1891	SULLIVAN, MARY E (MAHONEY)	61		CEREBRAL HEMORRHAGE	IRELAND
15-Aug	1886	SULLIVAN, MAURICE	66		CANCER FACE	IRELAND
17-Jun	1854	SULLIVAN, MICHAEL	10		SPINE DISEASE	IRELAND
29-Jul	1855	SULLIVAN, MICHAEL	35		DROPSY	IRELAND
26-Apr	1857	SULLIVAN, MURTAGH	75		BRONCHITIS	IRELAND
29-Mar	1855	SULLIVAN, TIMOTHY	21		KIDNEY DISEASE	BOSTON
7-Jul	1889	SULLIVAN, TIMOTHY	26		HEART DISEASE	IRELAND
9-Jun	1891	SULLIVAN, WILLIAM	33		PHTHISIS	BOSTON
20-Oct	1856	SUTTON, JAMES	52		HEART DISEASE	ENGLAND
24-Jul	1897	SUTTON, JAMES		10	FERMENTAL DIARRHOEA	LYNN
28-Jul	1896	SWARTZ, ABRAHAM		6	INFANTILE	BOSTON
29-Jan	1890	SWEENEY, ALICE (COTTER)	75		NEPHRITIS	IREALND
13-Jun	1890	SWEENEY, ELLEN (O'BRIEN)	55		PNEUMONIA	IRELAND
2-Nov	1863	SWEENEY, JOHN	26		AMPUTATION OF FOOT	NEW YORK
21-Mar	1888	SWEENEY, MARGARET	65		HEART DISEASE	IRELAND
22-Sep	1892	SWEENEY, PATRICK		5	MENINGITIS	BOSTON
17-Sep	1881	SWEETZER, JOHN	78		OLD AGE	NEW HAMPSHIRE, PORTSMOUTH
13-Apr	1887	SYLVESTER, JOHN	31		PHTHISIS & PNEUMONIA	CHARLESTOWN, MA
29-Jun	1884	TABER, GEORGE	48		RHEUMATIC GOUT (9 YEARS)	IRELAND
30-Dec	1862	TALLEC, SARAH (KELLEY)	24		DROPSY	IRELAND
29-Oct	1800	TALMADGE, ENOS	20			
4-Sep	1859	TANDY, THOMAS	34		DIARRHOEA	ENGLAND
2-Apr	1864	TARR, JOHN	64		SMALL POX	MAINE
17-Aug	1819	TASKER, MARIAH	56			
13-Sep	1856	TATE, MARGARET		5	SPINE DISEASE	RAINSFORD ISLAND
30-Jul	1892	TAYLOR, ANN (JONES)	50		ELEPANTIASIS	ENGLAND
21-Jan	1883	TAYLOR, DANIEL	22		NECROSIS OF ILLIUM	NOVA SCOTIA
16-Jan	1827	TAYLOR, THOMAS	26		SMALL POX	MERIDITH, NH
2-Nov	1858	TEDDER, JOHN	51		PARALYSIS	MARBLEHEAD, MA
11-Jan	1885	THOMAS, GEORGE A	36		PHTHISIS (6 YEARS)	GEORGIA
18-Sep	1888	THOMAS, JAMES	29		PHTHISIS	USA
8-Mar	1861	THOMAS, JOHN	48		PARALYSIS	VERMONT
12-Mar	1856	THOMAS, WILLIAM HENRY HARRISON	16		SMALL POX	NATICK, MA
8-Sep	1806	THOMPSON, BENJAMIN			DROWNED	
20-Mar	1860	THOMPSON, DELIA	28		CONSUMPTION	IRELAND
12-Feb	1864	THOMPSON, DORA	22		BRIGHTS DISEASE	MAINE
2-Jul	1891	THOMPSON, ELLEN (CURTIS)	63		CANCER OF UTERUS	IRELAND
14-Oct	1863	THOMPSON, FRANCIS	21		DIARRHOEA	IRELAND
7-Sep	1856	THOMPSON, GEORGE	44		PNEUMONIA	IRELAND
16-Apr	1864	THOMPSON, HENRY	20		SMALL POX	MARYLAND
23-Aug	1859	THOMPSON, MICHAEL	30		TYPHOID FEVER	IRELAND
2-Sep	1896	THOMPSON, RUTH		28 DAYS	FERMENTAL DIARRHOEA	BOSTON
22-May	1892	THOMPSON, SARAH (RYAN)	49		BRONCHITIS	IRELAND
2-Dec	1862	THOMS, ALEXANDER	43		BRIGHTS DISEASE	SCOTLAND
19-Apr	1888	THORNTON, SUSAN	65		HEART DISEASE	IRELAND
4-Aug	1890	THORPE, JOSEPHINE	37		EXOPHTHALMIC GASTRE	NORWAY
26-Aug	1819	THURSTON, JOHN	26			
9-Dec	1860	TIERNEY, PATRICK	35		BRAIN SOFTENING	IRELAND
10-Sep	1881	TILL, SAMUEL C	33		PHTHISIS	HADLEY, MA
1-Jan	1860	TINGLER, ANNA A	2		SMALL POX	BOSTON

MONTH	YEAR	NAME	AGE YEARS	AGE MONTHS	CAUSE OF DEATH	BORN
10-Jun	1879	TISDALE, JOSEPH H	49		PNEUMONIA	IRELAND
27-Jan	1892	TONER, ELLEN	40		CANCER SARCOMA	IRELAND
9-Oct	1859	TOOMEY, JOHN	34		LUNG GANGRENE	IRELAND
12-Dec	1892	TOOMEY, MARY (MOORE)	60		FRACTURED FEMUR	IRELAND
16-Jan	1890	TRACEY, ANN (DENNING)	71		CANCER OF UTERUS & BLADDER	IRELAND
22-Sep	1864	TRAINER, MARY	40		APOPLEXY	IRELAND
19-Dec	1854	TRAINOR, THOMAS	22		CONSUMPTION	IRELAND
20-Jul	1837	TRASK, JOANNA	1	1	SMALL POX	
28-Jul	1896	TRAVIS, WILLIAM		3 MONTH 18 DAYS	PNEUMONIA	BOSTON
16-Apr	1861	TRISTE, MARY (DOLAN)	50		ULCERS & DROPSY	IRELAND
23-May	1839	TROTT, JOHN	40		SMALL POX	
2-Sep	1855	TRULSON, JONS	19		DYSENTARY	SWEDEN
8-Sep	1863	TUBMAN, JAMES		9	STARVATION	BOSTON
12-Aug	1873	TUCKER, JOHN	62		OLD AGE	NEWBURYPORT, MA
9-Jan	1828	TUCKERMAN, WILLIAM			SMALL POX	
13-Jan	1888	TURNER, MARY (MCCOY)	49		BRONCHITIS	IRELAND
14-Jun	1880	TURNER, OTIS	52		CIRRHOSIS OF LIVER	ROXBURY, MA
31-Oct	1855	TURNER, SAMUEL	27		CONSUMPTION	ENGLAND
19-Sep	1857	TWOHIG, CATHARINE	16		TYPHOID FEVER	IRELAND
8-Apr	1860	TYLER, HIRAM	17		CONSUMPTION	NEW YORK, BROOKLYN
19-Jan	1860	TYNES, MOSES	28		SMALL POX	VIRGINIA
SEPT	1827	UNKNOWN, SAMUEL				
14-Mar	1859	UNKNWON, FEMALE	35		SHIP FEVER	GERMANY
20-Nov	1864	UNKNWON, FEMALE	60		EXHAUSTION	
14-Jul	1855	UNKNWON, MALE	45		APOPLEXY	IRELAND
29-Nov	1890	VANMELKEL, PETER F	71		PARALYSIS	BELGIUM
25-May	1860	VARGUS, FRANCIS	40		SMALL POX	AZORES
18-Aug	1898	VAUGHAN, DOROTHY		4	MALNUTRITION	BOSTON
28-Apr	1865	VAUGHN, JOHN	20		SMALL POX	IRELAND
19-Sep	1857	VEDITO, ROBERT F	32		CONSUMPTION	NEW YORK
4-Jun	1859	VESSELSTOCKS, JAMES	50		LUNG CONGESTION	NETHERLANDS
13-Apr	1860	VINT, SARAH	27		TABES MESENTERCIA	
2-Aug	1898	VINTON, FREDERICK		2 MONTHS 23 DAYS	INANITION	BOSTON
20-Aug	1898	VINTON, JOSEPH		3 MONTHS 15 DAYS	FERMENTAL DIARRHOEA	BOSTON
2-Oct	1858	VIOLA, LAWRENCE	40		CONSUMPTION	ITALY
10-Aug	1861	VITOUT, JOSEPH	30		LUNG GANGRENE	WESTERN ISLANDS
Sept	1803	VOSE, JEREMIAH	26		FEVER	
19-Jan	1864	WADE, MARY J	18		SCARLETINA	NOVA SCOTIA
2-Sep	1815	WAIT, JAMES				AMESBURY
25-Apr	1861	WAKEFIED, CAROLINE E (WARD)	31		SYPHILIS	MAINE
4-Aug	1862	WALDEN, WILLIAM	35		PHTHISIS	SWEDEN
4-Mar	1825	WALES, JOSEPH	21		CONSUMPTION	
10-Apr	1882	WALKER, CHARLES H	54		PHTHISIS	BRIGHTON, MA
6-Sep	1896	WALKER, JOSEPH R		1	MILK INFECTION	BOSTON
6-Sep	1828	WALL, MARY	1		SMALL POX	
8-Jun	1854	WALLACE, MARTIN	25		SHIP FEVER	IRELAND
6-Sep	1895	WALLACE, MARY		7	MENINGITIS	BOSTON
30-Jun	1864	WALLACE, WILLIAM	28		PHTHISIS	NEW BRUNSWICK, ST JOHN
10-Apr	1882	WALSH, CHARLES H	54		PHTHISIS	BOSTON
21-Dec	1854	WALSH, MICHAEL	22		SMALL POX	NEWFOUNDLAND
23-May	1863	WALTER, ELIZABETH (COUISE)	20		SMALL POX	ROXBURY, MA
28-Mar	1875	WARD, JOHN	30		RHEUMATISM	RANDOLPH, MA
16-May	1862	WARE, ADA	19		TUMOR INTERNAL	NEW YORK
17-Aug	1890	WARNER, ANN	68		BURNS	SCOTLAND
24-Feb	1865	WARREN, GEORGE H	25		SMALL POX	MAINE
17-Sep	1835	WARREN, JOSEPH		11	SMALL POX	
27-Jan	1865	WASHBURN, CHARLES	32		SMALL POX	NEW YORK
1-Apr	1862	WATERS, MARGARET (DRURY)	60		PHTHISIS	IRELAND
1-Feb	1864	WATKINS, SARAH (WOODRUFF)	18		PHTHISIS	NEWBURYPORT, MA

MONTH	YEAR	NAME	AGE YEARS	AGE MONTHS	CAUSE OF DEATH	BORN
5-Oct	1890	WATSON, ELIZA	53		SENILE DEMENTIA	NEWFOUNDLAND
6-Jun	1866	WATSON, ELIZABETH	50		APOPLEXY	VIRGINIA
23-Jun	1837	WATTS, ELIAS	40		SMALL POX	
27-Nov	1857	WATTS, JOHN	34		SYPHILIS	VIRGINIA, NORFOLK
2-Dec	1857	WEBB, SYLVESTER	57		CONSUMPTION	AZROES
10-Nov	1856	WEIR, JOHN	35		DIARRHOEA	SCOTLAND
20-Jun	1888	WELCH, BRIDGET	80		SENILITY	IRELAND
7-Oct	1892	WELCH, ELIZABETH (O'NEIL)	76		SENILITY	IRELAND
27-Mar	1864	WELCH, ELLEN	25		SMALL POX	IRELAND
26-Apr	1863	WELCH, HENRY	39		PHTHISIS	IRELAND
5-Apr	1887	WELCH, ISAAC N	77		HEART DISEASE & SENILITY	MAINE, KITTERY
23-Sep	1865	WELCH, JAMES	64		BRIGHTS DISEASE	NEW YORK
15-Mar	1890	WELCH, JOSEPH	28		TUBERCULOSIS	NEW YORK
7-Aug	1862	WELCH, MARY	30		BRAIN INFLAMMATION	IRELAND
22-Sep	1856	WELCH, MARY (O'CONNELL)	69		TYPHOID FEVER	IRELAND
3-Sep	1856	WELCH, WILLIAM	1	2	DYSENTARY	BOSTON
13-Aug	1894	WELLINGTON, ALICE	22		PHTHISIS	BOSTON
5-Sep	1857	WELSH, FLORENCE		1	MARASMUS	RAINSFORD ISLAND
5-May	1857	WELSH, JAMES	50		APOPLEXY	IRELAND
9-Aug	1857	WELSH, PATRICK	19		CONSUMPTION	MICHIGAN
4-Nov	1876	WELSH, THOMAS	79		OLD AGE	IRELAND
28-Aug	1819	WENDELL, ANSELL	21			
29-Jul	1885	WENDELL, HENRY	42		PHTHISIS	IRELAND
10-Jun	1883	WENTWORTH, BENJAMIN	74		BRONCHITIS	DORCHESTER, MA
21-Sep	1882	WEST, CHARLES	65		DEBILITY	PENNSYLVANIA (HARRISTOWN)
21-May	1864	WEST, SARAH	18		SMALL POX	BOSTON
5-Jan	1887	WEST, THOMAS	75		DEBILITY	IRELAND
4-Sep	1896	WEST, THOMAS W		9 MONTHS 7 DAYS	MILK INFECTION	BOSTON
4-Jul	1888	WHALEN, MARY	23		EPILEPSY & GASTRIC ULCER	BOSTON
12-Jul	1856	WHEELER, CHARLES		9	SCROFULA	CANADA, MONTREAL
4-Jul	1896	WHEELER, MORRIS		6	MENIGITIS	BOSTON
1-Jan	1893	WHELAN, MARGARET (BELL)				
20-Aug	1897	WHITE, HENRY		8 MONTHS 22 DAYS	GASTRO ENTERITIS	BOSTON
20-Sep	1891	WHITE, MARY E (BLANCHARD)	35		PHTHISIS	ABINGTON, MA
6-Aug	1856	WHITE, SARAH (HOGDON)	29		PNEUMONIA	ENGLAND
12-Oct	1861	WHITMORE, SARAH (BALDWIN)	21		TYPHOID FEVER	MAINE, EASTPORT
30-Jun	1886	WHITTEMORE, SAMUEL	76		SENILITY	SHARON, MA
30-Mar	1882	WILD, CHARLES	65		HEART DISEASE	NEW HAMPSHIRE, CORNISH CITY)
1-Aug	1864	WILDER, MARY	67		DYSENTARY	ENGLAND
18-Sep	1827	WILDER, SAMUEL				
5-Aug	1891	WILL, GEORGE	75		HEART DISEASE	FRANCE
18-Apr	1887	WILLCUTT, JOHN	82		PNEUMONIA & SENILE DEBILITY	BOSTON
23-Jul	1896	WILLIAMS, ABBIE		10	MILK INFECTION	BOSTON
2-Jul	1858	WILLIAMS, BRIDGET	30		CONSUMPTION	NEW BRUNSWICK, ST JOHN
22-Sep	1860	WILLIAMS, CAROLINE (JONES)	17		SYPHILIS	NOVA SCOTIA
20-Feb	1892	WILLIAMS, ELVIRA (CLARK)	68		BRONCHITIS & ANAEMIA	MAINE
15-Nov	1864	WILLIAMS, FLORA (GRAY)	22		INTEMPERENCE	VERMONT
17-Sep	1897	WILLIAMS, HAROLD		1 MONTH 22 DAYS	FERMENTAL DIARRHOEA	BOSTON
28-Sep	1877	WILLIAMS, JAMES	81		OLD AGE	BOSTON
9-Oct	1891	WILLIAMS, MARGARET (CAMPBELL)	64			IRELAND
23-Jul	1865	WILLIAMS, MARIA	30		GANGRENE	MAINE

MONTH	YEAR	NAME	AGE YEARS	AGE MONTHS	CAUSE OF DEATH	BORN
5-Sep	1890	WILLIAMS, MARY A (CHAPMAN)	46		NEPHRITIS	MAINE, PORTLAND
28-Mar	1892	WILLIAMS, PRINCE				
31-Jul	1895	WILLIAMS, SKOLASIKA		5	DIARRHOEA	BOSTON
18-Oct	1863	WILLIAMS, VICTORIA	17		TYPHOID FEVER	ALABAMA
19-Nov	1893	WILSON, MARY E (BROWN)	73		GANGRENE	NEW BRUNSWICK
11-May	1878	WILSON, SAMUEL	67		APOPLEXY (23 DAYS) & PARALYSIS	BOSTON
28-Sep	1862	WINCHELL, RUFUS	57		DYSENTARY	NEW YORK
9-Apr	1856	WINCHTON MARY	41		CONSUMPTION	IRELAND
28-Dec	1865	WINSLOW, MATILDA	45		PHTHISIS	NEW BRUNSWICK
22-Apr	1856	WINTER, CALARA (SHAW)	20		SMALL POX	VERMONT
3-Jul	1896	WIPLER, MARGERY		4	ENTERITIS	BOSTON
25-Aug	1829	WISWALL, GEORGE	20			PORTSMOUTH
27-Feb	1856	WITMAN, CHRISTOPHER	38		HEART DISEASE	NOVA SCOTIA
23-Jun	1865	WITTER, ELIZABETH	64		PARALYSIS	NOVA SCOTIA
28-Jul	1888	WOOD, MARGARET (JOHNSON)	38		PHTHISIS	NEW BRUNSWICK
5-Oct	1893	WOODBURY, HARRIET (MARSH)	75		SUICIDAL DROWNING	NEW HAMPSHIRE
18-Sep	1885	WOOSTER, DANIEL	72		BRONCHITIS	GERMANY
29-May	1893	WORCESTER, ELIZABETH			APOLPLEXY	WORCESTER, MA
10-Mar	1864	WRIGHT, JORDAN	22		SMALL POX	NOVA SCOTIA
28-Dec	1854	WRIGHT, THOMAS	39		SHIP FEVER	ENGLAND
2-Jul	1883	WYE, SAMUEL	70		PNEUMONIA	DELAWARE
25-Oct	1885	YAHN, BERNHARDT	51		PHTHISIS	GERMANY
17-Jul	1802	YELL, JAMES			YELLOW FEVER	LYNN
20-May	1855	YEWELL, THOMAS	35		APOPLEXY	NOVA SCOTIA
26-Nov	1854	YOUNG, MARTHA	34		SMALL POX	NORTH CAROLINA
3-Sep	1854	YOUNG, THOMAS	46		HEART DISEASE	IRELAND

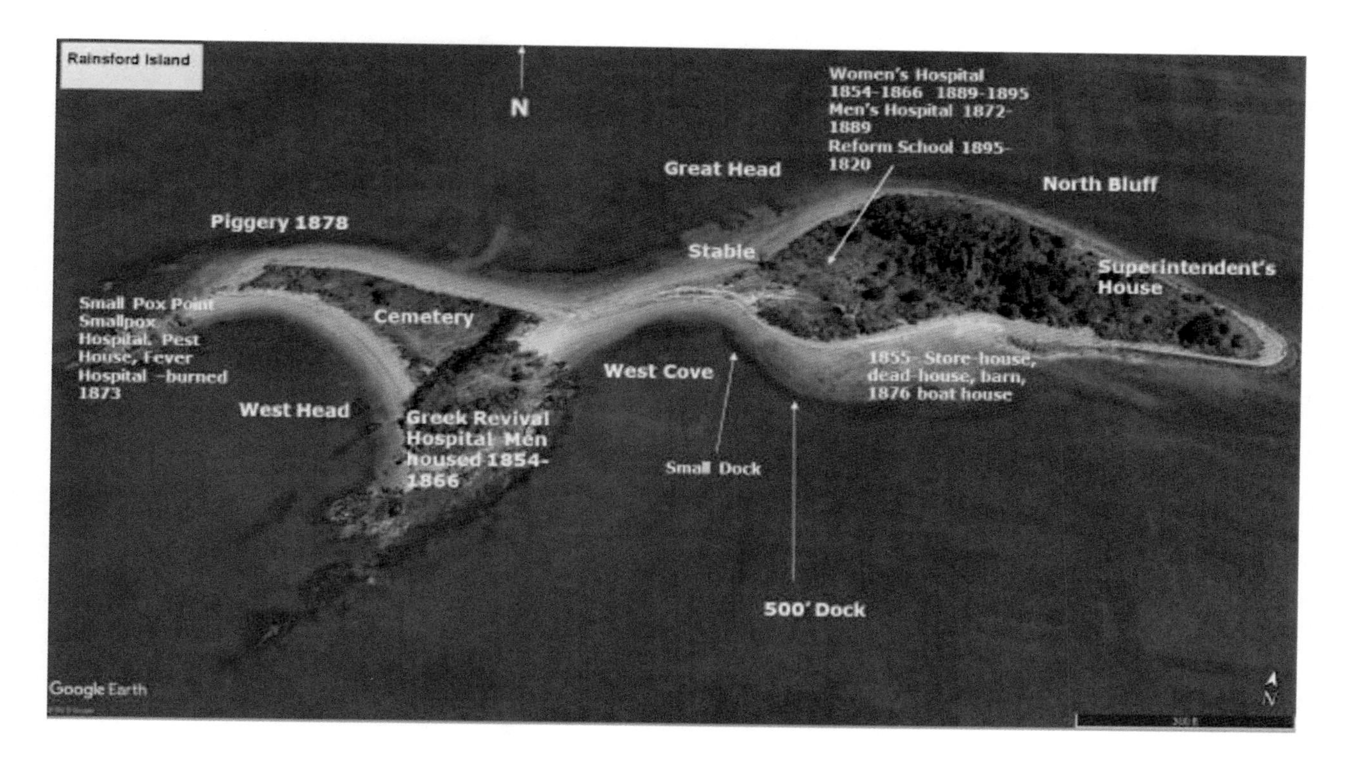

Google Earth

1880-89 - Digital Commonwealth - Creative Commons Attribution Non-Commercial No Derivatives License (CC BY-NC-ND).

1935- Dock - Digital Commonwealth - Creative Commons Attribution Non-Commercial. No Derivatives License (CC BY-NC-ND).

Great Head – New England Magazine, Vol 17, p. 332 1898 Suffolk School for Boys circa 1897. Brick building present during the Men's era 1876-1889 then women 1889-1894.

1910-1920- Winter View from Mansion Hospital. North Bluff in background.
Flickr.com - City of Boston Archives, taken by Frank B. Conlin. In the Public Domain.

1910-1920 - View from North Bluff. Mansion Hospital on West Head in the background.
Flickr.com - City of Boston Archives, taken by Frank B. Conlin. In the Public Domain.

1910-1920 - View from North Bluff. Entire West Head in the background.
Flickr.com - City of Boston Archives, taken by Frank B. Conlin. In the Public Domain.

1910-1920 - View of bluff from Mansion Hospital on West Head. Flickr.com -
City of Boston Archives, taken by Frank B. Conlin. In the Public Domain.

1910-1920 - Stables – Flickr.com - City of Boston Archives, taken by Frank B. Conlin. In the Public Domain.

1910-1920 Superintendent's house - Flickr.com - City of Boston Archives, taken by Frank B. Conlin. In the Public Domain. (Building erected in 1819. Boston Globe, July 28, 1932, p. 2.)

Alice North Towne Lincoln – Boston Post July 5, 1903, P. 1

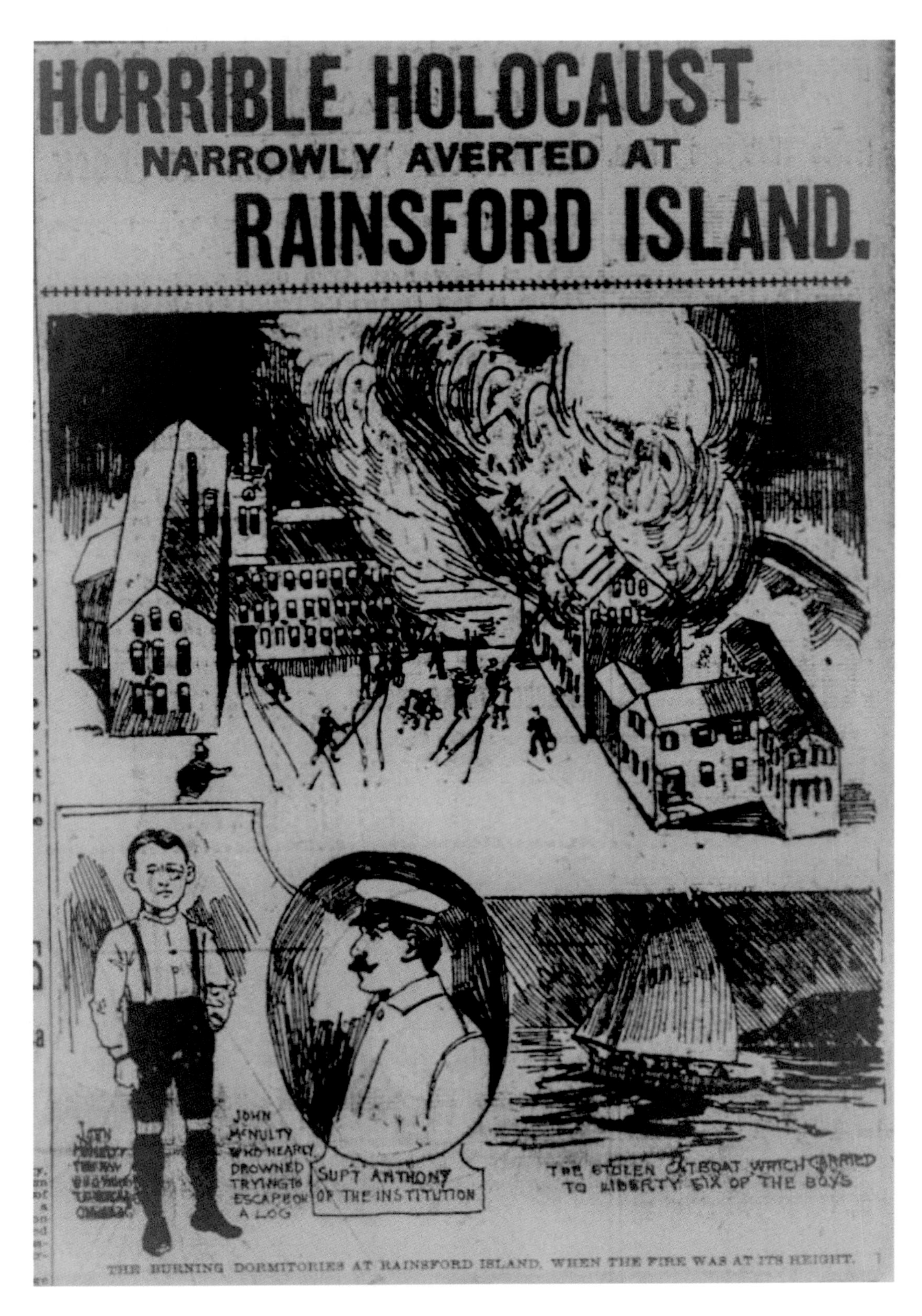

HORRIBLE HOLOCAUST

NARROWLY AVERTED AT

RAINSFORD ISLAND.

THE BURNING DORMITORIES AT RAINSFORD ISLAND, WHEN THE FIRE WAS AT ITS HEIGHT.

Boston Post, August 20, 1899, P. 1

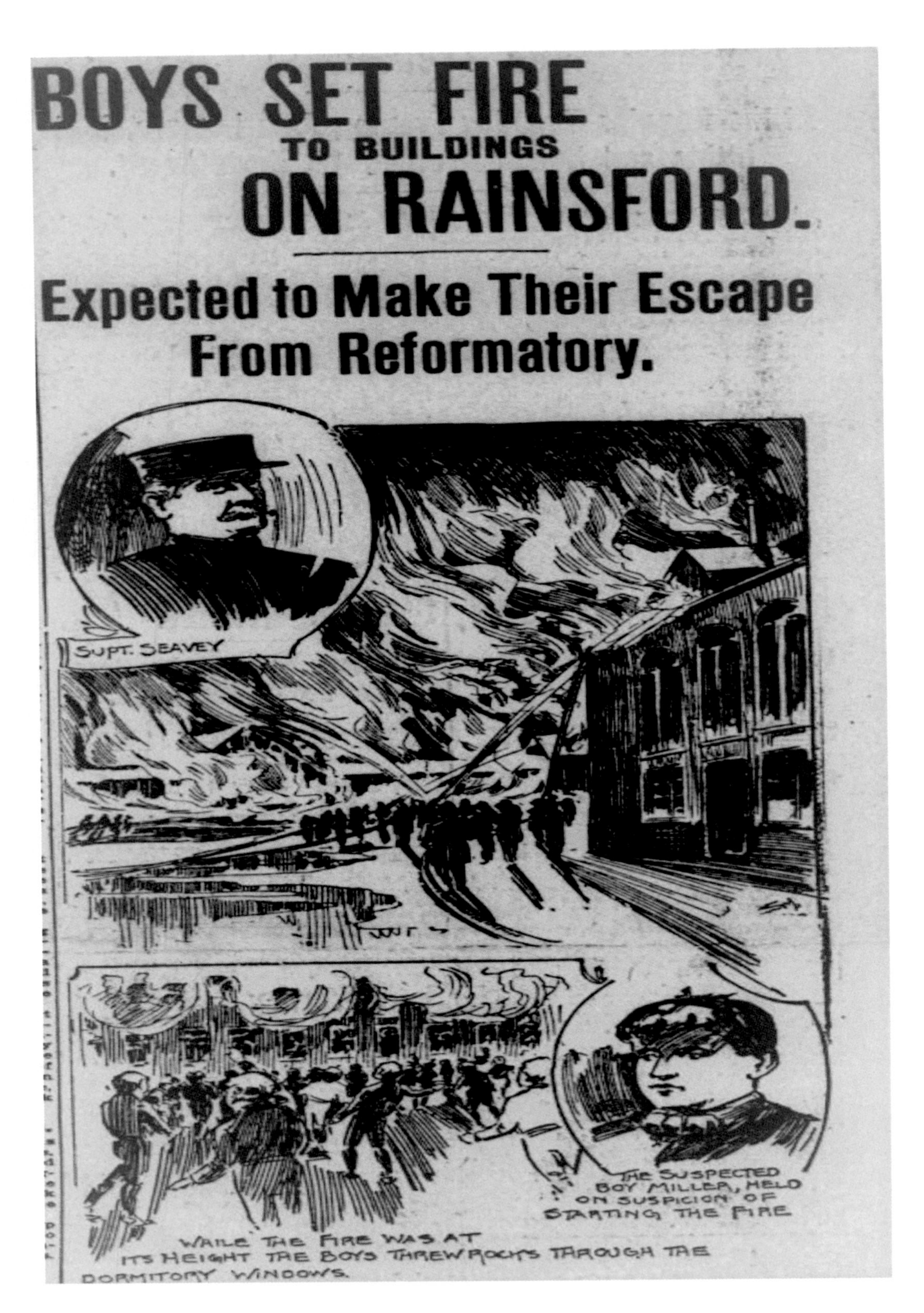

BOYS SET FIRE TO BUILDINGS ON RAINSFORD.

Expected to Make Their Escape From Reformatory.

SUPT. SEAVEY

THE SUSPECTED BOY MILLER, HELD ON SUSPICION OF STARTING THE FIRE

WHILE THE FIRE WAS AT ITS HEIGHT THE BOYS THREW ROCKS THROUGH THE DORMITORY WINDOWS.

Boston Post, March 21, 1900, P. 1

5 TRAPPED AND SAVED FROM BUILDING ABLAZE

Two Boys and Three Women Rescued in $35,000 Fire on Rainsford Island—Lives of 170 Persons Endangered by Rapid Sweep of Flames

RUINS OF THE SEWING ROOM OF THE RAINSFORD ISLAND REFORM SCHOOL.
Two boys and one invalid woman were carried from the burning building. The building was a 2 1-2-story wooden structure and the locker building was a 1 1-2-story affair. Both were entirely destroyed with a loss of $38,000.

Boston Post, February 14, 1919, P. 1.

North side of Isthmus approaching North Bluff, taken by Corinne Elicone.

North side of Isthmus approaching North Bluff, taken by Corinne Elicone.

West Head Cemetery, taken by Corinne Elicone.

West Head Mansion Hospital, taken by Corinne Elicone.

West Head Mansion Hospital, taken by Corinne Elicone.

West Cove - Remains of 500' pier pilings on shoreline, taken by Corinne Elicone.

Doc Searls - February 2, 2007

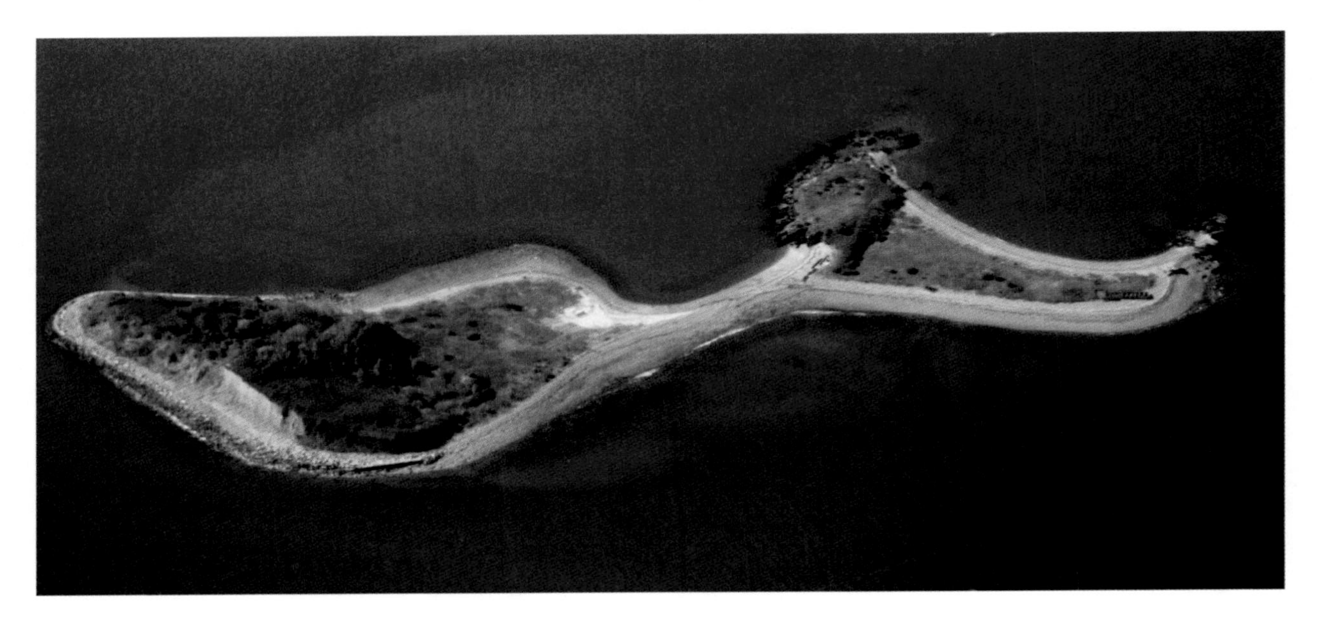

Doc Searls – May 8, 2008

Doc Searls - February 2, 2007

Doc Searls - May 31, 2009

Made in the USA
Middletown, DE
04 January 2021

28192256R00093